Praise for Entering Hekate'

"*Entering Hekate's Cave* by Cyndi Brannen is the book on shadow work I wish I had years ago. Brannen seamlessly blends the craft of a witch with the therapeutic goals of cocreating healthy mental spaces. I loved seeing how she aligns the benefits of crystals with the tougher parts of that internal journey. I will be coming back to this book for years to come."

—Amy Blackthorn, priestess of Hekate and author of
Blackthorn's Botanical Wellness

"Cyndi Brannen's best book yet, *Entering Hekate's Cave,* blends the practical and psychological with the transcendent and magical to help you journey to the deepest part of the psyche and truly know thyself. With rising interest in shadow work, this is just the book we need—timely, sensitive, well-researched, and rooted in lived experience."

—Nicholas Pearson, author of *Crystal Basics* and *Stones of the Goddess*

"With *Entering Hekate's Cave*, Dr. Brannen has firmly placed herself among the great psychospiritual researchers and teachers of our time—this book can rest proudly on the shelf alongside titles by Jean Shinoda Bolen, Marion Woodman, and James Hillman. With this work, Brannen secures her place—and Hekate's—among the best resources for trauma-sensitive and spiritually oriented healing for our times."

—Carmen Spagnola, RCH, somatic trauma recovery practitioner
and author of *The Spirited Kitchen*

"Cyndi Brannen takes us on a journey of the soul in her book *Entering Hekate's Cave.* In this masterful tome, we follow Hekate's guidance as we look into our shadow selves so that we may transform our spirit and step into our personal power. This book gives us a world of information and practical techniques that will help the reader connect with Hekate and her various epithets, each giving us strength to fully embrace our inner light."

—Chris Allaun, author of *A Guide of Spirits*

"In *Entering Hekate's Cave*, Cyndi Brannen offers a unique view and approach to the necessary spiritual work of soul healing and becoming whole. She not only succeeds in providing the reader with the means to do that but also does so from a distinctly Hekatean perspective. In fact, the book's guidance harkens back to experiences and gnosis I underwent myself in the early stages of my devotional relationship with Hekate. Beyond the confines of tradition or history, Brannen manages to marry ancient wisdom and modern innovation. This book will be especially valuable to those who engage with their spirituality from a psychological aspect, though most everyone would be well served by Brannen's work."

—Stefanos Chelydoreus, author and creator of
The Greek Witch and *The Equine Serpent*

"With *Entering Hekate's Cave*, Cyndi Brannen has once more shown herself to be a teacher, guide, and priestess of deep unfolding. This book leads us through the most integral part of the journey that we must all explore if we seek to heal ourselves whole. Step by step, Cyndi guides us through Hekate's Cave, reclaiming the fragmented parts of souls, our integral power, and the capacity to know and understand intimately the potency of Hekate's many aspects. Through ritual and sacred practices, the reader will find deep transformation and healing on each and every page."

—Elena Rego, creator and owner of The Witches Box
and The Holy Witch

"With a powerful but kind voice, Cyndi Brannen has given devotees of Hekate a gorgeous tool for exploring the mysteries of the Goddess to an even greater depth. Wisdom, beauty, and strength—all are found in this excellent book."

—Courtney Weber, author of *Hekate: Goddess of Witches*

Entering Hekate's Cave

The Journey Through Darkness to Wholeness

CYNDI BRANNEN

WEISER BOOKS

This edition first published in 2023 by Weiser Books, an imprint of Red Wheel/
Weiser, LLC

With offices at:
65 Parker Street, Suite 7
Newburyport, MA 01950
www.redwheelweiser.com

ISBN: 978-1-57863-791-1

Library of Congress Cataloging-in-Publication Data available upon request.

Cover design by Sky Peck Design
Illustrations on pages v, vi, xviii, 10, 11, 13, 20, and 47 courtesy of Margie Stingley
Illustrations on pages viii, xi, 1, 8, 43, 53, 54, 60, 62, 66, 77, 81, 92, 108, 117, 124,
    143, 149, 150, 164, 175, 197, and 209 courtesy of Cyndi Brannen
Illustrations on pages 4, 6 23, 31 45, 55, 61, 67, 70, 79, 93, 98, 109, 112, 113,
    125, 129, 145, 165, 170, 172, 173, 177, 183 199, and 203 courtesy of Cyndi
    Brannen and Margie Stingley
Interior by Debby Dutton
Typeset in Adobe Garamond and Incognito

Printed in Canada
MAR

10 9 8 7 6 5 4 3 2 1

None of the immortal gods or mortal folk heard her cry, nor the olives shining with fruit—except the daughter of Perses, tender-hearted Hekate, veiled in light, heard from her cave . . .

—from "The Homeric Hymn to Demeter," *The Homeric Hymns: A Translation, with Introduction and Notes* by Diane J. Rayor (Joan Palevsky Imprint in Classical Literature)

To those who have journeyed through darkness with me.

Contents

She is the darkness, and she is the fire.
She is the cry of "enough."
She is the sigil written in stone.
She is the silent walking away of the betrayed.
She is the lonely raising arms to the moon.
She is the lie told to live the truth.
She is the secret circle drawing down her moon.
She is the poison that heals.
She is the bold stare into the mirror.
She is the blood shed to bring rebirth.
She is all those who dare to become.
She is the power that is our right.
She has returned.
Answer her call.
The time is now.
Speak the truth.
Be healed.

Acknowledgments

There is a saying that goes: "When the student is ready, the teacher will appear." This phrase is often labeled as Buddhist. However, the more likely origins of the quote lie in Theosophy, a school of thought that has been greatly influential in modern spirituality. The passage can be traced back to a treatise by Mabel Collins entitled *Light on the Path*, first published in 1885. In it, she writes:

> To hear the Voice of the Silence is to understand that from within comes the only true guidance; to go to the Hall of Learning is to enter the state in which learning becomes possible. Then will many words be written there for thee and written in fiery letters for thee easily to read. For when the disciple is ready, the Master is ready also.

This book would not exist without my students, who have taught me how to become a better guide for their journey through darkness to wholeness. True "fiery" learning, when we listen to the voice of silence, awakens courage, commitment, and a desire for transformation. It is their energy that is evidenced in this book—my students who challenge, inspire, and support each other. The rituals and exercises in this book have been tried and tested by hundreds of them. I teach this cycle every year, and I am perpetually humbled by their fortitude and grace.

All educators have their own teachers. I wish to acknowledge those within mainstream psychology who trained me. Without my background in applied social psychology, the work I do today would not be possible. I am also grateful to the work of C. G. Jung (although his views on gender, race, and sexuality are problematic) and others who followed in his footsteps. In particular, I consider Marian Woodman and James Hillman to be two "ancestors" with whom I have what they might call an "imaginal" relationship. To me, they are my spiritual allies, and I often ask questions of them, especially regarding the dark journey toward wholeness.

In my personal cave are many who hurt me and many on whom I have inflicted wounds. Thank you for the pain, through which I found a deep wellspring of healing. I couldn't teach and write about the healing journey sincerely without having suffered and caused harm.

My amazing editor, Judika Illes, is an author whom I have long admired, and I am pleased to work with her. Her understanding of my work and her expertise on areas related to it are appreciated. It is a gift to know her. The entire team at Weiser Books is fabulous, and I am grateful to them for taking a chance on this very different book. I also wish to thank their highly skilled editorial team and their wonderful marketing team.

To my team at Covina, from the staff to the senior students who volunteer as guides, thank you for being in my collaborative container, helping others along their way to wholeness. Margie, thank you for being my artistic collaborator. Your artwork has rendered life to these pages. You spend a lot of time rummaging inside of my head to extrapolate my ideas and bring them to life. No easy task. Here's to the Temple of Good Enough.

Angela and Liz, true soul sisters, you make me feel heard and held. Thank you, Angela, for being my coconspiritor in putting Medusa's head back on. To Liz, who always brings truth to the table, I need you to know how much appreciation I have for you and your hard pants. Thank you for being my midnight editor. Long live The Widows of Herakles.

My boys are my champions, sounding boards, and cocreators of our wonderful family. Dear Teej, at whom life relentlessly throws hard-hitting fastballs, thank you for being a constant source of inspiration and for your unconditional love. You are my favorite Cancer-Virgo, and e'er will be. Aidan, child of Saturn in many ways, I adore your boldness, tenacity, and ability to see the big picture. My absolute favorite thing in the whole world is when the three of us talk for hours on end. This is why I secretly look forward to power outages. ACT forever.

Introduction: The Call

In complete darkness,
I tumbled down, down, down.
Until I landed at the bottom.
Broken open,
Out poured my soul,
Which formed into a key,
Held by a mysterious woman,
Who held her lantern high,
Whispering,
"Follow me."

To enter Hekate's cave is to embark on the journey back to the soul. This is a lunar quest, illuminated by the goddess's torches, following the rattle of her keys, and embracing the shadow within—an adventure that is equal parts exciting and daunting. In depth psychology, the concept of wholeness implies that we are intentionally integrating the shadow with the soul. The radical acceptance of our light *and* darkness is the path of truth. This is not the popular hero's journey where all is bright, with conquest as the goal. There is no waiting maiden or adoring crowd. Instead, we journey toward healing and understanding into the mysteries of the deeper world. The journey is inherently feminine, which is to say that it is associated with the traditional energies associated with this principle—intuition, introspection, and emotions.[1]

If you're a bit timid about the possibility of traveling with me through Hekate's cave, congratulations. I am always much more concerned about readers who are ready to dive in without any hesitation. At the same time, however, you may be feeling pulled into the cave. Call it intuition or survival instinct. Perhaps what you've been doing hasn't worked. Perhaps you have an inner calling to become much more than you currently are. There may be past traumas that simply won't let you go. Whatever it is that led you to this place, know that I'm right beside you. I sense your curiosity and your intrigue, as well as your well-placed fear of what the cave symbolizes.

Indeed, Hekate is a challenging figure. This mysterious spirit often arrives unannounced and unwanted in our lives. She shakes us to the core. She stands before us with torches flickering and keys rattling. Hekate is for everyone, whatever your beliefs about God, the universe, and the deeper world. She is the light in the darkness within each and every one of us, no matter our gender, occupations, or anything else. This light is yours to experience in the pages of this book, from the theories and research to the natural magic and rituals.

Hekate guides us toward wholeness. She appears in dreams as a mysterious woman, causing a thrum when we stumble onto an image of her, or invoking a sense of wonder when we say her name. This is how she comes to us. I myself never set out to become enchanted by this ancient goddess. Yet, here I am, well over ten years into answering her uncanny call. My first encounter with Hekate was surreal. While folding laundry late at night, I heard a voice inside my head say: "It's time." Somehow, I knew that this voice belonged to a woman who called herself Hekate. I had almost no knowledge about her. I thought I was finally losing my mind. I was terrified. Yet, reflecting back on that night, I realize that that was the moment I began the journey of *finding* my mind—and the rest of me.

Hekate abides at the crossroads. When we are at personal thresholds, we can always find her if we are brave enough to look. That long-ago event was a fault line. My marriage and career had self-destructed. My health was in tatters. I was depleted in every way imaginable. And let's be clear—I was not then seeking Hekate. I just wanted my life, and that of my children, to be better. I wanted to show up in my own life. Somehow, there was a crack in my control-freak consciousness that let something—someone—deeper sneak in.

I was in the basement that night—literally and spiritually. That is often when we give up clinging to the vestiges of whatever is keeping us bound. Desperate, alone, and without clarity, we find the courage to see Hekate. In the years since, I've heard of countless similar stories. It is not Hekate who comes to us, but we who find ourselves in her domain. We are deep in the Underworld—addiction, chronic illness, shattered hearts, and worse—and then, something happens within us that causes us to pause in our miserable wanderings and instead see a pale glimmer of light. That is Hekate's torch—the indomitable illumination of our own souls. We reach the bottom in order to see it. There's no point in wasting our time wishing that healing could be any different. It is simply thus. The only way out of hell is through it.

We make a choice when at this crossroads. We can stay in our aimlessness, or follow Hekate into her cave to find respite from the vast hellscape we're in. In her cave, we find the nourishing darkness, the warm, wet womb of the Mother Goddess.

Before my own crossroads moment in the basement, I had dabbled in the deeper world while building a career as a research psychologist specializing in helping women manage life's stressors. But my work seemed to be missing the same thing I was missing in my personal life—meaning. While analyzing a data set of women acting as caregivers for severely disabled loved ones, I realized that those who found meaning in what anyone would consider incredibly stressful scenarios fared much, much better than those who didn't. That this was my own central issue became clear only when I looked in the rearview mirror. I was breaking away from my career and a failed marriage, but I was moving toward an unknown destination. I didn't know at the time that this journey would lead to a lengthy sojourn in my own personal Underworld. I went deep into the cave in order to heal into my unique wholeness.

In my previous books, *Keeping Her Keys: An Introduction to Hekate's Modern Witchcraft* and *Entering Hekate's Garden: The Magick, Medicine, and Mystery of Plant Spirit Witchcraft*, I explored how practices related to my experience and that of my students led to improved well-being. This book follows a similar theme. I've spent the past decade researching Hekate's history and collecting data on how others experience her. What emerges is that Hekate can be understood in diverse ways. This book focuses on exploring her as a Great Mother figure who is Anima Mundi, World Soul. This harkens back to the most ancient writings about her, as in Hesiod's *Theogony*.

Ultimately, to heal into our unique wholeness includes venturing into the dark womb of Hekate's cave and allowing our own sacred creativity to flow forth. The Underworld journey is not optional if we are truly to become our whole selves. We live in a world in which we are mesmerized by artificial light. Sometimes called "toxic positivity," this obsession forces us to comply with a purely "love and light" approach to life. But that's not the way life works. For as long as we deny the nourishing power of the healing darkness of the cave, we remain stuck. "Don't worry, be happy" doesn't work. We end up worried, sad, and beating ourselves up for not being carefree bliss beings.[2]

Journeying through Hekate's cave heals us from this toxic positivity. When I faced and integrated the shadow aspects of myself with loving-kindness, rather than belittling them, I was able to accept the trauma of the past. This journey, rooted in depth psychology and merged with practical personal development strategies, has yielded transformative results for me and for hundreds of my students. If you are finally ready to get over what blocks and binds you, perhaps this book is for you.

When we are at a crossroads, or already in the Underworld, Hekate can rise up out of the deeper world, showing up in the cracks of our lives. She sends her emissaries—angels and hungry ghosts alike—to do her bidding. They occupy our dreams, invade our imaginations, and drop their uncanny hints until we pay them heed. Although their faces vary and their methods may be disparate, their message is always the same: Wake up! They intrude on our quiet minds until we hear them speak. And when we do, they tell us stories that unsettle us. They bring back the past, show us our own faults, and generally shake us to the core. That is the work of

Hekate in action. She scares the life *back into* us. She is the spirit of the sacred feminine that calls us to embark on the journey of the soul.

I've been supporting others in their shadow work for over a decade, as well as continuing my ongoing work on myself. My twenty-five years in various areas of social psychology, from attachment to cognitive behavioral applications stretching "down" to depth psychology, along with my studies in comparative religion, mythology, mystical traditions, and philosophy, have led me to create a path that blends psychology, spirituality, and ancient wisdom. My journey has led me through training in shamanism, tarot, astrology, energetic healing, herbalism, and other forms of traditional wisdom. That is the path I present here.

This journey is one of reclaiming the soul through encounters with Hekate and with the numinous, defined more commonly today as the transcendent. "Numinous," a term advanced by C. G. Jung, refers to all that which is beyond everyday life. It is symbolic and archetypal. Transcendence occurs when we venture into the numinous, temporarily going beyond the limits of our regular existence. Much of who we are has been stolen from us by a variety of influences. Our shadow selves harbor all the pain associated with these acts of thievery, from our feelings of being "less than" to supposed psychological disorders. I say "supposed" because many diagnosed ailments aren't actually clinical problems, but rather problems of the soul. When our true selves can't perform the assignment we were born into this incarnation to fulfill, we encounter all manner of difficulties that often appear as anxiety, depression, and other problems. I'm not denying that these ailments have a clinical dimension. But, more often than not, the symptoms we experience are associated with shadow power. Only by healing the shadow will we ever become whole. That is work accomplished in Hekate's cave.

As I was researching Hekate's history, I stumbled onto a collection of fragments known as The Greek Magical Papyri.[3] The words on the pages thrummed with a vitality all their own, beyond what I'd read in any other ancient texts. They transported me back across the centuries so that I was standing beside the authors. I could see their desperation, feel their heartbreak, and hear their anguish in their words.

World-wide, dog-shaped, spinner of Fate, all-giver,
Long-lasting, glorious, helper, queen, bright,

Wide-aimer, vigorous, holy, benign,
Immortal, shrill-voiced, glossy-locked, in bloom,
Divine with golden face . . . [4]

Over time, I collected the various titles and epithets used in these texts to describe Hekate and other goddesses. These names have their own resonance. They are archetypes that extend beyond any single mythic figure. Borborophorba, the Filth Eater, is the feminine spirit who consumes what no longer serves. Anassa Eneroi, the Death Queen, walks with us through the valley of grief while showing us how life endures beyond the grave and presenting the promise of rebirth. Drakaina, the serpent goddess, symbolizes the awakening soul.

Hekate can be our guide into our personal darkness. The ancients wrote about her as Enodia, the guide along our way. She was the one who abided at crossroads, thresholds, and roadsides, offering protection and respite. No hand-holding, hovering goddess, she neither coddles nor encourages constricting positivity. Hekate illuminates our darkness so that we can find our own way to wholeness. No wonder she is intimidating *and* comforting.

In this quest for wholeness, we become Persephone descending to claim our rightful throne, however that may look for us. We emerge from Hekate's cave initiated into our own soul, embarking on a new adventure with our true center as compass. Through explorations of our interior life, our relationships and the past, and natural magic and ritual, we cast aside the burdens we've been carrying for far too long, creating the space for our dreams and desires to flourish.

The chapters in this book each focus on an archetype—an ancient title of Hekate that is attributed to her and to many other expressions of the sacred feminine. These archetypes contextualize her place within mythology and other imaginative sources. Into that context, I weave sound psychological techniques for healing into wholeness.

This book also offers natural magic—including the crafting of talismans, candle magic, working with avian companions, and connecting to stone spirits—as a means to pass through the three "main gates" in Hekate's cave—the release of burdens, the retrieval of soul fragments, and the rebirth of the soul. I've also included references to plant spirits that can be most helpful. Every chapter contains practical exercises for connecting to the written content. I call these "practica" to indicate the application of knowledge. To practice is to learn. It is not perfect; it is a process. Do these exercises to the best of your ability. Abide in the Temple of Good *Enough*. Make your affirmation, "I am good. I am enough." There are also three ceremonial rituals to solidify these practical exercises: The Ritual of Catharsis, The Soul Retrieval Journey, and The Rebirth Ritual. You may want to dedicate a journal to this real work.

This book is also part memoir, recounting my own journey through a difficult upbringing, sexual trauma, addiction, disease, and more. I will not lie and tell you that the journey through darkness to wholeness is easy. What is more difficult, however, is staying depressed, stuck, and numb, or drowning in the past. Yet there is also great joy along the way as we lean into the mysteries of the deeper world. Here we find a sense of "homecoming" that brings peace of mind. Here we find a lightness that accompanies the heavy work done right. A natural balancing occurs. This is how we heal into wholeness and find that meaning I lacked long ago.

I am frequently asked whether Hekate is "real." This question opens the gates to a discussion about the nature of reality. The need to control everything is related to the conditioning around being literal. Hekate and her deeper world speak an entirely different language, rich in symbols and meaning. To me, this world is as real as the physical one—perhaps more so, because that is where I've found healing and purpose. To me, the mysteries are meant to be mysterious. Fundamentalism occurs when the numinous is subjected to the dogma of the literal. Be curious about Hekate and her world. Resist demanding literalness of what is inherently meant to be symbolic.

Think of it like this. Even in our closest relationships, with full disclosure among equals and excellent reciprocity, we never truly know the entire contents of another's heart and mind. Mystery is always present. In other words, understanding other humans is always challenging, and often elusive. Why should knowing the heart and mind of a deity be otherwise? We work to establish meaningful relationships based in mutual trust, respect, and affection because this is of value to us. I would argue that applying this approach to our association with the forces we know as deities and spirits deepens our understanding of them and the unseen world. We can say that we are "working" with these forces, and we certainly do, as a metaphor for how we collaborate with other humans. It's not adequate to explain the process, however, because it is inherently mysterious. Yet we can enter with an open heart, wise mind, and strong back as we enter Hekate's deeper world. And we can emerge whole.

May we journey well together.

Her Reflection

She crouches in the corner,
Shivering from eons of damp neglect.
Then Titaness, with eyes shooting fire-arrows.
Next, ancient stone mother with snakes for hair.
Daughter.
Crone.
Mistress of life,
Bringer of death.
The transforming
Wild goddess.
Trembling, dancing.
Relentless thrumming.
Whispers, shouts.
Cave and mountain.
River and desert.
Pulse of the universe.
Go ahead, she says,
Remain.
With your doom-scrolling, panic-inducing nonsense.
Plucking eyebrows, yet
Avoiding the mirror.
I'll still be here.
Getting water all over the bathroom floor.
Sitting at your desk.
In the corner of your bedroom,
Black eyes shining watching you slumber.
Legs stretched out from a kitchen chair,
Watch out, don't trip.
Until. You. See.
That it is a reflection.

Chapter 1
Anima Mundi: The Deeper World

Great Hekate,
Gods, goddesses, guides, and spirits,
Elements, directions,
Animals, plants, and stones,
All that is, was, and ever will be,
Guide me along my way.
Protect my journey,
And bless my path.
As I speak it, it becomes so.

Hekate comes to us wearing many faces and bearing many names. For me, the most resonant is her role as Anima Mundi, the soul of the world. This appellation comes from a few different ancient sources. In particular, a collection of ancient fragments discussing the nature of the universe, known as The Chaldean Oracles, refers to her as such. Hesiod, in his description of the gods, defines Hekate as a benevolent goddess who oversees all that is. In my thinking, all the spirits flow forth from the World Soul, be they plant (as I wrote about in *Entering Hekate's Garden*), correspondences, or entities. In particular, these spirits can be seen as representations of archetypes, which are foundational pillars of the universe. The many titles of Hekate, which I have used as the chapter names in this book, are symbolic of the underlying archetypes. Archetypes lie at the very core of everything. They are living, breathing, and conscious forces that are enlivened through stories and depictions of gods and goddesses. In fact, myths are all archetypal stories.

C. G. Jung pioneered the exploration of archetypes as a means of connecting to the deeper world on the journey toward wholeness.[1] When we explore ourselves, the deeper world, and the external world through an archetypal lens, we begin to develop wisdom about the nature of existence. Archetypes are symbolic forms that cannot be further reduced. They thus embody a force and power that is purely of them. They combine in myriad ways to create all things.

Archetypes speak through symbols. Consider how the key represents much more than opening a literal lock. Or how the serpent is symbolic of the soul. In fact, we can find symbols in just about anything—from corporate logos to dream images. And we can better see the many faces of Hekate by recognizing and understanding her archetypes, which each carry the energy of transformation.

When we answer the call of Hekate, we ourselves take on one of her ancient archetypes found in The Greek Magical Papyri—Nyssa, the sacred turning point, the initiation, the very beginning, and the amplifying energy of the starting gate. As we deepen our connection to Hekate and progress upon our journey toward wholeness, we become our own High Priestess (or other sacred title of your choosing), whose archetype, beautifully demonstrated in the tarot, is that of the full realization of the sacred feminine and connection to the moon, the mysteries, and, yes, the archetypes themselves. We may activate the archetype of the Queen, the sovereign monarch ruling from a position of power "with," instead of over, valuing intuition, being introspective, and standing sovereign within our truth. The Queen, of course, can be divided into other archetypes, as shown in the tarot—the benevolent ruler, the evil queen, and so on.

Contemplate, for example, the fluidity of the archetype of Hekate as the Triple Goddess. She is the transcendent bringer of magic, medicine, and mystery. She emits the energy of transformation in all of her many forms. Hekate's many epithets (titles and traits), dreams, the cards, astrology, plant medicine, magical correspondences—these are all archetypal.

As you read this book, the archetypes in each chapter will work on you in different ways. They will come to you in dreams. You may find yourself embodying them. Always look for them to turn up in unexpected places. Learning to see with the eyes of the soul opens your field of vision so that you can see how archetypes are always working on, and through, us.

The Nature of Archetypes

Archetypes are numinous, tricky to describe, and profoundly experiential. In fact, it is impossible to grasp the essence of an archetype fully, be it one of those presented in this book or any other. This is because, when we engage with an archetype, we bump into something that truly transcends human understanding. Archetypes have vibrations and essences. Each has a soul that can take on a thousand different faces. Deities like Hekate and Persephone can be understood as archetypes and as composites of archetypes, as can many other spirits. To understand and seek archetypal connection is to embark on the journey of the unconscious, which is the entrance to the world of spirits.

My teaching and writing are embedded in archetypes, especially those connected to the sacred feminine, the planets, and the elements. Hekate's many epithets are archetypes as well. She is Keeper of the Keys, the archetype of the divine one who guards the gates of the journey inward. She is the Torchbearer who carries the spirit of the light in the darkness, the inner flame, and the primordial fire. Art, literature, and music can evoke the spirits of archetypes. Many of the ancient texts I've encountered while researching this book awakened Hekate to me in profound ways. *The Orphic Hymn to Hekate* summons her as a benevolent, yet powerful spirit:

> Lovely Hekate of the roads and of the crossroads I invoke. In heaven,
> on earth, then in the sea, saffron-cloaked, tomb spirit reveling in
> the souls of the dead, daughter of Perses, haunting deserted places,
> delighting in deer, nocturnal, dog-loving, monstrous queen, devour-
> ing wild beasts, ungirt and repulsive. Herder of bulls, queen and mis-
> tress of the whole world, leader, nymph, mountain-roaming nurturer
> of youths, maiden, I beseech you to come to these holy rites, ever
> with joyous heart, ever favoring the oxherd.[2]

If you felt a thrum reading this ancient verse, that was an encounter with Hekate and the archetypes associated with her. Engaging in this hymn evokes the archetypes of Queen and Leader. What others do you find?

As demonstrated in the verse, archetypes often have specific features, such as Hekate being three-formed (heaven, earth, sea) and having companions, like animals (dogs, deer, oxen) and plants (saffron). They can also be associated with certain places; Hekate's association with roads and crossroads is an example. When connecting with an archetype, we often use these characteristics to call upon them, which is what we do when we create altars (more on those later).

Jung viewed the primal archetypes as anima, feminine energy, and animus, the masculine principle. Hekate, as Anima Mundi, represents the primordial force of the feminine, the soul of the cosmos. Animus balances anima, and we are all comprised of these two archetypes in various combinations. To become whole, in Jung's view, included embracing both anima and animus, within and without.

I've often been asked about Hekate and masculine archetypes. My viewpoint is that Hekate, as Anima Mundi, is the centrifugal core from which all archetypes flow—even masculine archetypes. In fact, Hekate's torch, as well as those of Persephone and Demeter, contains what is sometimes called "Pluto's Fire," referring to the sacred masculine. The distinction between feminine and masculine is a complicated one in our modern age, however there is value in examining them as archetypal forces.

In depth psychology, anima is the sacred feminine. It emanates as intuition, feelings, and the inward journey. It is the Mother in all her forms, yet, at her soul, she is the purity of darkness with her torch blazing bright. Animus projects rationality, thought, and the expressed self. In tarot, anima is represented in cards like the Queens, the Empress, and the High Priestess. Animus is found in the Magician, the kings, the Emperor, and the Hierophant. We all have both anima and animus within us to varying degrees.

The foundational force of an archetype, and its power within each of us, derives from what Jung called a shadow and a self. Thus, all things are dark and light, neither of which is undesirable. But too much of either can be harmful. The Dark Mother is deeply dark so that she can accept our darkness. The Dark Father disturbs our carefully constructed defenses so that we can be freed from them.

According to Jung, both archetypes and individuals can put on "personas" that are themselves archetypes. This is a bit like playing a role or putting on a costume. But we can take on the persona of an archetype that perhaps does not fit with our true nature. For example, we can put on the cloak of "worker" to cope with a job we dislike. Archetypes can thus be projections that may or may not reflect the true nature of the object of the projection. If you have ever been incorrectly labeled with an archetype, you know how upsetting this can be.

Archetypes come to us in dreams, imaginings, visions, and synchronicities. We ascribe them to ourselves, to others, and to our experiences. For example, it is said that we are currently living in the Age of Hermes. Hermes is an archetype for both the god and his planet (Mercury). He cannot be reduced further, yet he contains other archetypes as well, including traveler, trickster, guide, communicator, and *chthonic* (earthly). He is also associated with another archetype, the element of Air. In earthly Zodiac, which is a collection of astrological archetypes, he is associated with Gemini, symbolizing the tension between freedom and restriction and also Virgo, reflecting his more ordered and nurturing aspects. This friction is also evidenced in the two of swords in the tarot. Indeed, tarot cards are a collection of archetypes. Because of these many layered meanings, our understanding of an archetype is often intuitive and spiritual, and thus difficult to define using rational logic.

The phases of the moon, the planetary positions and connections, calendar dates and months, the seasonal shifts and their midpoints are all representative of different archetypes. Corresponding an archetype associated with Hekate to the lunar months can thus deepen our understanding of the Wheel of the Year, which is itself an archetype and part of the deeper archetype of Kairos, the rhythmic time of the deeper world, and Chronos, the linear time of the surface world.[3]

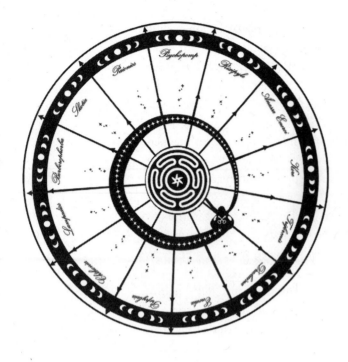

Time is a Wheel,
Bending,
Stretching,
Walking the circle.
Spinning backward,
Illuminating the past,
Finding wisdom and healing,
Reclaiming what's always been mine.
Creating the present,
Knowing it is an illusion.
A moment,
Now.
Pushing me back,
Pulling me forward.
The crossroads of what was
And what will be.
Turning to the future,
I cast my desires upon
The Wheel of Time,
Predicting what may come.
Time is my Wheel.

Symbols and Sigils

Archetypes are expressed through symbols, material manifestations of their energies. Common ones for those being called by Hekate are finding a key in an unexpected place, a black dog appearing out of the blue, and other rather mysterious occurrences. Jung called these events synchronicities. We connect to Hekate and her deeper world using symbols, like those placed on an altar or a candle representative of her sacred flame. There are historical symbols of Hekate like torches, keys, and animals, which I discuss in *Keeping Her Keys*. Making sense of the symbols we receive, be it through synchronicities or imagery in meditation or ritual, can be challenging.

Keep in mind, however, that the deeper world is neither linear nor literal. It speaks through emotions and intuitions more so than rational thought. Sometimes the meaning of a symbol we receive in dreams, meditations, synchronicities, or magical connections makes perfect sense when we explore what it means to us. At other times, we are befuddled.

Here are some ways you can begin to make sense of symbols and reveal their layered meaning:

- Consider how you received the symbol—its color, its shape, its motion, its size, its background setting.

- Describe your emotional reaction to the symbol. Were you excited? Calm? Nonplussed? Angry? Fearful? Happy? Content?

- What were you doing when you received the symbol? Dreaming? Meditating? Reading the cards? In ritual? Walking? Shopping?

- Where were you? Symbols can show up in specific locations that are themselves symbolic.

- How was the symbol given to you? Did it just appear, or did someone or something pass it to you? What did the giver do? "Jumper" cards in readings and uncanny synchronicities are two other ways in which symbols can be given.

- Why did you receive the symbol? In dreams, what did you do (if anything) to get it? In meditation or ritual, what were you thinking? Did you have a specific intention? What did you ask the cards?

- When did you receive the symbol? In dreams, pay attention to how old you are and the timeframe for the dream setting. Time of day can also be important. Was it morning? Nighttime? Twilight? Sunrise? Look to astrology for help with synchronicities.[4]

- Describe the physical qualities of the symbol. Is it smooth, rough, or unfinished? Hot or cold? Old or new? Worn or shiny? What color(s) is it? What shape? Does it have any numerical aspects?

- What else happened when you received the symbol? Did you get an auditory message? Did you have the "goosies"? Did you feel any other bodily sensations? Did a song pop into your head? Did someone say or do something that felt connected with the symbol? Did the symbol appear more than once?

- What does it feel as if the symbol means to you?

- Have you had any prior experience with the same or a similar symbol? Do you have ideas about what it means based on this? If yes, explore your age, your environment, or any activity that might be associated with the symbol.

- What had you previously learned about the symbol from secondary sources, like books or the Internet? Does this resonate with your impressions of the symbol? If yes, how so? If no, set the research aside and follow your intuitive perception of the symbol.

- Weave the various aspects of the symbol together into a form by sketching or printing out a picture of it (if you can find one), and then layer on your impressions.

- If you received the symbol in meditation or ritual, create a physical form of it to go deeper into relation with it.

Sigils: Enchanted Crafted Symbols

Sigils are enchanted symbols usually formed by blending together aspects of other symbols like letters, astrological glyphs, and common images like hearts, stars, and moons. They evoke the spirit with which they are attuned. Sigils have been used in magic since Neolithic humans scratched them out on cave walls.

Each of the chapters in this book, beyond the introductory ones, is enhanced through a sigil. All thirteen are pictured below. Before looking ahead to find which goes with each chapter, spend some time exploring them. What emotions surface? What images come onto your mind screen? Are there memories that come through?

Sigils are used to convey meaning, evoke emotions, and spur us into action in all parts of our lives. They can be drawn by hand or created using technology. They can be constructed using ink, paint, herbal infusions, and chalk, or by shaping earth, ash, and salt, or by pouring water or oil.

The most common approach used to create sigils today is to reduce a claim or intention down to its basic structure. It can be helpful to start by creating an acrostic of the focus of your working. For example, in chapter 15, I describe crafting a talisman using the word "real." You can leave the letters in their original form in the language in which you wrote them, or you can use a different language. Or you can use symbols associated with each letter. Strengthen the sigil by fumigating, anointing, or smudging it with the ash of botanicals associated with communication or plants that are specific to your intention.

When working with sigils, consider what emotions come up for you. What plays out in your mind? Can you find the components that comprise the sigil—shapes, number of forms, symbols? What energy do they contribute to the sigil? Engaging in the sigil will amplify your connection to the archetype it evokes. Reproducing the sigil—making it into an altar card or adding it to your journal—can help to align your work with the spirit of the sigil.

Natural Magic

We can connect to Hekate in her many guises through natural magic—crafting of talismans and such using archetypal symbols, sometimes called correspondences.[5] These include plants, stones, and colors. Correspondences possess spirits of their own and are connected to the archetypes that govern them—for instance, a planet. These are known as "signatures." The four elements and the Three Worlds are the seven archetypal forces of which all matter is created.

Symbols are themselves a type of correspondence, like the crafted images known as sigils that summon archetypes and guide us into the mysteries of the deeper world. We use correspondences in our rituals and ceremonies. Our altars are created using them. We can wear them and decorate our homes with them. Understanding the standard correspondences of botanicals further deepens our understanding of their properties. The common correspondences in addition to the elements and planets include zodiacal signs, colors, stones, and animals.

Generally speaking, the spirit of any one of these can be evoked to add depth to a working. Combining colors with a botanical and/or stone and associating this with an archetype renders a very potent form of natural magic. Of course, Hekate has correspondences that have traveled with her across time—certain symbols and certain plants—as well as more recent ones. We have our own unique correspondences as well.

In fact, all things have spiritual as well as material properties—one seen, one hidden. This is the dualistic nature of all that is. That which is not visible draws from the deeper world of archetypes. The two worlds can be described as *form* and *force*. When we work with spirits that have material form—like stones, botanicals, and animals—we bridge the two worlds by taking the physical object and pulling out its mystical properties, thereby creating the third space that is truly the crossroads of modern life (the physical) and the deeper world (the etheric).

Opening up to the spirit of a correspondence is the first step in working with one. The next is to attune yourself or your intention to the spirit. This happens when the energetic signature of a specific correspondence becomes aligned with your purpose or your personal vibration. All spirits have a vibrational essence that is a mix of the archetypal energy plus unique features, including characteristics and stories. This is why our definitions of a correspondence can vary greatly. For example, you may start to work with a correspondence based on the standard properties, but then find that it speaks differently to you. Follow that intuition.

Throughout this book, I invite you into the world of natural magic through altars, talismans, incantations, and other types of sacred creativity. As you contemplate the journey, you can prepare by choosing a winged companion, a sacred container, and a candle, and establishing an altar.

Allies of Spirit and Flesh

Spirits of all sorts have been my companions since I was a small child. I value my spirit guides, from ancestors long dead to my animal and plant spirit companions. I've been helping people connect with, understand, and work with spirit allies of all sorts for several years. They bring a richness to our lives that is difficult to explain until you've felt it. Mine have led me on journeys to other worlds and to the deepest reaches of my inner temple.

Spirit allies are our protectors, companions, and advisors from the deeper world. They are emissaries of the deeper archetypes. Goddesses and other deities awaken in us when the time is right. For many, they are primary allies. As you read through this book, the sacred feminine archetype will come to you, perhaps in many different forms. Allow her to be who she is meant to be for you.

Other forms of spirit allies include beings like angels and ascended ones, ancestors of blood and spirit, and spirits of the natural world. Some may once have known the physical self, like ancestors of flesh or spirit. Others may always have been in spirit form.[6] Some, like beloved animals, are both corporeal and spiritual. Plants and stones are spirit allies.

The tarot, or oracle cards, are collections of spirits. Major arcana cards and the court cards of the minor arcana make excellent spirit guides. Other types of spirit guides can communicate with us through the cards. Listen well. They are already trying to get your attention. Spirits come to us in dreams, send us signs in the physical world, and whisper to our intuition.[7]

Allies can take many forms: deities, angels, animals, departed loved ones, ancestors of spirit, ascended masters, plant devas, past selves, and even quirky little monsters. As in any other relationship, talk to them, be kind to them, and don't use them. They aren't spiritual vending machines that can dole out favors whenever you push their buttons.

Generally, the universe is on our side. But there are harmful spirits out there as well.[8] Keep yourself cleansed of toxic waste and protected. Scrub your body with salt and keep an open dish by the entrance to your home, amplified with a herb like lavender or, better yet, juniper. Some spirits are fierce but still on our side. Shadow allies are our protectors, for instance. Although they can be very intimidating, they are not harmful. You'll know the difference based on your reaction. Are you frightened of them or are they just frightening in general? Think of them as your spiritual bodyguards.

Hekate's Aviary

I recommend developing a close alliance with a winged companion for your journey through Hekate's cave. Avian allies were often associated with Hekate and her companions in art, myths, and religious practices. One beautiful story describes how a beloved goose led Persephone to discover the mysteries of the cave. In this myth, scholars posit that Herkyna, which means "guard dog" or "she who wards off," is an epithet of Hekate. In Lebadea in central Greece, where this story originated, people associated

Herkyna with a *herkos*, a term that was used to describe fences and other types of confining spaces, including a type of net used to catch birds.

In the story, Herkyna encounters Persephone (who was then still Kore, the Maiden) outside of her temple holding tightly onto a goose, which is symbolic of us trying to domesticate our wild soul. As long as we are holding it tightly, it cannot lead us where it wants us to go. We can imagine that Hekate (Herkyna) was counseling Persephone that the way to become a truly sovereign goddess was to let her soul go where it needed to go. Perhaps Hekate was explaining to her that the only way to become whole is through the journey through the sacred cave.

When the goose escapes into a cave, Persephone becomes distraught and travels into the cave, eventually retrieving it from under a stone. As she does this, a river springs up, symbolizing the river that we cross in order to be reborn—the emotional healing found through transcendence. Persephone crosses the river, compelled by a force greater than herself. When she comes to the entrance of a temple, she is met by two serpents coiled around a scepter, forming the caduceus, an ancient symbol of healing and wisdom that was carried by many deities, including the great soul guide and communicator Hermes. Today, the caduceus is used to symbolize the medical profession.

The goose then leads Persephone to Trophonios, an oracular spirit whose name means "nourisher of the mind." Thus, by following the goose into the cave, Persephone finds wisdom. The goose symbolizes Persephone's soul longing for freedom. She begins by trying to contain her true nature, and finishes transformed into wisdom.

This story inspired me to focus on avian allies as our companions on our journey through the cave. Birds associated with Hekate include those from antiquity, like owls, raptors, goldfinches, and geese. Corvids (crows and ravens) often appear with messages. She can also be associated with vultures, as they are agents of her role as Borborophorba, the Filth Eater (see chapter 9). Bats, although not birds, can also be used as avian companions during the journey since they fly and live in caves. The raptor family is symbolic of sovereignty, perspective, and slaying what binds—hawks, for example, Circe's namesake.

Expanding to mythological creatures, dragons often show up as allies, although they are technically not birds. Dragons are Medea's preferred familiar, and Hekate herself was called Drakaina (She-Dragon or She-Serpent). The phoenix may materialize for you as well. But heed this creature's appearance, for it can be a harbinger of a fiery transformation.

The goddess herself can take on wings, enveloping us in her nourishing embrace. Then there are her *angelos*, the awe-inspiring agents of her bidding, her protectors, and the conveyers of her messages. In mythology, Hekate is mothered by Asteria or Nyx. The quail was sacred to the former, and the latter was often portrayed with wings. Insects, particularly bees, butterflies, and moths, are often messengers as well.

Gone are the flowers,
Forsaken are the fields.
Crow and I remain.
Gone are the timid,
Afraid of freedom.
Hawk and I remain.
Gone is the light,
And those who need it.
Owl and I remain.
Together we stand,
Answering Hekate's claim.

Any of these fabulous winged creatures can be our allies as we journey through darkness to wholeness in Hekate's cave. Your avian companion will find you—perhaps in dreams or perhaps on your daily commute. Or perhaps you already have a special winged companion. From the whirring, wheel-inspiring wryneck to the mysterious owl, birds are wonderful allies. However your avian ally comes to you, explore the archetypes it represents; create talismans to honor it and to summon its energy.[9]

The Cista Mystica

The *Cista Mystica*, or sacred box, is a container to hold your symbols, sigils, and other objects—a sort of sacred suitcase for storing the souvenirs you accumulate as you journey through the cave. Consider this container an enchanted box, a form of what is sometimes called sympathetic magic, meaning that it is something physical that is connected to the deeper world of archetypes. Sacred boxes were a vital part of the ancient temples to Hekate, Demeter, and Persephone.

While Cista Mystica specifically refers to a sacred container, it also expresses the idea of the Inner Temple that is symbolized by the cave and was also found in a larger form within ancient goddess sanctuaries.[10] Known as the *megaron* (from the Greek root for the word "cave"), it was the place where sacrifices were made.[11] This most likely stemmed from earlier practices of using caves as temples. In fact, the megaron was a central feature of the ancient Greek world. In temples, it referred to the inner area and featured a hearth. The same term was also used to describe the central part of a palace or a house, with one side being open.

You can create your own Cista Mystica as a sacred container for the symbols that come to you through your cave journey. Mark the completion of each chapter by choosing a symbol from your work therein and add it to the container. The form and design of the Cista Mystica is entirely up to you. Every year in late summer, my students, my staff, and I create a new Cista Mystica. They are incredibly varied, from the more expected lidded wooden box to small bookshelves. I recommend putting two symbols in it to start out—one that is symbolic of your journey so far and one that reflects who you are becoming.

Hekate's Stones

The journey into Hekate's cave is the blending of torch and stone. Stones are born of the essential fire that fuels all of life, deep within the earth. The spark ignites, the lava flows, and the stone is birthed. The torch begets the stone, and the stone is stronger than anything else. This symbolizes the power of the cave; it cannot crumble. Hekate is steady and true.

Stones have energetic properties based on their mineral composition, their crystalline structure, their archetypal connections, and their mythic associations. In addition, their color also has energetic properties. This creates an archetype of their own that is reflected in their standard associations. Some, but not all, stones have their own unique personality that may or may not correspond to the standard properties.

Crafting a talisman out of stone is a beautiful way to connect with the strength of Hekate and her cave. Having a "touchstone" as a magical talisman dates back thousands of years. In ancient times, obsidian, jasper, and other stones were etched with images of Hekate to create what were often called "magical gems." Use your stone to link you with the healing energy of Hekate and her cave. Whenever you are stressed, connect with the stone to be nourished by her healing.

Throughout this book, I make recommendations for stones and crystals that will augment the rituals and exercises. I've stuck with the ones I teach most often: amethyst, black obsidian, clear quartz, fluorite, garnet, moonstone, red jasper, rose quartz, selenite, shungite, smoky quartz, and tiger's eye. Stones often show up in our lives just when we need them. Be open to random rocks and sparkly crystals that present themselves to you. On the other hand, using these stones as correspondences may lead you to research their properties. Follow your intuition. My first choices for books are *Crystal Basics: The Energetic, Healing, and Spiritual Power of 200 Gemstones* by Nicholas Pearson and *The Book of Stones: Who They Are and What They Teach* by Robert Simmons and Naisha Ahsian.

Although these stones have many properties, I've selected one for each archetype discussed in the coming chapters as a correspondence for the overall energy found therein. Unless I've specified otherwise, any of the subtypes of the stones listed can be used.

- Triformis: fluorite for learning and expanding awareness.

- Drakaina: amethyst, which is an excellent helper for awakening the soul, is also especially good for encouraging meditation.

- Enodia: smoky quartz as a talisman symbolic of transitions.

- Propylaia: rose quartz, to help you set (and maintain) boundaries.

- Chthonia: black obsidian—a real powerhouse. I've placed it in this lesson because this is when we first enter Hekate's cave, invoking this stone spirit as an ally for the entire journey.

- Lampadios: tiger's eye for balance, awakening intuition, and prosperity.

- Borborophorba: red jasper for protection and endurance during the catharsis process.

- Skotia: clear quartz for clarity of vision and purpose in the deepest dark of the cave, and to unify the energy of the previous stones into a harmonious field.

- Paionios: rhodochrosite for self-acceptance and healing, especially the relational kind—the stone for our time with the Healer archetype.

- Psychopomp: mysterious shungite for soul retrieval because it works at the root in a granular way, creating space and absorbing the returning soul shards.

- Rixipyle: garnet to calm you down when the energy of the Chain Breaker can have you in a tizzy. It stabilizes the body, mind, and soul.

- Anassa Eneroi: rainbow moonstone for rebirth and your initiation into the mysteries of the cave. Rainbow moonstone brings joy, offers protection, and is stunningly gorgeous—a perfect symbol for completing the journey and being reborn into your unique wholeness.

- Kore: selenite helps keep you in alignment as you emerge into your new life. A selenite wand is especially useful.

Geology and mineralogy speak to the scientific side of this practice. Learn the basics about the different types of rocks and delve into crystalline structure if you're so inclined. Those structures correspond to various sacred geometric shapes, which is fascinating. Piezoelectricity is the name given to the electrical currents found in many stones.

The mineral composition of stones can be related to planets and deities as well. For example, the granite that is ubiquitous where I live is classified as plutonic rock, so named after Pluto himself. There are some great books about stones, including those by Nicholas Pearson.

I always encourage a mixed-methods approach. It's important to know the established properties, methods, and applications for anything, including working with stones. However, when it comes right down to it, intuition is just as important. If a rock speaks to you, work with it. Seeing the world through your Third Eye is also a great way to get past the glamour of sparkly objects. Seeing the soul of a stone is much more beautiful.

Working with stones that occur naturally where you live is one way of practicing real stone-spirit magic. This can start with just being more en up to the possibilities around

and call out to the spirits of the

Don't miss those stones that want

ot paying attention. Purchasing sec-

e a spirit a welcoming home. This also

es will disappear on their own.

with which I have a relationship, from my

h a big hunk of smoky quartz to my new

ragon. Carrying stones in your pockets and

cks in your bra!) attunes them to your energy.

ers as you go about your daily business. It's like

Crock-Pot—little effort = great results.

The Altar

Your altar provides a home and working platform for your sacred objects—the Cista Mystica, your bird symbol, your stones, and your candle. Altars to Hekate are often built on a tray, in keeping with the ancient altar known as an *eschara*. You can add other objects as you journey through the cave. Some of these I'll discuss in the following chapters; others will be unique to you.

Assembling these objects on your altar can leave you energized. There is something more going on than just arranging objects on a tray. Think of this as an awakening. Knowing that your life needs to change drastically is an awakening. For many of us, this comes after a long period of living according to others' terms. We have been invalidated through word and deed long enough. I liken this awakening to a serpent stirring in the very center of your being.

The first step of any journey is to become aware that there is the potential for one. Something in the wind changes, bringing in the scent of a different way of being in the world. To me, this is the awakening of the soul that exerts a pressure on us to change. As it awakens, the serpent—an archetype of the Triple Goddess—hisses that we are much more than the past, this moment, and our embodied self. It tells us there is a deeper world where wholeness is found. Perhaps dangling a key from its tongue, the serpent makes us uncomfortable in our own skin and the numbness evaporates. We become unsettled. We often call this anxiety, but it's different. This unsettlement is the desire for something *to change*.

The serpent can be seen as the soul opening its eyes, forcing you to expand your field of vision. As your vision improves, things start to become clear. Unsurprisingly, this awakening often brings forward your intuition and your connection to the deeper world. You can see the shimmer of Hekate's torches, illuminating the way to her cave.

Rituals

Rituals are a way of connecting to the deeper world through words and actions. And yet, rituals are part of everyday life as well, from how we make our coffee in the morning to our bedtime routine. Spiritual rituals are beautiful ways to step into the deeper world. These can be spontaneous, like when we are struck by awe when contemplating the moon, or planned, as with the rituals in this book. Intentional spiritual rituals can be completely intuitive or ceremonial, with specific guidelines and certain objectives. The actions and words in the rituals I teach are carefully developed to guide the seeker gently to a state of transcendence, opening the way to the deeper world of archetypes, and perhaps even transcending regular consciousness.

The three rituals in the coming chapters have been well honed by hundreds of students. Consider them spirits unto themselves, carrying with them support and wisdom. Do the best you can with what you have when undertaking them. Reside in the Temple of Good Enough. You are good, and the ritual will bring goodness. You are enough: completely worthy of the transcendent, and of Hekate. Whatever you've been able to do as preparation is enough.

> *My body is the temple,*
> *My mind is the altar,*
> *And my soul the shrine upon it.*
> *My life is the ritual.*
> *I am sacred ground.*

Entering Hekate's Cave

The Sacred Fire

Imagine having your sacred container and your avian ally beside you as you face Hekate's cave while contemplating the journey to come. As you peer inside, you see a distant light—a glow from Hekate's torches that beckons you into her nourishing darkness. Something about this resonates deep within you, and you feel curiously compelled to enter this subterranean refuge of the goddess. That is the call of the numinous, which resonates with your soul.

Candles are symbolic of this illumination. Any candle that speaks to you, even if it is battery powered, is suitable. I recommend having a fresh candle to light as you begin this book, and then lighting it each day as part of the rituals and exercises I discuss. The three central rituals in this book —the Ritual of Catharsis (see chapter 9), the Soul Retrieval Journey (see chapter 12), and the Rebirth Ritual (see chapter 14)—are all augmented with a special candle.

After each ritual, continue to light the candle as you feel led. A favorite part of the rituals I teach is transitioning from one cycle to the next by illuminating the new candle with the flame of the old, and then extinguishing the former one.

Practica: Threefold Ritual

All the rituals that I teach include three "keys"—cleansing, protection, and invocation. The last component can take many forms, from a general blessing to a specific focus. I call this basic structure the Threefold Ritual. Here's an overview that you can adapt according to your needs.

Stand in front of your altar, place your hands on your root, pointing down, and say:

> I banish all that blocks and binds; I enter into this ritual with sincerity and trust.

Take time to sink your roots into the ground beneath, releasing all that harms you while tethering yourself to the earth. Now place your open hands at your heart center and say:

> I am protected from all harm.

Allow your heart center to open, connecting you to the natural world. Say:

I bless myself, my beloveds, and this ritual.

You can ignite any incense at this point. Place both hands pointing up with thumbs on your forehead. Stretch up your branches to the Starry Road above, connecting to the energy of the cosmos, and say:

I come seeking guidance.

You can specify your invocation from here.

Spend time in this presence, allowing visions and messages to come through. When you are ready, pull down the branches of your higher self over your forehead. Pull your middle self over your heart center. Finally, pull your roots and your lower self up from the earth.

Practica: Ritual Incantation

Incantations render life into an object crafted using natural magic. While I thoroughly believe that such words are best spoken from our own souls, here's an incantation template that you can customize for your talismans and more. It is based on candle magic.

Light the candle and hold it at your heart center over the object, saying:

Sacred Flame, bring this to life.
It speaks of the mysteries, of healing, and wholeness.
In the name of Hekate and her allies, Sacred Flame,
Render life to this.
Spirit made flesh.

While encircling the object in a counterclockwise direction three times, recite these words:

Cleanse this, Sacred Flame.
Spirit made flesh.

Bring the candle back above the object at your heart. Then circle it three times in a clockwise motion, saying:

Protect this, Sacred Flame.
Spirit made flesh.

Bring the candle back above the object at your heart and say:

Awaken as companion on the journey,
Helpmate and guide,
Blessing us both.
As I speak it,
So it becomes.
Hail Hekate and her allies.
Hail the Sacred Flame.

Practica: Working with Stones

When you get a new stone, open yourself up to its spirit. See your energy currents reaching down into its crystalline structure. What is there that needs to be removed? There are many ways to go about this. Psychic surgery to remove the blight is one approach. Fumigating the stone with smoke from an ethically sourced sage wand or sweetgrass braid can be very effective. Once cleansed, let the stones further recover on a bed of soil, sand, or salt. Drawing the moon into stones is another way to help them release the past. They've come a long way to meet you; treat them as you would any welcome, weary traveler.

Connect with the stone spirit by holding it in your hands. See your Third Eye opening, unleashing a cord toward the stone. Feel the connection; relax into the moment. Give the stone space. Don't smother it energetically, unless, of course, that is what you are trying to do. Ask the stone spirit: "What is there for me to know about you?" Listen to any messages. When you are doing this simple technique, you may find that you are being pulled to a deeper connection with the stone spirit.

Practica: Quotidia Candle Ceremony

I teach a three-part daily practice that is symbolic of the triplicity of Hekate. It is known as *Quotidia* (from the Latin for "daily"). It begins with lighting a candle and reciting a mantra or prayer.[12] I recommend beginning your journey in Hekate's cave with a new candle adorned with symbols that feel right to you. Do this whenever it is right for you. The time before dawn, just before the day begins, is when I do my own sacred practice. Lighting the candle in darkness evokes the feeling of the cave. I encourage you to create this ambiance.

Simply light the candle, recite your chosen sacred words, and allow yourself to soften into the flame. Elevate the energy by circling the candle three times counterclockwise, envisioning any harmful energies from body, mind, and surroundings being cleansed away. Then circle it three times clockwise for protection. End by holding it at your heart center and feeling its nourishing blessing within and all around you. Spend time connecting with your avian ally, allowing its wisdom to speak to you. I'll talk to you about the other two parts of this daily practice—meditation and the Enodia Oracle—in coming chapters.

> *I light this candle to ignite my soul fire, flame that burns within.*
> *I light this candle connecting to the Sacred Fire of Hekate.*
> *By moving it counterclockwise, I banish and cleanse.*
> *Circling it clockwise, I am protected.*
> *I hold it at my heart, knowing I have all I need to be healthy and whole.*
> *I extinguish this candle of the soul fire,*
> *Knowing that this light cannot be put out,*
> *And that it is always burning bright.*
> *As I speak it,*
> *It becomes so.*

Chapter 2
Kleis: The Keys

I claim the Key of Catharsis,
Letting go of what blocks and binds.
I claim the Key of Retrieval,
Calling back what was lost.
I claim the Key of Rebirth,
Emerging whole.

For centuries, long before the Greeks learned of her, Hekate was understood as an expression of the archetypal Mother of All—presiding over the natural rhythm of the universe. She was Kleidoukhos, the Keeper of Keys to all things.[1] She held the keys to the everyday world and the deeper realm, as did all faces of the Great Mother.[2] This spirit was known by names including Inanna, Cybele, and Demeter. Isis, one expression of her, was known as "She of 10,000 Names." What is shared by these figures is that her womb is the font from which all life springs, and to which all return.

The ancients performed important rituals in caves, perhaps symbolizing the Mother's great uterus. The waters that gush forth are the force that fuels life, death, and everything in between. Inspired by these ancient rites, I've developed a series of three gates through which seekers pass on their way to wholeness. These gates focus our energy on the three key components of psychospiritual healing—catharsis, retrieval, and renewal. The gate of catharsis is traversed by letting go of what burdens us, thereby creating space for what we've lost along our journey. The gate of retrieval is where we retrieve parts of ourselves that may have become lost. Finally, at the gate of rebirth, we re-emerge from the interior womb of healing.

The River Road

The source of this healing power is the natural world, of which we are a part. Our culture sees medicine as only curative and as disconnected from the natural world. It can be challenging for those programmed by today's society to see the goddess as healing and to understand her as the bestower of this power. But Hekate restores the true knowledge that medicine is all that is good for the mind, body, and soul. Over the thousands of years that humans have tried to comprehend her, Hekate was assigned many roles in an attempt to understand her healing power. Yet there is a force far greater than our limited mortal understanding that calls us to pass through her gates and enter her depths.

From her cave deep within the earth, Hekate stirs her cauldron of stars, which pour forth to become the river that creates the ocean and then evaporates to reappear as the stars that fall back to earth as rain. We can enter this river, which leads us to the healing darkness of her cave, but first we pass through the gate guarding the entrance.

This force leads us down a River Road that pours from her cauldron in the heart of her cave. It calls us to the crossroads, where we stand on the bank of this river—a river that is a road, a road that is a river. We see this River Road through the eyes of the soul. And this looping road always leads us back to where we are meant to be. Our souls long to dive deep into this river, but our shadows may tell us that the water is too deep. It is not. We are strong swimmers.

Have you ever felt that you are constantly swimming against the current? That no matter how hard you try, you get nowhere? That is the opposite of swimming in this deeper river that is the flow of Hekate. When we finally live from soul, we become more connected to our beloved goddess; we enter into the flow of her river. We need to learn skills for shifting from battling the current of the false river toward competency in navigating her deeper waters. We can choose to tread water and circle her crossroads in endless laps. Or we can choose to pass through Hekate's gates and enter her cave. The cave journey is where our souls learn to swim.

You've almost certainly already been immersed in this deep river that leads to the cave. In those moments when we forget ourselves, when time becomes nonlinear and all the nonsense of the exterior world is washed away, we are in the flow of this deeper river. This may happen while in a dream, during a transcendent experience, when doing sacred crafting, or when out in the natural world. Reflecting upon these times can help us to see how connected we truly are to Hekate and her deeper world.

Hekate's cave symbolizes the dark, wet womb of the primordial goddess. When we dare look at its watery entrance, our connection to her is reflected back. When we enter the first gate, we begin to release the past. We see with the eyes of the soul that we are *agape* (pure love) and *phoberos* (fear), light and dark, the past and the potential, breaking free of burdens, being cleansed in the surface to explore our own depths. It is a return to whence we came. The waters are deeply cleansing, releasing us from the past.

But first, we learn to be comfortable with our image reflected upon the water's surface. We may envision the water as a cascade flowing over the entrance to the cave; we may know it as a great well. Or we may see the entrance to the cave as a submerged portal. In ancient times, the entrance to the Underworld was seen in these ways. This realm is mystical, archetypal. We cannot confine how we perceive it to one narrow vision.

Keeper of the Keys

Hail, Hekate Kleidoukhos,
Keeper of the Keys of the Universe.
Accept my gratitude for your
Protection, guidance, and wisdom.

There are many ancient titles for Hekate that evoke her power to crash through our humdrum existence and compel us to dive into her depths—Chain Breaker, Earth Shaker, Gatekeeper. But perhaps it is her role as

Kleidoukhos—Keeper of the Keys—that intrigues us the most, since these are the keys to our own souls. As we come to the river that leads to the cave, we hear them rattling and know that we have a decision to make. Do we refuse to pass through the gate, or do we embark on a journey inward? Because these gates *will* open, whether we enter intentionally or not.

Entering the cave with purpose, rather than remaining unconscious in our own lives, makes all the difference. The gates that block us from entering were constructed by our shadow selves. In a sense, they keep us protected. They shield us from harm. Yet they also block us from our center. When the soul breaks through these barriers, the gates to Hekate's cave open and a warm glow, or even a raging inferno, takes up occupancy within us. This is the soul responding to the sound of her rattling the keys to our souls.

I had lived outside of my own life for most of it. Perhaps you can relate. Life happened to me instead of me happening to it. But gates will open and, if we are aimless wanderers, they invariably open onto Underworld journeys that don't lead us through the cave. They lead us through the shadow realms of Tartarus, where we loop around repeating the same patterns of dysfunction.

The day I decided to show up in my own life, I uttered what I consider to be the most powerful prayer: *Help Me!* That unlocked the journey back to my own soul, down Hekate's River Road and into the cave. As she always does, the goddess shook me to the core. Becoming unbound from the chains of the past is an upheaval. I let go of almost everything that others thought were signs of living a good life. What I found was truth and wholeness beyond anything I'd ever known. To take up a key offered by Hekate is to lean into her mysteries. We become voyagers in her deeper world, where we realize that there is no separation between the symbolic and the literal. We occupy our embodiment and live fully in the soul.

It was this merger of everyday life with the transcendent that inspired me to call my work Keeping Her Keys. I have always been a seeker of the mysteries. Hekate—who was called Anima Mundi, the World Soul, by ancient philosophers—signifies that which I stretch into. She guards the mysteries of all life with her cosmic keys. In this role, she reflects my sovereignty over my own life—the coming together of the mystical and the mundane. It is here that I find the crossroads of modern life and the deeper world.

One of the most wonderful gifts of the Keeper of Keys is how our vision expands to see her signatures in our lives. Her archetypal role as Kleidoukhos positions Hekate at the crossroads of all there is. She is the Gatekeeper who permits entrance to those who seek her with an open heart and mind. To those familiar with Hekate, this role is intuitive. We know, deep in our souls, that keys are one of her main symbols, along with fire and her Wheel. To us, these keys represent her primal role as World Soul. They unlock her mysteries. They free the binding. To the ancients, the goddess was multifaceted, unhampered by restrictions placed on her by the powerful. As Keeper of Keys, she held the knowledge of all things.

Trusting ourselves to go into Hekate's cave is daunting, yet there is a light within that resonates with the archetypal symbol of the goddess as Torchbearer. Imagine she holds two torches high up, illuminating her quivering keys, standing just beyond reach, on the other side of the gate at the entrance of the cave. The River Road is numinous, shifting, spiraling in currents of energy. Her torches reflect upon it, igniting the water with luminescence. The pale moon shines above, and the creatures of her garden take heed of her presence.

Sacred Darkness–Artificial Light

To the ancients in the area around the Mediterranean, caves were very sacred places. Unlike temples, where rational order prevailed in religious ceremonies, caverns were mystical places for deep communion with the spirits, and were of particular importance as a place of connection with the gods and goddesses.[3] Hekate's priestesses held court in them—for instance, the Sibyl of Cumae and the Pythia.[4] There were also pits within temples that symbolized the cave and the Underworld (megaras) where she was venerated and where offerings were left. We also know that chthonic altars, known as *eschara,* were used as well.[5] In fact, the Underworld itself can be seen as analogous to the cave, although the cave represents one "chamber" in the vast expanse of the spiritual subterranean. But the deities of the Underworld, like Hekate and Persephone, were associated not only with death and spirits, but also with healing and wealth.

Thus, the cave can be seen as a place of sacred darkness, a place where we awaken to our own souls, a place where we turn toward the primordial *hieros pyr,* an ancient epithet of Hekate that means the sacred fire that burns deep inside of us. Our journey through this life—the difficulties, the pain, and our quest for wholeness—calls us into the sacred darkness of Hekate's cave. Venturing into the cave takes great courage. We live in a world that denies the healing power of the womb of the archetypal Great Mother. But this sacred darkness is nigh in our world, with great upheaval and change everywhere. We can return to the dark, wet womb from which we came to save not only ourselves, but also our planet. The Mysteries at Eleusis offer insight into how the mysteries of the cave were understood in ancient Greece (see chapter 6).[6]

Phoberos, which means "fearful," is one of the titles from The Greek Magical Papyri that evokes a force far greater than us. It carries the dual meaning of being afraid and of instilling terror. In *Keeping Her Keys,* I presented an exercise that offered a way to explore both love and fear. There is power in this exercise, and it has become a favorite of many. Phoberos represents our shadow selves, the parts of ourselves that we fear. But the thing about fear is that what we often fear the most is our own ability to be fearsome. While our shadow turns our fear toward our true selves, it is also the power-seat of our ability to be toxic to others.

> *There is a light so deep inside of me*
> *That nothing can extinguish.*
> *It has burned through a thousand lifetimes,*
> *Always leading me back to the center.*
> *My soul fire knows the way,*
> *As it responds to the dim light of Hekate's torches.*

The world, with its chaos, hassles, and pains, diminishes the illumination of what enlightens our inner depths. Think of this as a false solar energy, whereas Hekate offers her lunar torchlight as a way to the truth. It is to be expected that we fear the dark when we've buried so much in there. As a culture, we are conditioned to believe that the artificial light offered through the quick dopamine hits of social media and consumerism is a salve. Instead, we become numb to all but the incessant anxiety these things elicit. When Hekate calls us, she cleaves through numbness and pain, shaking us up. She holds the mirror under our noses and asks us if we truly are content to remain trapped in the fluorescent glare of what caused the distress in the first place.

We live in a time when darkness is denigrated, and we are encouraged to live purely in artificial light. This denial of the need to descend into our depths to be whole, sometimes called "toxic positivity," has led to a society that is obsessed with falsity. We see it everywhere, from social media to children's toys. Our world has become so blindingly bright that we cannot breathe. But the paradox of telling us that positivity is the key is that this only makes us more fearful. We are afraid that, if we give voice to our fears, we will be judged negatively. Yet it is only by stepping out of this glaring light and recognizing the fears that are harbored within the shadow that we can overcome them.

In psychological parlance, the soul is viewed as the depths of the psyche. The work of the cave is thus to turn inward, away from the artificial light. This is not to deny the importance of the brilliant sunlight, but as an antidote to too much falsity. The shadow flourishes in the artificial light of continually being in character because it is ignorant of the soul until we turn to it with love. This is a daunting process that we may fear in and of itself. However, the way to wholeness, what is called individuation in depth psychology, invites us to turn inward. Only by turning away from the solar glare do we connect to Hekate and her deeper world. We bring into our consciousness our inner phoberos, which is conditioned by society.[7] Then we embark on the road to wholeness, overcoming the fragmentation of the shadow (differentiation).

Fear of Uncertainty

There is a fear of uncertainty that is ingrained in many of us. We need to control as much as possible. But embracing our sacred wildness means accepting uncertainty. Our incessant need to control is often born out of our deep-seated anxieties. Perfectly understandable. I certainly will always be a recovering control freak. But I'm inviting you to get gentle with this part of yourself. Understand where your anxieties are coming from, and then reassure yourself that uncertainty is a natural part of life that is to be expected.

Another fear we have been conditioned to accept is fear of the sacred feminine. That which is feminine—that is to say intuitive, emotional, generative, and destructive—is vilified in today's society. This is evidenced in the denial of the true female form.[8] We see photoshopped images of women with plastic surgery, vast amounts of makeup, and stuffed into confining clothes, for example. It seems as if every few weeks there is another research report on the damning impacts of social media, especially on girls and women.[9]

Entering the cave separates us from this madness. You may stand alone. Perhaps you're reading this book in secret, lest your housemates find you are interested in Hekate and her mysteries. I applaud your courage. There is a light within you that is designed to withstand the artificial light of the world. Fluorite is the stone that helps to illuminate that light within.

All this programming leads us to fear our own power—that which is intuitive, eternal, emotional, and without restriction. We also become fearful of our ability to evoke fear in others, and we ignore our rightful rage. Anger, anxiety, and even guilt all have their correct place. When we use them to fuel our remorse or righteous rage, we grow in strength. But in the shadow's hands, they immobilize and weaken us.

When we enter the cave, we choose love and embrace our fears. We are both agape—pure illuminated love and trust—and phoberos—the totality of all fears.

Practica: Self Reflection

Societal conditioning and invalidation by others may cause us to be uncomfortable with our appearance. The journey through the cave will show you that you are splendid, exactly as you are meant to be, while offering healing for maximizing your authentic appearance. The shadow tells us we are not appealing; the soul says we are reflections of the goddess.

This practice can help you see a reflection of your true self. I recommend sitting with reflective water—out in nature if possible. Or use a bowl or even a mirror to contemplate your true beauty. Allow your gaze to soften, opening up to what I call "soul vision." Feel the power of these dualities within you. Reflect on them in your journal.

Chapter 3
Triformis: The Transformation

Triformis.
Triformis.
Triformis.
Eternal, ever-changing
Triple Goddess.
Transform me.
Becoming real and true
As I follow you.
Mistress of Transformation.
I walk with you.

The archetypal view of the sacred feminine as three-formed is found across times and cultures, and Hekate as the Triple Goddess is an image that enchants the mind and heart.[1] It is she who sees past, present, and future. In modern times, she's often depicted as Maiden, Mother, and Crone, although the historicity of this is debatable.[2] She wears many faces yet is always familiar. Her eternal nature is as constant as her perpetual transformation.

Hekate morphs into the vision we need to see. At the cultural level, she is twisted into forms that can be frightening or benevolent. She shape-shifts, at times with dizzying speed, even before our eyes can make sense of her last presentation. Yet she is the great unifier, which can seem contradictory given her shifting, transforming nature. She embodies the maxim: the only thing constant is change itself.

It is in the spaces between these shifting forms that we find wholeness. The three heads or bodies sometimes used to depict the Triple Goddess speak to the healing of the split between self, shadow, and soul. Because Triformis is one, we become whole. The threads of time—those tiny fibers in her great Wheel of Time from which our lives are woven—stitch us back together when we journey through shadow to soul, leading us to our authentic, empowered selves. Hekate is stone, blood, and air. Fixed, pulsing, and fleeting. As we integrate the healing of soul retrieval, we face our own reflections, finding that we are the same. We *are* Triformis. We are continually transforming. The question here, as we approach the cave, is how do we transform into our most authentic selves?

Our awakening to Hekate and her deeper world often comes when we feel defeated, enslaved by pain, and in the thrall of shadow. We see here again the triplicity of the goddess, for we are shadow, self, and soul. Our dance of wholeness is that of Triformis, as we weave the three together. I'm often asked why many who have endured great trauma and hardship are drawn to Hekate and her mysteries. Certainly, she is soul; she calls us back to our own. Beyond this, I feel it is her power of transformation that reverberates with those who have been grievously injured by the outer world. In our rituals and magic, we find the strength to heal ourselves because we see the *possibility* she embodies. The separate lines merge into one sigil that thrums with potentiality. The simple piece of string becomes a talisman that we wear to guide us forward in truth.

But there is always uncertainty. The Fates keep Hekate's Wheel of Time to themselves, allowing only glimpses into their secrets. The ego—the small "s" self—craves certainty because it pushes back against the transformation underway. There can be great tension between self and soul during the integration process. The self wants everything to be orderly and linear, while the soul knows that disarray and circularity are the essence of the Triple Goddess. Transformation is an alchemical process in which we weave what was lost back into the formula that is our own personal philosopher's stone. Triformis is the ultimate alchemist who holds the key to the heart of her Wheel, where the essential stone/soul is contained in her fire.

The Triple Goddess

Come here to me, goddess of night, beast-slayer,
And heed my prayers, Selene,
Who rises and sets at night, Triple Headed, Triple Named.
Mistress of Night and the Underworld, sacred.
'Round whom the star-traversing nature of the universe spins.
Give heed to me, Lady, I ask of you.
You have established every worldly thing,
For you engendered everything on earth
And from the sea and every race in turn.
Of winged birds who seek their nests again.
Mother of all, who bore Love, Aphrodite.
Lamp-bearer, shining and aglow, Selene.[3]

There are two distinct forms of the Triple Goddess—one that portrays her as having three aspects contained within herself, and another that portrays her as part of a trio. Historically, when she is depicted with animal characteristics, the creator of the images is attempting to capture how deeply she is connected to the natural world.[4] But Hekate is also part of many goddess trios, from her alliance with Persephone and Demeter, to her familial triplicity with Circe and Medea. She is also entwined with Artemis and Selene as they preside over the moon.

Hekate is often depicted holding her keys, brandishing her torch, and raising her blade in three-formed statues and images. In fact, this is one of her most iconic images. She is shown with either three heads or three bodies in many ancient and contemporary depictions. This image of the Triple Goddess has been with us since at least the fifth century BCE, when her eponymous statue overlooked Athens.[5] Looking down from her tower, she could see in all directions, conveying her role as guardian over the city state. Over centuries and across cultures, her tripartite figure has been used in various works of art. Sometimes her heads are those of animals, reflecting her different attributes and her connection to the natural world.

While this may have been the intention of early images depicting her with animal heads and of the words calling her by different bestial epithets, as in The Greek Magical Papyri, later depictions of Hekate that described her with animal heads may have been designed to portray her as nefarious and diminish her veneration.[6] As Triformis, we see Hekate portrayed as the mighty Triple Goddess, as the Great Mother, and as a hideous figure connected to "primitive" people. Today, as the sacred feminine has once again gained footing in popular culture, she has transformed yet again.

Considerable attention has been given to the meaning of the triple-headed goddess beyond her ability to see everything. Today we can interpret this image as symbolic of the contemporary interpretation of Maiden, Mother, and Crone. Historically, Hekate has been linked to maidens and mothers by some writers, perhaps indicating that she reserved the role of Crone for herself.[7] Certainly, her wisdom has endured throughout the ages and across traditions. This is the healing power of Triformis—she who is always changing yet remains the same.

There are many ways to interpret the Triple Goddess. The structure I used to create my own practice synthesizes her many epithets, historical depictions, and personal gnosis into three aspects:

> Hekate's three overarching roles as Guardian, Guide, and Gate-keeper merge Her portrayal in many ancient texts. From the ancient connection with the moon to the modern neo-pagan version of the triple goddess, the common thread is Hekate in the roles of Guardian, Guide, and Gatekeeper. This reflects Hekate's long history as a Three-Formed Goddess but adapts the ancient epithets to our modern understanding. The ancient epithets associated with this model of Hekate are Enodia, Lampadios, and Kleidoukhos. Enodia literally means "of the way" or "at the crossroads" and is most indicative of Her role as a guide for our earth-bound journey. Lampadios means "Lamp-bearer," representing Hekate as the light in the darkness of the Under World. Hekate as the Keeper of the Keys sits at the gate

of the Upper World, protecting Her mysteries and waiting for us to reach out for each new key along our life's journey.[8]

She is the Gatekeeper who grants entrance into her mysteries, she is the Guardian who keeps us safe as we do the inner work, and she is the Guide who leads us onward.

In my studies of modern shamanism, I learned about the Three Worlds and the three selves.[9] To me, these map onto the threefold nature of Hekate, and I incorporated them into my teaching. Eventually, these keys became the foundational meditation of awakening the soul serpent (see chapter 4).

The Three Worlds are threads that rest within each of the *loci spirita* (energy centers) of the root, heart, and crown. They weave together when we allow them to work on us through our meditations and rituals, and whenever we explore the deeper world that is Hekate's domain. They are braided together within Hekate's Wheel, a million tiny threads of individual lives, times, and places. These are the threads that the fateful sisters spin (see below).

These worlds are energetic realms that are connected to the material world. The Upper World refers to the celestial realm; some call it heaven. I tend to refer to it as the Starry Road. The Middle World is the force of everyday life. This is where we live and is somewhat similar to some ancient philosophers' view of the material world. The Lower World is the realm of some spirits, including animal spirits. This world meshes well with the ideas of the Underworld in certain historical traditions, as in the religions that honored Hekate in ancient times.

We explore Hekate's Three Worlds through her cave, her garden, and her temple. When we map these onto the Wheel of Time, the cave connects with the time of decay, the garden symbolizes the return of the growing season, and her glorious temple embodies the months when all the world is in full bloom. The night is her cave; the morning until midday is her garden; the period between midday and sunset is her temple. These worlds are reflected in us in the intuitive lower self, the active middle self, and the intellectual higher self. In terms of our totality, the three realms of Hekate can be seen to correspond to the soul, the shadow, and the self.

Hekate, Persephone, and Demeter

Hekate, guide and protector.
Wise woman speaking truth to power,
Protecting the vulnerable.
Persephone, began as the nameless girl.
Became benevolent queen who turned the seasons,
And guide of souls.
Demeter, knew the pain, tried to protect her daughter,
Raged until balance was restored.
Together, the whole trinity,
The above, the below, and the in-between.

The goddesses Hekate, Persephone, and Demeter were entwined through myths and practices in the ancient world in a glorious web of mystery. Hekate emerges from her cave to console the maiden Persephone, thereby demonstrating the healing powers of the darkness. All three goddesses are certainly at work within us and through us. We can be Persephone, thrust into misery. We can be Demeter, raging against unfairness. Or we can be Hekate, acting as mediator for others in distress. In Persephone's mythology, Hekate comes to her when no one else will, and she also gives advice to Demeter in her sadness. There is some evidence that all three were venerated in the same temples, and some scholars believe that Hekate played a central role in the mystery cult at Eleusis. Most important, all three offer healing for the soul. They come to us to show us how to persevere and go deeper into healing. They teach us that wholeness is found in their mysteries. In fact, we can integrate the lessons of their myths into our own healing journey.

As mediator, Hekate helps to negotiate the terms of Persephone's time in the Underworld and takes on the responsibility for being her guardian. She continues this role as Persephone's guide back and forth from her subterranean life to the solar world, thus turning the seasons. This journey to and from the Underworld represents our own journey into Hekate's cave, for Persephone found her wholeness only through facing her own fears, accepting her circumstances, and eventually becoming the benevolent queen of the depths.[10]

In fact, our journey *is* that of Persephone. We set out as the bone-weary traveler who has suffered greatly, seeking the respite of the cave, all the while knowing that the path forward will be rocky at times. Our Demeter, focused solely on the outer world, rests while we explore our interior landscape, to be reunited when we emerge from the cave born anew. Their soul healing is embodied in this reunion into wholeness.

A psychological analysis of the Hekate-Persephone-Demeter triad reveals that each is contained within us, as different aspects of the sacred feminine. Hekate is the soul, the mediator between the psyche (Persephone) and the persona (Demeter). Demeter had an interior life, and Persephone certainly had an external one. Hekate walks between the worlds, as does our soul, guiding us along the way.

Moreover, in the Homeric *Hymn to Demeter*, Persephone is depicted as Kore, the Maiden, while Demeter is described as Mater, the Mother. Hekate, as the embodiment of wisdom, can be seen as the Crone. As symbols of the natural cycle of the world, Kore (young Persephone) is potential, Demeter is the vibrancy of the green world, and the mature Persephone (which means "destruction") is death. Hekate is the force that binds them.

When we look more closely at these three goddesses, we discover that they all achieved radical self-acceptance. Demeter relinquished being a mother. Persephone let go of her innocence. Hekate stepped away when her role as mediator had ended. Thus, the journey of the cave is one of self-acceptance—*radical* self-acceptance. For as long as we reject what we know to be true in the center of our being, there is no wholeness.

Self-acceptance is a vast construct that includes terms like self-confidence, self-efficacy, self-esteem, self-reliance, and self-trust. Of course, the often used term "self-love" is part of it as well. To be honest, however, this term befuddles me. It's slippery, in a way similar to the term "balance." But let's get clear, because clear is kind. Self-acceptance is where we start. Have you ever loved someone but not accepted that person for who he or she is? Sounds shadowy, doesn't it? Self-acceptance is the "heart" of Hekate's eternal fire, which also burns within us. It is the soul fire where truth abides. Part of overcoming the conditioning we've all endured is to practice radical self-acceptance. Through honoring the self, we illuminate the way back to the soul.

The Wheel of Time

Hekate creates the Wheel of Time according to her own laws. We may call her Wheel the *strophalos* or *iynx*.[11] Many place it on their altars or have it tattooed on their skin. This symbol consists of innumerable wheels that represent each cycle, both annular and that of individual lives. The secrets of Hekate's Wheel are known only to her and her most trusted companions, the Moirai—Lachesis, Clotho, and Atropos.

The Moirai, another face of the Triple Goddess, are the sisters who rule fate. Often portrayed clothed in white, Lachesis uses her rod to measure the thread of life spun by her sister Clotho. She determines the length of a person's life, which includes the details of the life lived. At the end of life, the third sister, Atropos, cuts the life thread. The Moirai can help us to weave ourselves into harmony with our fate.

The Moirai are selective with whom they share their secrets, even to those who sincerely seek them, as they do Hekate's bidding. Prophecy was so important to the ancients that one of the Moirai, Lachesis, was specifically associated with the casting of lots and petitioning for assistance with divination. Hekate shares the mysteries of her Wheel of Time with them alone, offering her prophets mere glimpses into the enormous arc of the universe. Yet we are literally tempting fate when we use our divination purely for predicting the future.

While the Moirai guard the secrets of the Wheel of Time well, they do share their wisdom that time is indeed circular. The saying that those who forget history are doomed to repeat it is 100 percent true, as is the maxim that we remain stuck in the past until we are willing to live in the present. Time is not a linear progression up a steep staircase, although our culture tries to convince us otherwise. Rather, the future is an arc, stretching out to form what will someday be ancient history. Our culture is addicted to "more"—always moving forward, always acquiring. Up, up, and away with our arms loaded with things we don't even want. That is the only acceptable transformation. Triformis looks at this insanity and shakes her head. If we are pointing in only one direction, we miss the wisdom of the other directions and ignore the present moment. But as Eckhart Tolle has taught us, there is great power in now.[12]

I am The Weaver,
Stitching myself whole,
Back to soul,
I call upon The Weavers, guide me,
As I journey through my destiny.
Singing songs of freedom and connection.
Dancing toward wholeness.
Spinning, whirling,
In countless colors
Until I am my unique tapestry.

This is where we meet Hekate as we prepare to enter her sacred cave, at the crossroads between past and future. Wholeness may seem like a distant goal, yet the power of transformation is thrumming in our veins. Time is a wheel, with wholeness being both distant and present, and we stretch to the past for the wholeness that was forsaken. The ego, which is dominant at the societal level, wants transformation to be a quick jaunt up an easy flight of stairs. But this simply isn't how growth usually works. This can lead to a worsening of the split in our interior tripartite nature. Shadow becomes amplified; self shifts into ego; the soul is ignored. The most potent healing of the Triple Goddess is this shift from actor to director.

Hekate, like many other goddesses, has different epithets identifying her as three-formed. She is one, but many. She is constant, but in flux. Like the general will of the universe, she is ever-expanding.[13] But while we can romanticize the goddess in whatever form she presents to us, there is no idealizing the transformation process. Change is never linear. We go two steps ahead, and then circle back. One of my biggest beefs with self-help books is that they typically paint transformation as an effortless process.

Transformation is hard, but it is the kind of hard that is worth it. Isn't it worse staying stuck in pain and pouring all your energy into containing the largeness inside of you? Isn't being afraid worse than any possible risks? The picture-perfect images on social media are designed to make transformation look effortless. But real change is messy, as is spiritual growth. The cave is a dirty place. However, you've taken the bravest step by embarking on this journey. Whatever comes ahead, know that you did the biggest hard thing by opening this book.

My soul is wise and strong. I listen to my intuition. I am resilient.
I have claimed my key, and opened the gates locked around my soul.
I am sacred.
I am so much more than any situation or how others see me,
Including the false voices in my head.
I am supported and loved beyond measure.
I am the creation and the creator.
I am awakening.

Regression, Progression, and In-Between

Transformation includes regression, progression, and occupying—with stillness—the space between the two. Regression, in particular, typically happens after soul retrieval (see chapter 12).[14] Simply put, regression is the return to earlier stages of being. We do this spontaneously when we feel threatened, reverting back to the way the traumatized child within us would react. Our society often calls us into damaging regression, taking us back to childish beliefs and behaviors, like small children who refuse to do what is in their own best interest. This sort of regression is an attempt to gain control over a situation. How many times have we reverted to tantrums or sullenness when we felt overwhelmed?

In the context of healing, regression occurs when we adopt the psychology and behaviors of the age we were when the split occurred. This regression has the potential to be part of the healing process when we hold space for it. For example, we may start to change our appearance to resemble how we looked back then. Or we may do things like sleeping with a stuffed animal if our retrieval brings back the memory of a beloved plush protector. Our behavior can become more childish, including temper tantrums and being uncharacteristically selfish. Those we are close to may notice these differences.

Conscious regression may also include talking to your younger self about your dreams and desires, and this is vital for a successful integration.[15] Let your younger self know that it is held and heard, allowing it to take up the space it was long ago denied. Give it a seat on your Inner Council and listen to it (see chapter 8).[16]

A curious incident transpired while I was writing the original draft of this chapter that wove together the Triformis archetype with the thread of my life. I was with a group of moms, one of whom was sharing about the intense slut-shaming and other types of bullying (including violence) that her daughter was experiencing. It was heartbreaking. Another mom launched into a story about how she knew a girl who was experiencing similar suffering. Initially, I thought that this was "story-matching," which can be a defense mechanism that invalidates another's narrative. Yet now it seems that she may have been trying, although perhaps in a very imperfect way, to let the other mom know that her daughter was not the only one.

Positioned as I was, physically between the two, I was literally holding the space between the one who was seeking support and the one who claimed to have all the answers. Without forethought, I blurted out my own shaming when I was in the tenth grade to the point of having to leave the school. I offered to speak with the daughter. In my case, if I had said anything to my own mother about the bullying, I'm confident I would have gotten a hard slap across the face, something with which I was all too familiar whenever I tried to speak truth. Then I turned to the rest of the moms, who were looking more than a bit uncomfortable, and said that this is why women who have been bullied are often uncomfortable with women who either have never known chronic shaming or are unconscious of their trauma. Their fake niceties often only add more shame to the pile. They judge us as too sexual, too fat, too lazy, too weird. Enough. It stops here.

Just before this discussion, I became aware that the mothers were discussing me in an unfavorable light while I was in the bathroom. Hours later, when I arrived back home, I crawled immediately into bed with a chunk of fluorite. I fell into the web that is Hekate's Wheel, traveling back once more to that girl who had been bullied. I spent time with her, feeling her wounds in my body, which is the same body that suffered bullying and all that went with it. I gave her the power of the stone and stayed with her until we found the bright lights in that devastating time. As a child, I had loved reading, writing, drawing, music, calligraphy, flowers, nature, and school. There was beauty within the chaos in my childhood. The bullying was just one symptom of the chronic trauma that started not long after my arrival in this life.

And that is the power of the thread of the Moirai. In my courses, we weave bracelets symbolic of our journeys, adding charms and symbols that represent the pieces of soul with which we've been reunited. I encourage you to create your own symbol that empowers the weaving together of the past and the present. Heal the split by stitching it back together with the mysteries of those fateful sisters who know all.

Three Worlds–Three Selves

Roots stretch deep into earth, grounding.
Heart open to receive, strong back supporting.
Crown stretches up to the heavens, allowing.

In my teachings, I emphasize the correspondence between the many faces of the Triple Goddess, the Three Worlds of Hekate, and our three selves. Hekate presides over the Starry Road by which we ascend to her temple. From there, we descend into her subterranean cave to heal into our unique wholeness. The balance of the two is found in her garden. These Three Worlds—the Upper World, the Lower World (or Underworld), and the Middle World—are located within us at the crown, heart, and root. Through the process of unifying these locations, we become whole, fully attuned to the "river under the river" that is Hekate's deeper world.

We access Hekate's healing powers through plant medicines, stone allies, archetypes, ancestors, and more. They come to us in dreams and in synchronicities. They show up during meditations and rituals. Hekate always illuminates the dark. Contrast this to the energy of Apollo, who is always associated with the sun's rays. Spiritual author and former monk Thomas Moore wrote about Hekate in the context of an Underworld journey, on which we can choose to either heal from the past by turning inward to the soul or spend our lives trying to escape our hungry ghosts.

Hekate is a lunar spirit, a soft source of strength when life is thick with feeling and there seems to be no way out of confusion. This patroness of your darkness doesn't shed brilliant light on your problems. Instead, her torch gives you hints, intimations, and suggestions. After a while, you may feel comfortable with the wafer-thin intuitions you experience. You may not need explanations and solutions, but only indications that everything is essentially all right and that you can handle whatever comes along. Hekate's torch illuminates the pervading darkness with a dim lunar light.[17]

Practica: Triple-Goddess Altar

You can work with the imagery of the Triple Goddess by setting up your altar with a crossroads arrangement and adding beautiful fluorite to amplify the energy of learning and expansion. The Triple Goddess takes up all the space she wishes, and fluorite is wonderful for helping us to do likewise.

Chapter 4

Drakaina: The Awakening

Drakaina

Hail, Drakaina, the Serpent Goddess,
Hail, Drakaina, Eternal She-Dragon of Myth and Might.
Hail, Medusa, Great Gorgon Guide.
Hail, Drakaina, Mother of the Great Serpent that is all of life.
Teach me of your mysteries,
Show me how sovereignty is spoken,
So that I honor my moods, desires, and needs.
Hail, Drakaina!

Drakaina is an ancient title of Hekate and other goddesses that can be translated as "serpent" or "dragon."[1] The archetypal serpent goddess rattles, shakes, and spins. She roars and flies in her dragon form. And when she does, it awakens our own inner dragon. Ever since Eve listened to the snake, the sacredness of the serpent has been misunderstood. Yet before that story was told, the serpent was a potent symbol of the Mother Goddess. In my work, I've witnessed countless dreams of serpents, and even synchronous sightings of them in their physical form. Invariably, these envoys of Hekate arrive when we are at the crossroads. The serpent is symbolic of the soul, which can rest under a rock until we turn our attention inward. The serpent teaches us that we can shed our false skin. And this is the awakening of Drakaina.

There are many vivid images of Hekate with snakes in the ancient texts—having a crown of snakes, being girthed in them, and wearing them down her back. Clearly, snakes are favored by her. As we learn about Hekate's mysteries we realize that snakes are not to be feared, but are powerful Upper World allies. They provide much wisdom and are a reminder that all things have the potential for danger. Perhaps more important, they show us that we can "shed our skin" and be born anew. Thus, the snake and the key are powerfully connected.

I see an unexpected snake visitor as a particularly good omen. There is possibility of healing and of the numinous. Serpents remind us that there is duality in all things—from creation to destruction. Moreover, snakes are exceptionally clever animals. Their powerful intelligence is reflected in two ancient symbols—the caduceus and the ouroboros. The former is the well-known symbol of medicine, with two snakes wrapped around a central pole. This is an ancient talisman of healing and power associated with Hekate's frequent companion, Hermes. The ouroboros is associated with Hekate in both ancient texts and objects, including several magical coins. These coins were used as a manifestation tool. I've made several of these coins for use in my own spells and to carry as talismans. The image of the snake eating its own tail teaches us that all life is circular. Through the infinity of the ouroboros we can connect with Hekate as the key of the universe, infinite and eternal.

Serpent symbolism is complex, as you can see from the various aspects above. This is why I consider them Hekate's most potent animal ally. Snakes are associated with Hekate in diverse ways, reflecting her multifaceted nature. Find your way through serpent energy to the images with which you can connect.

As you explore the serpent, Medusa may find her way to you.[2] In her myth, she was punished for being the victim of sexual violence. Her penalties were her serpentine hair and the uncontrollable power to turn others to stone. In this tale, we see how society vilifies the victim, something that continues to this day. Even when all the evidence demonstrates the guilt of their attackers, women may end up being the ones on trial.[3] In a sense, we have snakes in our hair. Indeed, those of us who suffer from conditions brought about by trauma are often ostracized, as if our wounds were venomous and destructive. When we heal from these wounds, we put Medusa's head back on as well as our own. The wisdom gained from this restoration tilts the energy of the world toward justice.

Serpent Healing

Serpent healing may come to us in dreams. We wake up looking for the bite marks, drenched in sweat. That is how the serpent goddess's strong venom often works. She rattles us until we pay attention to what our souls are trying to tell us.

My own serpent dream started with me wearing a hat of snakes. I was perfectly comfortable with them. My only concern was that the unidentified person who was supposed to be taking a picture of me with my serpent crown was not up to the task. Cut to the next dream scene—me sleeping in a nest of snakes. They were all around me at roughly the positions of the bodily meridians of Traditional Chinese Medicine. One was snuggled right into my nether regions. I had no fear of the snakes. I wasn't even curious about why they were there. I just felt comfort, acceptance, and a vague feeling of complete surrender.

The paradox of surrender, however, is that this is how we become our most powerful. In my own dream, an unidentified person showed up and asked me about all the snakes. I was nonplussed and explained that they were not a big deal, although one kept chewing on my hair. I stood up and draped myself in them. I tried to move the one in my crotch, but it wasn't budging. Again, none of this bothered me. I felt powerful. And I woke up feeling quite content.

Prior to the dream, I'd felt quite stiff every morning for several months. I live with the effects of chronic early childhood trauma every day in the form of relentless bodily inflammation. One of my personal mantras is: my body is a temple of pain, and I am the High Priestess. This discomfort settles down once I get moving, but waking up aching all over, as if my skin were too tight for my body, is not an ideal way to start the day. Since my early twenties, I've endured too many allopathic medical treatments to list. I've sought various botanical and energetic solutions. I meditate. I breathe. I eat the right things. All of this helps me live a truly beautiful life, but I am never without physical pain.

So I took this serpent healing seriously, following up by rolling around on the floor with a big hard foam tube underneath me. This can become a bit comical. Once I caught my hair in it and ended up in quite a predicament. But the practice was a means for me to integrate the serpent healing. My inner serpent goddess, Drakaina, had called and I answered. The soul and the serpent are one and the same.

Drakaina, and other faces of the dragon goddess, sends her serpents as powerful harbingers of mysticism, the mind, and being in the universal flow. They are healers of our harmful thoughts. They can poison the dysfunctional ways in which we see ourselves and others, revealing the truth. I call forth the energy of her serpents to activate my own divinity within. In fact, modern neuroscience tells us of the importance of our physical inner serpent—the vagus nerve—for healing body and mind. Drakaina is mystical and embodied. That is why garnet is an excellent stone for connecting with the energy of Drakaina.

Serpent energy is deeply connected to healing from past sexual trauma. Survivors of sexual trauma often detach from their physical bodies. We avoid the crime scene that is ourselves. Sexual violence has been part of my journey since I was raped when I was thirteen. My first husband, whom I married when I was nineteen, was a master of sexual manipulation. Overall, my relationship with sex has been complicated, to say the least.

Like many who grew up in an invalidating environment, I had no internal models for what healthy sexual relationships looked like. I struggled throughout the years with sex, often choosing partners who were undeniably poisonous. The dream I described above came months after what was the worst in a lengthy series of unfortunate sexual encounters. Uncharacteristically, I went to a large, private, winter solstice ritual. At the event, I met a man who later violated me in truly horrible ways, but in a manner that left me thoroughly confused about my consent. Like many victims of sexual violence, I was left troubled by how I may have contributed to the situation. This was about much more than a toxic affair. It broke me down, way down to the bottom, reminding me of past trauma, but in a way that forced me to know that this had to be the absolute last round of this business. I had reached the end. My serpent goddess slept no more. I see Drakaina rising in the "me too" movement.[4] She compels us to shed the shame, and even attack when threatened.

This healing can be a physical sensation of movement at the base of the spine that tells us that the serpent goddess is awakening within, like an incoming kundalini activation. The concept of kundalini comes from a spiritual tradition that works with energy centers, called *chakras*, located along our bodies. These energy centers affect our health and how we interact with the world. In this tradition, the essence of the soul is seen as a coiled serpent resting on our root.[5] Once awakened, the serpent stretches out across our other energy centers, fully activating our life purpose and our power. A kundalini awakening can appear to be spontaneous, but it is always the result of profound spiritual work. It can manifest as a physical sensation deep in our root, as dreams of snakes, or as a rapid acceleration of our spiritual life—for example, amplified awareness of and connection to the deeper world, including our psychic and healing abilities.

Serpent healing occurs when we let the serpent of our truth poison that which blocks our way, so that many false ways of seeing ourselves die. When this happens, we lose interest in what doesn't nourish. Radical change often results—from leaving our careers to changing our addresses. But this happens only if we let our divine inner snake goddess do her work. She longs for the safety of the cave where she can rejuvenate. When the serpent goddess beckons, it is a call to her sacred cave. Like the dragons of legends, she carries the power of fire on her breath. She can heat us up until we flee to her cave to cool down.

The Power of Stillness

The serpent pays attention, but doesn't strive for it. The awakening serpent brings the vision into focus, allowing us to see things as they truly are. We often get caught up in the busyness of modern life, in a spiral of continual, meaningless motion. But the serpent is still. It watches and waits. Snakes attack only when threatened, or for food. They are not out to get us.

A consistent phenomenon I've observed in students over the years is a confusion about what we are supposed to be "doing" during awakening. We can strive to do all the right things, hoping that healing and wholeness will come from following a list of instructions. We may even feel—and I certainly did once upon a time—that we need to do the correct things, or else the forces of the deeper world, whether we call this Hekate or by another name, will "get us." This is not true. It is in our stillness, and in our paying attention, that we find the essence of our unique awakening. Be calm like the snake; save your energy. Snakes may appear to meander, but they always know where they are going. Our journeys are like this—going sideways and even loop-de-loop until we come to the entrance of the cave.

The serpent can inspire great fear, and rightfully so. Certain species are incredibly lethal. While the evidence for an evolutionary basis for a fear of snakes is shaky, many of us do acquire a serpent phobia.[6] Even when we consider that, for many of us, the probability of encountering a venomous snake is practically nil, we're still terrified of them. But we are not statistical machines living our lives based on data about probable outcomes and normative risks. Decision-making is an intricate process.[7] Yet when fear is activated, we can be frozen in place, unable to move forward.

We can have a subconscious fear of the soul serpent within, not wanting to listen to the truth it speaks.[8] As we awaken, the serpent speaks to us of our desires and dreams, which are the components of the great work of our lives. One of my favorite descriptions explaining this fear comes from Marianne Williamson:

> Our deepest fear is not that we are inadequate. Our deepest fear is that we are powerful beyond measure. It is our light, not our darkness that most frightens us. We ask ourselves, "Who am I to be brilliant, gorgeous, talented, fabulous?" Actually, who are you not to be?[9]

Indeed, who are we *not* to overcome the fear of the soul? Isn't that what we are here for?

The journey through Hekate's cave to wholeness asks us to be still and to listen to the soul. To ask ourselves: What would I do if I weren't afraid? In my school, we have a perpetual sharing circle about overcoming our fears. Trust me, whatever it is inside of you that longs to get out is worth any perceived risk. We always imagine far worse catastrophes than are even remotely likely to happen.

I remember reading an article by Martha Beck in *O Magazine* many years ago in which she said something like: "Live your truth, consequences be damned." I kept the clipping on my bulletin board for ages, but it got lost in a household move in which I was busy living that truth—moving from what I thought was a "normal" home to my ramshackle cottage in rural, coastal Nova Scotia. I overcame my fear of not fitting in, and I know you can, too. And so does your inner soul serpent.

Light your candle, connect with a piece of amethyst, and settle into stillness. Take out your journal and let out all those dreams on the pages. Without judgment or expectation, give them the oxygen they deserve. You may want to keep this list in your Cista Mystica, or perhaps create a talisman or choose a symbol instead.

The Power of Meditation

Because of the importance of stillness, daily meditation is fundamental to the awakening of the serpent and the journey through darkness to wholeness. I know it's off-putting to contemplate sitting in stillness with the slow and steady soul. I know. I've been there. But I overcame this fear, and you can overcome it, too.

Meditation is simply the shifting of awareness to being present within yourself. It is moving the vantage point from the sense of self to your true self. From having thoughts to being aware of having thoughts. It is the shift from being an actor in the drama of your life to being the director. And this is why meditation is vital on your journey. It is the micro act of power that becomes the macro claim of sovereignty. When you become aware of your thoughts through contemplation (which is the beginning of meditation), you create unity within. You understand that you are both actor and director. I think common misperceptions about meditation make the practice seem intimidating. But meditation is not emptying the mind; it's *mindfulness*. It's sitting with yourself and seeing thoughts as within your control. It is by consciously shifting your attention to a mantra, or mental imagery, or music that these vibrations can better attune you toward wholeness.

Meditation can open the door to trance, where we can connect to the divine to receive guidance and inspiration.

Meditation can also be a fantastic way to learn to self-manage your energies. If you don't already have a regular meditation practice, I recommend that you start doing your research now to find one that works for you. Or try out the meditation below. Personally, Pema Chödrön's *How to Meditate* helped me finally break through in my practice. Learning to sit in stillness with your thoughts, your emotions, and your actions fortifies your inner serpent goddess.

Serpents have a strong spine and a soft front. This grounds them while connecting them to what is nourishing. And meditation can help you develop a similar attitude characterized by sovereignty and boundaries, coupled with curiosity and kindness. This healthy vulnerability was perfectly summarized by Zen Buddhist Roshi Joan Halifax:

> All too often our so-called strength comes from fear not love; instead of having a strong back, many of us have a defended front shielding a weak spine. In other words, we walk around brittle and defensive, trying to conceal our lack of confidence. If we strengthen our backs, metaphorically speaking, and develop a spine that's flexible but sturdy, then we can risk having a front that's soft and open, representing choiceless compassion. The place in your body where these two meet—strong back and soft front—is the brave, tender ground in which to root our caring deeply.[10]

Meditation can help you develop an open heart that accepts reality while entering into the mystery with curiosity.

But this is a process. Being too shielded prevents us from being open to believing ourselves—finding the message in the mess, the truth in the dream—and denies us the richness of this life. A student of mine contacted me in great distress, requesting a meeting because she was struggling. Notably, the lesson asked her to learn a meditation for awakening her soul serpent. When we met, she spoke of her challenges and then proceeded to discuss what she had been doing instead of the prescribed curriculum. She revealed that she had been performing daily healing on a very sick python. This snake had come to her through synchronicity, as these things do when we awaken Drakaina. In practical terms, daily meditation can open the way to these occurrences, while strengthening and softening us.

Meditation is critical for awakening the soul, and for the soul-making that comes along with it. The meditation below can help you raise into awareness the three epicenters of your being—the root, the heart, and the crown. The root, located low in the belly and at the base of the spine, is the seat of your emotions, intuitions, and sexual energy. The heart, situated in the middle of the breasts, is the crossroads between the outer environment and your inner world. The crown, at the top of the head, opens the gateway to the deeper world. Consider each of these locations as a part of the soul serpent—grounding tail, expansive heart, and stretching head wearing a gorgeous crown.

Practica: Unifying the Three Selves Meditation

Find a quiet place where you will not be disturbed. If you are feeling distracted, begin by counting down from thirteen, seeing each number on the screen of your mind. If you have one, bring a piece of amethyst with you to encourage meditation. I have a large, vulva-shaped hunk that I keep right above my office altar.

Begin with the lower-self center, which is located at the root, within your pelvis. Start by becoming aware of your current feelings. Are you stressed or at peace? Whatever emotions are within you, acknowledge them and sink deeper into them, as they become one unified field.

Next, explore the state of your physical being. Allow your root, through your sitting bones and feet, to become grounded to the earth beneath. Where are you holding tension? Release that gently down through your body, letting it dissolve into the ground beneath you. The power of Chthonia, the Underworld, draws in what no longer serves you and sends back to you beautiful groundedness.

The middle-self center is located at the heart. Breathe into your heart center, feeling the beautiful fire within you, allowing it to spread through your body. Stretch out this fire so that it nourishes all that is blessing to

you and burns away all that harms you. See this fire of yours connected to all the world around you.

The higher-self center is located at the crown. Here, you become aware of your thoughts, feelings, and embodied state. See your thoughts as fleeting images on your mind screen. Coming and going. You aren't attached to any of them. None are right or wrong; they just are. Non-judgment is the key to this stage of meditation. You stretch up toward the Starry Road, becoming attuned to the mystical energy above. Rest here in this space, allowing thoughts and feelings to come and go. Slowly allow yourself to go deeper within until you find stillness. Be in this place where your goddesses and spirits can speak freely with you.

When you are finished, relax your connection to the Starry Road, gently pulling your energy back into your crown. Separate from the world around you by pulling your energy back into your heart center. Disconnect from the ground by pulling up your energetic roots. Count back up to twelve, leaving that one bit of connection to your energetic self and the deeper world.

Chapter 5
Enodia: The Crossroads

It is to Enodia I cry when I am lost,
Shine your torches so that I may return to your sacred road.
I am the pilgrim of your truth,
Guide me to rebirth so that all that is false is shed,
And I am woven whole from the threads of my soul.

With a thrumming deep within, the soul serpent stirs, and the altar vibrates with potential. This is the momentum of the crossroads. You are offered a choice to proceed or retreat. There is the road behind you, and there is the road ahead that leads into the cave. I call this the Mother Road.

Hekate's association with roads stretches back to the earliest historical records.[1] In fact, Enodia is most often translated as meaning "in the road," although sometimes it is defined as "of the way." Perhaps the most descriptive version of its meaning is "she who stands on the road." This title of Hekate and other goddesses, including one herself named Enodia, is interconnected with her association with the crossroads. This appellation undoubtedly morphed into Hekate's Roman associations with roads, notably in the title of Trivia. In the Greek tradition, Trioditis refers to her specifically as goddess of the three roads.

In fact, traveling the road back to the origins of this title for Hekate is a rather long and winding journey. Enodia (sometimes spelled Einodia or Ennodia) was an ancient Thessalian goddess who became syncretized with Hekate and Artemis, and the Roman Diana.[2] There are also tangential connections between Enodia, Hekate, and Cybele, notably the evidence found in a rock throne in Rhodes.[3]

There is no way of disentangling the history of Hekate from Enodia or her frequent companions, Artemis, Persephone, and Selene. The practices of the ancients were no different from ours today. They adapted their daily rituals based on their understanding as individuals and as societies, demonstrating that there is a deeper archetype at work. Enodia is a spirit far deeper and more powerful than any name assigned to a face of the goddess. Enodia is the guide along the Mother Road, regardless of what else we may call her.

Goddess of the Roads

Use of Enodia as a title of Hekate is found in the fragments of one of Sophocles's plays, known as *The Root Cutters*, contained within what remains of a partial telling of Medea's story, retold by Euripides and the Roman Seneca.[4] When her attendants are petitioning Hekate's assistance for Medea's spell to murder Pelias, they call out:

> Lord sun and holy fire, sword of Hecate of the roads, which she carries over Olympus as she attends and as she traverses the sacred crossroads of the land, crowned with oak and the woven coils of snakes falling on her shoulders.[5]

While we may resist the urge to do away with the men who violate us, there is a strong association between women who refuse to be victimized and Enodia.

What can we take away from this fragment as it relates to our modern understanding of Hekate? Most important, it firmly shows her as being summoned using Enodia as an epiclesis (invocation) for the casting of a spell. It is an example of how being "of the road," as a woman, carried with it the force of fighting the powerful who harm others in their quest for glory. This contrasts with other goddesses—for example, Hestia—who had the good sense to stay inside the home. Demeter, of course, failed in

Entering Hekate's Cave

her attempts to stay wild herself and save her daughter from the will of the gods. In the story of Medea, we find the friction between wild woman and the so-called civilized world. This is the common thread among all those who bear the title Enodia.

This enmity between the wild and the civilized was a projection of those more powerful "southerners" who wrote the ancient plays and myths that featured Hekate and her female companions. Thus, Enodia is symbolic of the north, which is synonymous with dangerous wildness, including the mysteries of the cave. It is unsurprising that merely speaking the name Enodia evokes, even now, a deeper reverberation within the souls of all of us who seek to become unbound. She is the one who resists conformity, who uses natural magic to gain empowerment over the civilized world.

Another shared aspect of Hekate and Enodia is benevolence toward women and children, including assistance with pregnancy and child-birth. This reflects upon the power structure's suspicion of all things related to women's reproduction. How little some things change even after 2000 years! Enodia thus symbolizes both the womb and the road in and out of it. This is the sacred road that leads to, through, and from her cave.

And herein lies the mystery of Enodia. She stirs within the depths of the soul that call us to remember our own wild nature. It is the call to enter Hekate's cave. To Persephone, Hekate was Enodia as she guided her to and from the Underworld in order to change the seasons. Persephone had been robbed of her innocent wildness to serve as a cautionary tale for any girl thinking she could escape the marriage bed. Hekate helped broker a deal that permitted her to return to the wild world in exchange for taking on the heavy responsibility for turning the Wheel of the Year.

The Mother Road and the Cave

Persephone, Circe, and the wild women ancestors both known and forgotten all walked the Mother Road with Hekate. As resist-ers, decampers, and, at times, foolish rebels, we risk all to follow the torches of Enodia, because this is the only road on which we belong. Like Circe, who fell for Odysseus's charms, our knowledge of the cave can cause heartbreak.[6] When she refused to accompany him to the cavern entrance to the Underworld, she knew that her journey would be fundamentally a solitary one and that she would say goodbye to him willingly. His cave became her soul cave—a journey into the depths of sadness. As with Persephone, being allowed to walk the Mother Road often includes considerable negotiation. Artemis as Enodia managed to maintain her journey on the Mother Road with little incident. Selene's role along that path is to shine her light on our journeys, which occurs at night when the domineering eyes of the "civilized" world are firmly closed.

Enodia brings with her the reminder that there are those who will spin tales about us that paint us as evil and fearsome—or, to use that modern epithet for a powerful wild woman, a bitch. As we all know, when powerful men who are afraid of female power speak, they tell great lies. To walk the Mother Road, we learn to heal from those wounds. When we focus on traveling the road, when we follow the goddess's torches, we are only ourselves. It is imperative that, in these perilous times, we embark on the Mother Road journey with strength and commitment. All other paths lead to chaos and ruination.

Enodia's nourishing torches guide us forward into the mysteries of her wisdom as we enter the cave. This is the modern interpretation of Enodia as guide along our earthbound journey. Enodia is both the guide and the road. The road always knows where it is going, even though we pilgrims who travel it may not. There is a certain trust inherent when walking the Mother Road. We turn to our inner Enodia, which is the torch fire of Hekate within our souls, leaning into our intuition and reserves.

Hekate nourishes our fire as we tread her cavern road, healing and empowering us. She protects us from the nasty glares and the sordid lies that may be told as we veer away from the false dead-end roads of the civilized world. We walk the roads of her Great Wheel, the strophalos, which loop and bend, leading in unexpected directions, yet always take us back to our spiritual home—the crossroads.

Across cultures and traditions, the crossroads has long been understood as a spiritual portal. Hekate's association with the crossroads dates back to ancient times when offerings by people seeking her protection were left at these locations.

Indulge me for a moment with a walk back in time. Once upon a time there was a woman who had worked very hard to hide what she knew in her heart to be true, because she knew the sting of rejection when she

Entering Hekate's Cave

spoke of her truth. Unsurprisingly, she kept her ways secret from even those closest to her. She knew of Hekate's Wheel, of the crossroads, of the sacred fire within. She knew of the keys of magic, of medicine, and of mystery. She often stood before her little altar, candle glowing, with little sticks forming a crossroads. These were times of immense upheaval in her life, and there were moments when, instead of leaning in, she sprinted in the opposite direction. Still, she always came back to the crossroads of her goddess, where the keys are found and the soul-flame burns bright. Eventually, the cost of denying her truth became one that she was unwilling to continue paying. She leaned into Hekate's road.

Yes, that woman was me. And I have traversed several crossroads since then.

Practica: Creating a Crossroads Altar

You can create a crossroads on your altar using any objects that speak to your intention. Light your candle and contemplate all that you encountered on the road that led you here. Choose a symbol of this past for your Cista Mystica. Assemble the three "key" stones of Hekate—black obsidian, clear quartz, and red jasper—to evoke the energy of her healing crossroads.[7] I recommend smoky quartz for connecting specifically with the power of transiting a crossroads.

Practica: The Enodia Oracle

This two-card reading known as the Enodia Oracle consists of igniting the sacred fire using a candle, sitting in presence with the altar, and then practicing the Unifying the Three Selves Meditation given in chapter 4. Smoky quartz is a wonderful ally for this reading. Mine is never far from my personal oracle deck. You can use this oracle for guidance on your day's journey. I perform it upon rising, before the day awakens. Do whatever works for you, but do it. I say this out of love.

This simple daily reading changes everything, according to my students. We have a sharing circle in which we share our interpretations and support each other. This helps me to see how students are progressing in their readings, and how they are changing their lives. I encourage you to keep a journal of your readings, whether in a spreadsheet or a journal. Again, whatever works best for you.

As you draw the first card, focus on approaching and passing through a gate to start something new, then ask the card what you should approach that day. As you draw the second card, imagine shutting a gate or door, summoning up the energy of avoidance, then ask the card what to avoid.

Chapter 6

Propylaia: The Threshold

Propylaia

"Who is it that stands before my gate?"

"I have traveled far, Mistress. My journey has been a difficult one. Now I seek entrance to your cave so that I may heal."

"Ah, I see. Take this key. Keep it in your soul. It grants entrance to my mysteries."

Propylaia is an epithet given to Hekate in several ancient sources.[1] Literally translated, the title means "she who stands at the threshold." She is both the gate and the one that tends it. I believe her price of admission is a deep desire for healing and a willingness to give up the ghost of the past (see chapter 2). To those who saw Hekate as the Gatekeeper, this reflected a role often held by the mistress of a household. In particular, it was the custom for new brides to be given the keys to the household. Thus, the one who presided over the threshold and was keeper of the keys was generally seen as female. In the temple at Lagina, the temple key-bearers were often women.[2] This is not to say that men never held these positions of power. It is merely to point out that, in the strictly patriarchal society of the day, women had a unique association with control over who was let into the home or the temple.

As a gate goddess, Propylaia was venerated at the entrance to the Athens Acropolis, as well as in other ancient Greek cities.[3] For example, in Selinunte, Hekate stood watch on a monumental gate by the sanctuary of Demeter. In Eleusis, she was honored in a temple at the gates of the sanctuary. On Rhodes, Hekate was worshiped as Propylaia together with Hermes Propylaios and Apollo Apotropaios. In Lagina, the center of Hekatean worship, located in what is now modern Turkey, a statue of Hekate was erected when a new city gate was constructed. In addition, there was an annual procession in Lagina to honor Hekate in which a female led the Procession of Keys. A similar festival was held in Meletus.[4]

At sanctuaries, Propylaia presided over admission to where the most sacred ceremonies were held. The most revered of these rituals, like the Mysteries at Eleusis, were often held in caves. Here at this entrance, you see Hekate as soul, as ancient philosophers described her in The Chaldean Oracles. This Hekate is both gatekeeper and the key itself.[5] Sarah Iles Johnston, in her dissertation on Hekate as Soteira, theorized that the key was, in fact, that of the soul.[6] The cave as temple is symbolic of our own inner sacred chamber, which we enter when we cross into Hekate's territory.

The Wounded Healer

The archetype of the Wounded Healer, well portrayed in myths like those of Circe and Medea, shows us that we are all burdened by the past, yet still very capable of helping those in need.[7] Circe sang words of power for those she loved and struck down those who sought to bring harm. Medea rejuvenated her husband's family before his betrayal caused her to strike them down. Artemis, whom we can see as a very introverted goddess, favored the vulnerable and destroyed those who threatened her. Persephone became the benevolent queen after her own Underworld journey. We look to their stories to see how these eternal mythologies are living through us, and then learn to see how they are working on others as we mentor them.

To see our lives through this mythological lens is to understand that Hekate and her deeper world are always present. We are much more than our everyday experiences. Much of modern psychology and mainstream healthcare focuses exclusively on the surface, placing its emphasis on a cure that is bestowed upon us. In depth psychology, however, healing is cocreated by the guide and the seeker drawing from the depths of the soul. We explore not only myths but also the eternal archetypes they symbolize. And while we are made of flesh, we are also comprised of these forces.

The healing portrayed in the myth of Persephone became realized in the rituals in ancient Eleusis. In these rites, participants walked the road just as we do. Their first gate was catharsis, the second retrieval, and the final one rebirth. Most likely, Hekate was involved in these rites as the guiding link between the everyday world and the mysteries of the Underworld. And these ceremonies, like this book, were built around the principles of catharsis, retrieval, and rebirth.

The first part of these rites, which included the cleansing of the body and a ritual sacrifice, is a release in which candidates shed their surface selves, symbolized by the sacrifice of a pig. The sacrifice was then buried in the ground, representing the death of the former self. In the second part of the ritual, called *katabasis,* candidates traveled deep into a cave in search of Persephone. This trek symbolizes our descent into the darkness to find the light of the truth and to reunite with ourselves. This is soul retrieval. In the final rite, the candidate goes through rebirth, entering the temple as Kore, the eternal child/maiden/youth, representing the wholeness we achieve by dismantling the illusion of separation between us and the deeper world. The three rituals given in this book, which I call the Rituals of the Sacred Cave, replicate this cycle in a way that is safe for you to do on your own (see chapters 9, 12, and 14). These rituals have been performed by hundreds of students under my supervision, and I have put great care into adapting them for you.

These rituals open us up to the deeper world of Hekate. We see with the eyes of the soul serpent, exploring our dreams with curiosity and finding synchronicities all around us. Within the ritual, we may feel emotions and receive symbolic gifts. Render these etheric treasures into flesh however you feel led to do and keep them in your Cista Mystica. In them, we open the gate to the unconscious through techniques like meditation and the use of other trance-inducing techniques like breath work and plant-spirit medicine. We journey to connect to the sacred within us, through which we return to the goddess. She awaits. Through our journeying into her cave, we can transcend the regular mind to receive deep healing. This is the healing that leads to wholeness.

Imagination and Creativity

The goal of entering transcendence, whether in the deep trance states of our rituals or in our meditation, is to stretch beyond regular consciousness so that we reconnect to our inner torch, the soul. Imagination and creativity are the keys that open the gate to the deeper self, which always leads to the deeper world. Meditation is the daily journey into our cave-temple within that opens to the possibility of Hekate. It is the spark that kindles the torch within, which is tethered to the hieros pyr, the sacred fire of Hekate. Meditation burns away destructive mind tricks, from obsessive thoughts to the persistent voices of others. Thus, meditation trains the mind to create space for what nourishes us while banishing wasteful thoughts.

We fuel our inner torch by expanding what lights us from within—creativity and imagination. This is not to say that there isn't a structure that is foundational to rituals and meditations. It is merely meant to draw your attention to the lifeblood of these endeavors. Imagination expands the mind to allow the messages of Hekate—those signs that come to us in the dreamworld, our nightly spiritual journeys, which are often representations of her known symbols—to come into focus. This is achieved through daily practice. Think of your mind as your new Cista Mystica, eagerly awaiting what is to come. This vessel is sacred, and your offering to it is your imagination.

Consider your imagination a crossroads where you meet Hekate and her spirits. The more you visit this intersection, the stronger the connection becomes. Our awareness of the communications from the deeper world amplifies. We see the synchronicities and messages that the spirits are transmitting our way.

What also happens when we travel the imagination's road is that we resurrect memories of previous encounters with spirits. In particular, we recollect times when we dreamed of a mysterious woman, found an unexpected symbol, or other uncanny event. Perhaps, as I described in the introduction, you experience an uninvited visitation. Most of the time, the goddess shows up when we least expect it, especially when we find ourselves in a "dark night of the soul."

Hekate's torch is the divine immanence of the goddess, which also abides within you. When you "bump" into her, you are rattled. You feel deeply; your body is stirred up. The hairs on the back of your neck stand up. Your stomach turns; you cry a river into existence. One minute, you are having perfectly ordinary thoughts and the next, you find yourself in another place and time. This is the great awakening that her torch brings.

As soon as possible, journal about your experience. Record it on your phone. Make a quick sketch. Hekate is fond of symbolism, and our other guides often speak to us in riddles and symbols. Writing about them can help you unravel their meanings. Rose quartz is most helpful for the processing and integration of deeper-world experiences, as it both carries unconditional support and helps to enact firm boundaries.

Practica: Processing Encounters

You can use these prompts to help you understand encounters with Hekate and other spirits:

- What is my current emotional state?

- What physical sensations am I experiencing?

- What thoughts am I having?

- What did the landscape look like?

- Who were my allies? What did they look like?

- What did they say to me?

- What did I say?

- What symbols did I receive?

Once you've processed the journey, write down your own understanding of the experience and then seek other sources for standard interpretations. Drawing a card or two can help to clarify puzzling symbols and experiences. Once you've answered the questions, start to examine common themes across your emotions, experiences, and symbols.

Chapter 7

Chthonia: The Descent

Chthonia

Come here to me, goddess of night, beast-slayer,
Quiet and frightful, and consuming our offerings.
Heed my prayers, Lunar Queen,
Who knows suffering,
Rising and setting at night.
Triple-headed, triple-named, fearful, gracious-minded, and regal.
Mistress of Night and chthonic realms, sacred, black-clad,
'Round whom the star-traversing nature of the universe revolves.
You have birthed every worldly thing,
For you are the originator of all known and unknown.

—Inspired by The Greek Magical Papyri, IV. 2441-2621

Chthonia is one of Hekate's most ancient titles. Deities are considered chthonic if they abide in the Underworld, as opposed to ouranic deities, who reside on high. Hekate and Persephone are chthonic queens, while Demeter is an ouranic goddess.

It is Hekate's chthonic energy that often presents to us when we are at our lowest. This is a symbolic representation of our own "earthiness," an indication that we feel deeply when our internal Underworld calls us to deep healing. Chthonia comes at these moments and especially during autumn, when all is returning to the earth.

Earth goddesses like Gaia reflect the energy of the planet itself and the surface landscape, rather than the spiritual realm of the Underworld. Demeter, for example, can be considered an earth goddess, even though she is not chthonic, because she is associated with the land. But Hekate and other chthonic deities are of the cave, the bottom of the ocean, and the interior world. As such, chthonic deities are often associated with the moon, which symbolizes the psyche as the realm of intuition, the soul, and the shadow. Solar deities, on the other hand, are ouranic because they reflect the persona, the outer world, and the surface.

In antiquity, chthonic deities were associated with death, the afterlife, and spirits. As Stephen Ronan points out in *The Goddess Hekate* (1992):

> We can easily relate these to her character as a chthonic deity; for it is the earth which brings forth life, and into which the dead return and where they dwell.

Likewise, chthonic deities are connected to intuition, prophecy, and the mysteries. They walk under the pale light of the moon. To the ancients, they were also associated with wealth and protection. This is symbolic of the storage of food and treasures deep underground, especially in caves. And, as we have seen, the earliest temples were often located in caves. Thus, the chthonic deities were held in very high esteem by their followers in the ancient world.

Hekate has chthonic aspects as one dimension of her triplicity of universal dominion. The journey through her cave is chthonic, in that, as a consequence of it, we return to the embrace of the Dark Mother.

The association of Hekate, and all chthonic deities, as dangerous is an unfortunate consequence of the denial of the sacred feminine and the depths of the soul. The ancients knew that the gold lay deep within us and the earth. Any depictions of the sacred feminine as a purely ouranic spirit are most likely the product of our male-centric culture. The ancients understood that the Great Mother was both light and dark, night and day. But she was especially of the depths because of her capacity both to bring forth life and destroy it.

Today, we have been programmed to think that the dark is a place of danger and evil. Thus Hekate has become associated with things deemed out-of-bounds for civilized people. This is true for all the goddesses, but it is an error most strikingly made for those who were associated with the Underworld.

Yet Chthonia brings gifts as well. She is the velvet embrace, the stern guidance, and the unwavering protection we need for the journey through darkness to wholeness. The Underworld and Chthonia are entwined with the dead and restless spirits. As you venture into her cave, your own will likely come calling. In addition to the shadow, past versions of yourself, old relationships, people long forgotten, and even familial ancestors may appear. Chthonia also brings powerful dreams and visions and inspires great creativity as you explore your own rich inner life.

Hail, Chthonia,
Mistress of the Underworld,
Subterranean Queen,
Guardian who presides over
Mysteries,
Within and without.
I descend into your realness,
Sinking into the depths.

Descent and Deconstruction

The descent into Chthonia can happen due to life circumstances in which we suddenly find ourselves at the bottom. In our desperation, we cry out to Chthonia, even when we don't consciously know her name. Or we may consciously embark on the downward journey when we realize that it is time to heal into our wholeness. In either case, we are veering away from the societal addiction to the bright lights of artificiality. Descending into Chthonia is natural, as all living creatures need periods of healing in the dark. Even if we find ourselves in a metaphorical hell, the only way out is *through*. Refusing to admit that we are in dire circumstances, have been wounded, or suffer from addictions is the very definition of hell. Being stuck in the old ways of being that only made things worse is hell. But the cave symbolizes the womb. It is where we are reborn.

The soul is nourished by the Underworld. As the ancients knew (and so does the soul), the richness lies in the chthonic depths of Hekate's cave. As you descend into Chthonia, a natural shedding of what has held you prisoner occurs. You may experience radical shifts in thoughts, emotions, and actions. These revolutionary changes result from the stripping away of the false self that fed the shadow, which was born of pain, trauma, and invalidation. All these changes cause a massive awakening of your true self—the soul, your sacred anima.[1] This soul is seen as a serpent running through your etheric body and then into your physical body. It is bidirectional; what goes on in your corporeal form blends into the deeper self. Thus, the descent into Chthonia is about breaking down the illusion of separation that you may have held regarding your physical being and your soul. It also shatters the illusion of disconnection between you and the goddess. She abides deep inside of you, and you inhabit her archetype. This process of reunification can be intense.

This period of deconstruction can be challenging. Many things may percolate to the surface. The shadow is bound to tell you that you cannot even fit through the open entrance to the cave. But you will. We are on this journey together. If the passage feels too tight, we will get through together. Keep your stones from the previous chapters with you and add black obsidian now to help unlock the cave while protecting you from harm.

Temenos–Sacred Space

Temenos is an ancient term that refers to sacred spaces, but also refers to our internal sacred space when we hold the psyche as sacred.[2] This created sacred space reflects our personal boundaries and what we keep within them. Boundaries are rules that we use to safeguard what we hold dear— our sense of self, our dreams, and our personal needs. When we view ourselves as sacred spaces, it profoundly changes our perspective. The cave is sacred, our altars are sacred—and so are we. As we descend into Chthonia, we feel a strong need to get rid of burdens. Embrace this energy by exploring your personal boundaries as well as continuing to go into the sacred space of your daily practice.

The boundaries we set create our own personal temenos. They are how we safeguard ourselves while we traverse Hekate's cave. Think of your boundaries as your personal sacred space, a truly magical circle within which you live. You are a sacred vessel. Respect this space and surround yourself with others that reciprocate.

Our lives are sacred vessels as well—the ultimate offering. Work on protecting your interior temenos through exploring your personal boundaries, establishing and/or reinforcing wards around your home, and avoiding "negative airspace." Honor the space you've created, because you've worked ridiculously hard to create it. Toxic people and general societal anxieties are powerful projections that can infect you when you are unaware. Mind how you expend your energy. Avoid interactions with harmful people when possible. Keep "doom scrolling"—an obsessive attachment to negative news—to a minimum and focus on all that nourishes you.

All that said, while having clear boundaries is truly magical, it can be hard enforcing them as protective measures or to rebuild them after they are trampled. Discovering your own courage occurs here. Having difficult conversations with someone who has interfered with your personal sacred policies in the past is part of this real work.[3] On the other hand, having such a chat may be pointless; the work may be yours to do alone.

Having boundaries with family can be especially challenging. We've all sat at the holiday dinner where discussions about politics get heated. In my family, religion has been the hot-button issue ever since I was the peculiar child who loved nothing better than exploring nature with a squad of imaginary companions, both human and otherwise. Then I became the rebellious teenager who just wanted to be a popular girl. As a woman, I continued this campaign of differentiation from my family of origin by marrying a Catholic and becoming a psychologist. I could go on, but this is enough to give you a picture of how different I am from my family. In my twenties and thirties, I struggled with wanting to please them while remaining true to who I was.

What worked for me was seeing myself and my sons as residents on an island. I'm the gatekeeper. If anyone, including my family, is highly likely to cause unnecessary upset in my little queendom, they don't get admitted or are removed. When I'm with someone who has the potential to be intrusive, I say to myself (sometimes many, many times) that that person will not penetrate my magic circle.

Learning to take what others say at face value is another key component of establishing and maintaining healthy boundaries. If you feel called to go deeper into your boundary work, I recommend *The Dialectical Behavior Therapy Skills Workbook*.[4]

One insidious threat to our boundaries comes from microaggressions—those subtle pokes and digs that some people are gifted at making, especially toward people in a traditionally marginalized group.[5] Sometimes these are directed right at a person, but more often they are accomplished by talking about others behind their backs. If there were awards for this, my family would be wearing gold medals. I try not to share that podium, but being real here, it's something I work at every day. Conditioning is strong. Maybe it's right in my DNA. These slurs can come from others as well—from supposed friends, from work colleagues (bosses!), and even from strangers. They are all designed to undermine our personal sovereignty, because the people engaging in them feel disempowered themselves.

While we can learn to offset potential boundary disputes from those we know, it's almost impossible to predict when a stealth attack on our boundaries may occur. I was at a party talking to some people I didn't know well. Out of nowhere, a man started berating adolescent girls as sluts. A huge part of me wanted to explain things to him, but the wise woman inside me said to simply step away. I excused myself, giving him a stern look. The others all knew what I meant. Since then, I've avoided any contact with him. Telling him off would have felt good, but it would only have drained my own energy.

Energy and Attention

Energy flows where attention goes. This is one of my top five personal mantras. I had a student who always had a certain news channel on in the background during our live video classes. The TV was mounted behind her, so that we all saw the screen. I found this very disruptive, but I never said anything to her. I wondered why anyone would keep a news channel on while engaging in a class about spirituality. This inspired me to develop very clear boundaries about how my students can present themselves in a live gathering. But I never did spell it out to the woman with the TV.

It became clear that this woman was completely disinterested in actually doing the *real* work I teach. She just wanted attention. She got my personal telephone number and frequently called me. Another boundary violation. I answered once to explain that she couldn't call me, but she ignored that. Eventually, because of her incessant emails, messages, and calls, I had to completely block her from my public work and private life (she found my personal social media). And to think that I could probably have prevented all this tomfoolery if I had just told her the very first time I saw that TV behind her to turn it off or shut down her camera. Recently, someone had a similar TV setup in a video meeting, and I simply said to turn it off.

If something is bothering you, as this TV did me, explore why it does. Pay attention to the "ick" factor and your gut reactions. Those sensations happen because your body is telling you that your boundaries have been traversed. Then sit with these feelings to reveal why. Develop a strategy so you don't re-experience the negative reactions. If it does happen, be very clear that it is unacceptable. You can just leave, as I did at the party, or you can explain with kindness that the behavior has to stop.

Here are some examples of behaviors that indicate you have strong boundaries:

- Using your passion to guide you and inspire others.

- Being kind to others.

- Demonstrating integrity within yourself and to others.

- Being wary of others who come on too strong, too fast.

- Not seeking validation from another.

- Not tolerating unacceptable actions or words.

- Asking a person before touching them.

- Appreciating others' truths.

- Observing others' boundaries and noting inappropriate behaviors and actions.

- Respecting others.

- Saying "no" to unwanted attention of all kinds.

- Trusting your decisions.

- Understanding that others have their own disadvantages and problems.

Here are some examples of behaviors that indicate you have weak boundaries:

- Trusting or distrusting without reason.

- Touching people without asking.

- Being overly involved (enmeshed) in others' lives.

- Being involved in hurtful talk or actions involving others.

- Defining yourself by how you want others to see and treat you.

- Expecting people to read your mind.

- Disrespecting others.

- Having a rigid mindset.

- Jumping quickly into relationships or situations.

- Ignoring or minimizing others' experiences and opinions.

- Not listening to your own inner voice.

- Revealing everything about yourself to people you don't know well.

- Tolerating others' behavior that you find unacceptable to avoid rejection.

Boundaries and Self-Protection

One way to protect your boundaries is through energetic work. And perhaps the easiest way to do this is to cast a magic circle—a space within which you are safe from unwanted encroachments on your energy and your mind. A magic circle can also help you to avoid crossing others' boundaries.

When my youngest son was in preschool, he had major issues with respecting other children's boundaries, and he was very sensitive to others' emotions. We set to work creating his personal magic circle by training him to envision a protective white shield that grew from within him. This helped him to understand others' boundaries and to reinforce his own. He also slept with ancient Egyptian deities because the statues and images made him feel safe. You don't need to do that to reinforce your boundaries and not absorb others' energies, however. You can rely on whatever deities or images make you feel safe in your personal circle. As for my dearest youngest child, he is definitely a reincarnated pharaoh.

When I know that I'll be spending time with people who are energy vampires, I shield, set intentions, and make a list of all the things I will not say or do when I am with them. There are many stones you can carry with you to help reinforce your personal circle. Obsidian and other pure black stones are great for absorbing harmful energies. I like amethyst and rhodochrosite for self-acceptance, which encourages strong boundaries. I have a yellow citrine amulet that I carry at all times to facilitate healthy relationships. In the past, my weak personal policies have resulted in troubles with others, especially romantic entanglements. Citrine is great to augment my work in this area. Stones are amazing allies as we venture into Hekate's cave.

Protection is a part of the healing, but be mindful not to isolate yourself. It's easy for me to cut myself off from others completely (except for my offspring; I can't escape them). When I do this, I don't worry about violating my boundaries. But by doing so, I deprive myself of the richness of social relationships. Maybe you can relate to this. For me, understanding my own boundaries and those of others is a fascinating ongoing process. There is no perfect set of personal practices; they change over time and vary among individuals. Just do what feels right to you to keep you on your path.

Practica: Know Your Limits

Explore the times when someone has crossed the line with you. What was it that caused them to violate your limits? Make a list of absolute lines that others can't cross without consequences. Take these boundary definitions and turn them into affirmations. For example, if hate speech is a boundary for you, write a statement like: I will protect those who are marginalized. This moves the energy of the boundary from being dependent on the actions of others to your own sovereign principles. It's a form of reversal magic.

Practica: Your Personal Magical Circle

Thinking of boundaries as our personal magic circle solidifies their vital role in protecting yourself from harm. I've written extensively about casting magical circles—which are really just sacred spaces—in my previous books. A simple, yet profound exercise is to explore what is inside your personal magic circle and what is out of bounds. This exercise uses intuitive automatic writing. The key is to go with the flow, no editing or second guessing. Nobody will see your completed talisman unless you show them.

You'll need a candle, paper (canvas, wood, etc.), and art/writing supplies. We use this practice every year in Covina, where we elevate it to a true talisman through collages, painting, and so on. I've provided the basic steps below. Amplify this however you feel led.

Before you begin, draw a circle on a piece of paper, creating a template. Add stones of cleansing, protection, guidance, and inspiration, placing them around your template to form a sacred space.

Light a candle. Using the protocol discussed earlier, circle the flame counterclockwise around the paper, cleansing the space and summoning all that you need to keep outside of your circle, saying:

> I cleanse this space, claiming it as sacred. Sacred Flame, reveal to me all that which I need to keep outside of my personal magic circle.

Write, without editing, everything that surfaces in your mind that you need to keep out of your personal magic circle. Include serious things like hatred and invalidation, people who are toxic for you, and lighter items. When we do this as a collective exercise, we always finish up with the funny things we can't abide, from mint chocolate chip ice cream to creases down the front of pants. This calms the heaviness of the earlier items.

When you are finished, take up the candle and say:

> All this is beyond my circle; I have no space for it inside of my life.

Spiral the candle clockwise around the paper, saying:

> I protect my personal space; my boundaries are strong. Sacred Flame, remind me of what is sacred to me.

Now write everything that comes to mind, from music and movies to people and places. Include your deities, allies, cards, etc.—all that is sacred to you. Do this in a stream-of-consciousness style.

When you are finished, hold the candle over the paper, which has now become a talisman, and recite something like:

> This is my personal magic circle. All that blocks and binds is outside. All that nourishes is within my sacred space. As I speak it, so it becomes.

Extinguish the candle after contemplating your talisman, which you should see as a working document and a spell for maintaining your boundaries.

Chapter 8

Lampadios: The Illumination

With each step I take,
The unbearable heaviness of my false-skin,
The weight of the scars,
And the load of my burdens,
Is shed.
I leave it on the stairs,
One by one,
Piece by piece,
Stepping downward,
Dropping what needs to die
In my wake.
As the darkness approaches,
I am enlightened,
Seeing the glimmer of her torches,
Illuminating the journey.

Turn your gaze toward Hekate's torches, those guiding lights that lead us through her cave. This is Lampadios calling us toward her depths so that we can heal.

Lampadios (also Lampadephoros) is an ancient epithet meaning "lamp carrier." It refers to both torches and oil lamps that were used in rituals. Although these are different, they share the power of controlled fire. They hint at Hekate as the keeper of the primordial flame. Other titles meaning Torchbearer, including Pyrphoros and Dadophoros, are epithets associated with Hekate's broader role as illuminator—for instance, Phaesimbrotos (Bringer of Light) and Phosphoros (Light Bringer).

There are many ancient titles assigned to Hekate that illustrate her role as a goddess who lights the way. Indeed, her twin torches are one of her most iconic symbols. In the historical record, when Hekate arrived with her torch blazing, it was a portent that all would be well in the end. At times, she used her torches in mythical battles, like the one led by Zeus against the Titans. In one tale, she used them to light up an ancient city so that potential marauders were prevented from attacking. Usually, however, Hekate's appearance with her torches blazing was not connected to battle, but rather as a sign of her role as guide.

Hekate's dual torches have been written about and illustrated for over 2000 years. In The Chaldean Oracles, she is called the Hieros Pyr, the sacred fire.[1] She is also described as Anima Mundi, the World Soul, in these ancient fragments. It is through Hekate's sacred fire that all the material world is birthed and sustained. In myths, ancient rituals, and even plays, Hekate's fire is seen as all-powerful, as in this example from Sophocles:

Thou hallowed fire, weapon of Hecate the road-goddess, that she bears when ministering in Olympus on high and in her haunts by the sacred cross-ways on earth. (*Fragments*, Vol. 2)

In The Chaldean Oracles, Hekate is referred to as the hieros pyr of creation using different epithets, including the Flower of Fire (sometimes translated as the Rose of Fire) and the Lightning Striker. These are noetic epithets referring to her role as the cosmic World Soul. Less philosophical ancient writers evoked her fiery nature as well, as in The Greek Magical Papyri. Some scholars contend that the torch is a phallic symbol representing a Great Mother who presides over both the feminine and the masculine.[2]

The torch represents the divine immanence in all things. We are drawn to Hekate's torch because it is a kindred spirit to the light within us, and the inherent phosphorescence in the universe. If you've ever sat alone in a dark room with a lit candle, which I heartily encourage you to do, you may have touched upon this sort of energy. Softening into the candle, allowing your mind to rest, evokes a feeling that you can't quite describe, but that you feel and know. When you feel it, you are touching the divine immanence of the goddess.

Compare this to lighting a candle in a room immersed in artificial light. It's not the same at all. In modern times, we don't go around with torches to light up the night, but we can return to the power of Hekate's flame when we turn off artificial lights. We need the Dark Mother's healing in order to see our true inner light. There is no way for us to get to soul without entering the darkness. Tiger's eye is the stone to use for this part of your journey. Set a piece on your altar beside the candle to amplify your forward momentum into the cave and to help hone your intuition.

The divine immanence of the goddess has been denied in our culture for hundreds of years. Those who follow Hekate's torch to their truth have been persecuted, tortured, and murdered. We've been labeled as weirdos and pushed to the edges of society because of our refusal to deny her sacred flame. And what we are experiencing on the individual level is happening on a global scale.

When we turn inward to our soul fire, we illuminate the world because we are connecting with Hekate's torch. This takes bravery. We are finally admitting to ourselves that we carry within us the healing power of her fire. We are finally acknowledging the need to abide in both what's sometimes called the world of force and the world of form. Jung called these the "spirit of the depths" and the "spirit of the times."[3] The depths of the hidden world, the world of force, is where the torches of the goddess shine brightest. Lampadios comes to us in dreams, in remembering who we are, and in her unexpected messages and visions. She is the fire that burns within.

The Fire That Burns Within

In today's chaotic world, we've seen the false light of the dominant cultural and social structures crack wide open, allowing Hekate's darkness to break through. Most likely, you found the light of the goddess when you were experiencing a "dark night of the soul." And this is where we find ourselves as a planet. This is a tipping point—a *nyssa*. But if we peer into the darkness, we see Hekate's torch blazing, waiting for us to enter her cave. When we enter, the torch becomes a mirror of the spark that burns within each of us. We are being cracked open to our inner light.

Lampadios is often depicted with two blazing torches to illustrate her connection to the primordial fire. She shines the light for those willing to enter her cave. Perhaps the most striking modern-day depiction of this is the Statue of Liberty, who beckons the weary to her land of acceptance and opportunity. The torch-bearing goddess shines brightest when it is darkest. In our personal lives, it is only when she feels out of reach that she comes to us.

Turning toward Hekate's torch ignites our courage. Answering her claim brings empowerment and peace. We find firm footing that vibrates with healing essence. It brings with it a return to the womb, a reawakening of the sacred feminine. It is dark and wet, the perfect antidote to the barren dryness of modern life. The torch illuminates and warms, offering protection and guidance. As we heal, Hekate's fire becomes stronger within us. It melds with us. As a blacksmith shapes lumps of metal into beautiful treasures, it shapes our beings into our unique truth. The fire blossoms within until we are reborn from it. What you may be experiencing now is the brightness of those torches, illuminating patterns that are keeping you bound, casting a glow around possibilities long forgotten and clarifying the way forward.

When you turn toward Hekate's torch, you bring into consciousness that which needs attention. You fill the vessel of your mind, your internal temenos, with what is nourishing while continuing to illuminate what no longer serves. You experience the crystal clarity of standing within your center and allowing what wants to come forward to do so. This can be a huge transition; go easy into this process. Hekate's symbols are often how our conscious minds receive her healing. It shows up in dreams, in our imaginations, and in unexpected synchronicities. And while these traditional symbols are important, so are the ones that are unique to us.

Torches are hopeful symbols. They light the way forward and the way inward. Lampadios is thus the proverbial light at the end of the tunnel. But she is also much more than this. She is the firelight of the soul burning within. When we turn toward her torch, we awaken our own light. Hekate carries our soul-torch, lit from her primordial source, until we are able to reclaim it for ourselves.

At the heart of Hekate's Wheel is a star that represents the goddess's fire. Thus, when we enter into Hekate's cave, we embark on the journey within this Wheel that leads to her primordial fire. That is the healing her torches bring. They are the soul made material.[4]

One important aspect of the symbolic power of Hekate's torches is how they were used in history to demonstrate her governance over the Three Worlds—Upper, Lower, and Middle. The torch lights the Under-world, but is born from the primordial fire of the heavens above. Hekate's role as Enodia, the goddess of highways and journeys, signifies her illumi-nation along our earthly journey. To the ancients, she ensured safe passage along roads and through treacherous crossroads, in much the same way that she guides us through our personal lives. Hekate Lampadios guides us forward into the mysteries of her wisdom. To access this wisdom, we turn inward to the torch fire within our souls by leaning into our intuition and reserves. Hekate nourishes our inner fire as we travel her road, healing and empowering us as we go, protecting us from the nasty glare and the sordid lies we encounter as we veer away from the false dead-end roads of the civilized world.

You are the ground on which I travel,
And you are the way.
You are the shadows and the night,
And you are the nourishing light.
Bright shining sacred fire that beckons me deeper.
Eternal as the universe itself.

Three Torchbearers

Hekate, Persephone, and Demeter are all depicted as torch-bearing god-desses, reinforcing Hekate's role as the Triple Goddess and recognizing both their individual and combined powers. Persephone learns to use her torch to bring light to the Underworld. Demeter uses hers to light her way through her grief. Hekate uses hers as a torch of guidance. When we explore the historical significance of their torches, we see that they were associated with their diverse roles. Torches were often associated with chthonic deities, representing their ability to "see in the dark." Indeed, Persephone in her fullness as queen of the Underworld has been represented with torches as well, as was her mother, Demeter, creating yet another linkage between these three goddesses.

The torches of all three goddesses signify vigilance; they are always on the lookout. We see this in some of Hekate's other roles as well, including her self-contained three-headed self that looks in three directions at once. Demeter's relentless quest to find Persephone symbolizes our internal journey to our own unique truth. The power of the goddess to illuminate what is hidden is demonstrated at various times throughout the story. Near the beginning, when Persephone is distraught and Demeter is grieving, Hekate apparently leaves the young girl to take care of herself while she goes in search of Demeter. This symbolizes Hekate's role as mediator and unifier.[5] Demeter, who was raging against her daughter's betrothal, refused to accept reality. We've all had experiences like this, when our insistence on clinging to a situation we can't remedy leads to great upset. Ultimately, the way we heal is to bring this truth into our consciousness. Avoiding reality rarely helps. Hekate's torch can illuminate even the most difficult situations and can teach us to stop avoiding that which cannot be undone. Through Persephone's peril, we can see how our own naivete may have contributed to our troubles. We walk with Demeter in her outer expression of anger because our inner Persephone is suffering.

The relationship of these three goddesses is a testament to fidelity—to themselves, to each other, and to the unfathomable demands of that which we can't control. This may be the machinations of others, sometimes even of those who exist solely in our minds, or the whims of destiny. Like Persephone and Demeter, we can shine our own torch to light our own way, and also allow Hekate's torch to burn so brightly within us that we provide the same illumination for others going through their own cave journeys. This is the divine immanence of the goddess at work in the world.

Individuation and Sympathetic Fire

Kindling our soul fire ultimately allows us to shine a light for others as they pursue their own wholeness. This sympathetic fire can thus be a cocreation that nourishes us as individuals while supporting others. Contemplate how Lampadios creates this evocative emotional response within you. She compels you to enter her darkness so you can reach your own light at the end of the tunnel.

The goal of personal development within depth psychology is known as individuation.[6] Simply stated, this is the process of living from the center of our beings with healthy boundaries and openness. Being individuated means that we relinquish our dependencies on others. We no longer live according to someone else's expectations, rules, or desires, or what they think we are or should be. Going into the cave is part of this process since there is no wholeness without darkness. Consider the "terrible twos," in which tantrums kick-start a toddler's independence; consider adolescent rebellion. Adult individuation characteristics include leaving jobs, ending relationships, and defining what is meaningful to us. All come with great upheaval.

While this may sound as if the emphasis is on our solitary work, by becoming whole ourselves we become connected to others in deeply meaningful ways. We go through different individuation processes throughout our lives. The infant individuates from total physical dependency on the primary caregiver for survival.[7] In adolescence, we transition our attachment relationships from our parents to friends and romantic partners, and we establish our own journey, separate from our families of origin.[8] For Jung, the greatest individuation occurs when we fully become our own unique being, freed from familial and societal expectations.[9]

We experience sympathetic fire when we are inspired by the light that another shines. This can be a friend, a public figure, or a mythic character. Their torchlight reflects our own and amplifies the underlying archetype of foundational fire. When we are being led by shadow, this fire may burn us. We can find ourselves in repetitive relationships with people who tend the shadow's flames. But Lampadios shines her light on those relationships, illuminating dysfunctional patterns.

A consistent phenomenon I've observed in my students is that their relationships change dramatically as they lean into their inner torchlight. They report ending shadowy alliances that they've been unable to escape for years. "Friends of convenience"—those who perhaps lit their fire at one point, but certainly don't anymore—tend to fall away. Temporary loneliness may result, but without fail, students quickly find nourishing relationships that strengthen their inner flame.

Shadow, Self, and Soul

The great Marion Woodman wrote extensively on the interplay between aspects of shadow, self, and soul. In *Dancing in the Flames: The Dark Goddess in the Transformation of Consciousness* (coauthored with Elinor Dickson), she describes the process of turning to the Dark Mother in order to find the internal torchlight that allows us to see the light in all things, including our interior territory. We are shadow, self, and soul. We put on our personas, which are the outer projections of ourselves—some nourishing, some constraining. All these aspects blend into an internal construct sometimes called the ego.

The ego, in and of itself, is not destructive. Consider it to be your surface self. If you live purely in its shallowness, however, you simply cannot see your inner light, nor the torch of the goddess. It is opaque at best, pure murky miasma at worst. While the ego has an important role to play as the interface between you and external reality, if it is controlled by the shadow, you end up being projections of it rather than emanations of your true light. As you gain the brilliant clarity found in Hekate's cave, you gain the ability to dialogue with shadow, to see from the soul, and to intentionally create the self. (This is a tough subject; perhaps hold on to your tiger's eye as you read and make notes on this section.)

Think of your personas as roles you play—mother, daughter, partner, worker, student, friend, and so on. Some of these roles are true to your soul, others are simply part of life, and a few can be a burden. Your soul holds space for the personas that are nourishing, but can be brutal to those that aren't. When you turn inward to the torch of the goddess, she will guide you in which personas you should maintain, and which need to be let go. We see this in the story of Persephone, as she learns that she is both daughter and wife. Likewise, these personas of ours often need to undergo substantial revision until we find the right balance. That is the illumination of the cave. As Woodman tells us: "Hecate has the wisdom that allows Persephone to be daughter to her mother and, at the same time, wife to her husband."[10]

Whenever you engage with a persona, you enter into an underlying archetype—daughter, mother, or wife, for instance. But these archetypes need not be exclusive. You may be a "work wife," for example, or a teenage rebel trying to piss off the "mother."

One of my personal favorites of Hekate's titles is Pyriboulos, which translates as "she of fiery counsel." Indeed, Hekate's messages can be quite heated, and may even burn a bit. Yet they are always sage advice. She calls for us to shed our false skin, peeling away the layers of all that no longer serves. The shadow suit of certain personas cannot withstand the heat of her torches. Yet there are personas that we still need to assume, and some of these will be eager to oblige. When you go to work, you put on the persona suitable for that environment. You may play the role of the good daughter to avoid conflict, which can become constricting as you journey into your own wholeness.

Some of your personas may not fit quite right—like getting stuffed into a snowsuit that is too small when you were a child. You stand there rigid, unable to move, afraid that you'll pop the seams. But when you are standing before the torches of Hekate Lampadios, who reveals all falsity, that snowsuit becomes unbearable. Explore what personas are feeling too "hot" for you. Which ones work to feed your shadow rather than reflecting your authentic self?

The self (sometimes called the Self, with a capital "S") is widely understood as the soul, and also called the psyche. The soul, residing largely outside of our consciousness until we start to let the torch illuminate it, has a will all its own. How many times have you ended up in a predicament because you didn't listen to your intuition? That is the soul inviting you to listen to it. Or else. The soul comes to you with gifts—the visions and experiences you have of Hekate and the deeper world. This is because it is the connector between your regular state of being and your eternal, unborn self.

The soul is nonrational and nonlinear. It speaks through symbols, which is why it is helpful to explore what they mean when they break through into your consciousness. The soul holds the keys to the deeper world and what is to come. The soul sees the shadow and offers compassion and understanding.

We can honor the shadow through a number of talismans and rituals. One ancient talisman used for this purpose is the *maskelli maskello* (see below). Although the exact meaning of the term remains a mystery, it appears as part of the ancient *voces magicae* (magical names) in various texts, including The Greek Magical Papyri, where it is used to evoke the presence of Hekate. There is evidence that these power words are rooted in the Hebrew word *miskel,* which indicates a "song of wisdom." Certainly, contemplating our shadow is such an endeavor. When I first read one of the ancient spells containing this expression, I was enchanted. It opened up a door within me that called me into the depths of Hekate and spoke of memories from past lives. It was a transcendent encounter; I simply knew that maskelli maskello was about writing a hymn to the shadow. It is about revealing the mask within.

The shadow can be seen as a mask that we use to protect ourselves—but which simultaneously entraps us. In ancient rites evoking Hekate and her companions—as in Dionysian rites and in the Eleusinian Mysteries—worshippers often wore masks. Our shadow mask is one that we have worn unintentionally for too long. The time has come to take it off, with passion, kindness, and integrity. The act of projecting the shadow onto the mask removes its power over us. When we "name and claim" the pieces of our shadow, we start to be woven into wholeness.

Soul Vision

We all hold within us the innate ability to be in relation to Hekate, to the collective psyche, and to the world of spirits. This relationality also holds our psychic gifts. As you get deeper into the cave—as you are freed of binding personas and separate from the voices that don't nourish—your latent intuition rises to consciousness. Your inner compass gets stronger, and you may receive messages and insights from manifestations of certain archetypes. In particular, your daily oracle's meaning will become more apparent as you see the world as archetypal (see chapter 5). You may find that you receive symbols from Hekate and her companions. The sacred flame may form into images.

You may also start to experience visitations from ancestors, and even from etheric spirits like angels or saints. This ability is known by many names—psychic communication, mediumship, and channeling, for instance—yet most of these descriptions don't touch on the underlying ability. I call this ability *sibylika* in honor of the ancient sibyls who spoke prophecy and offered healing, reflecting their ability to communicate with the deeper world.[11] I also call it simply "soul vision," although it comes through in all our senses. Fairy tales offer us a way of seeing from the soul, revealing their deeper meanings. The great Marie-Louise von Franz's work on these tales is a fabulous way to enter into their mysteries. Her quote about our innate ability to see from the soul is a personal favorite:

> We could all be mediums, and all have absolute knowledge, if the bright light of our ego consciousness would not dim it.[12]

When we bring our soul vision to the forefront, it can illuminate how we've been drawing in information from the deeper world without even knowing it.

A side effect of leaving our soul vision unkindled is that we can accumulate the energy of others. Today, this is sometimes called empath overload, which can result in being burdened by the emanations from others. Often, we have become so accustomed to this that we aren't consciously aware of the noise in our heads from all these voices. While they can be deeply nourishing, they can burn scars into our psyche as well. These scars make us beautiful, but they can be very tender.

When we follow Hekate's torch, we become unavoidably aware of the ruckus in our heads that I call the "voice of others." This is a vast compendium of all those who hold space within us—our families, friends, and coworkers, as well as the voice of the collective conscious and the mores and values of our society. Now this isn't inherently bad. There are voices that support and love us, cheering us along our journey to wholeness. When we are low, having an imaginary conversation with one of these can be most helpful. Moreover, Hekate abides deep within our souls and often comes through as one of these voices. This can be how we receive her messages.

But because our own ability to connect to energy in many forms is strong, we can perceive these voices in a way that can be almost maddening. You know your dial is turned up too high when you are uncomfortable within the circle of mainstream society. But soul vision has always been at work, compelling us away from the cultural zeitgeist and drawing us toward the in-between where the soul is most content. We are inherently different from those who abide solely in what Jung called "the spirit of the times."

Think of it like this. There is a group, the collective of mainstream society, that has such a huge energetic pull that it typically overwhelms us. Most of those in that collective are focused on things like the latest Internet craze, celebrities, and so on. When we get stuck in this collective noise, we get sick because we are sensitive to the voices—both the noise that we perceive and its underlying energy. Simply put, we become strangers in a strange land. But the place we want to be is on the fringe of the collective, thereby reducing this noise. If you've ever been in a noisy room full of people, then left and come back, you'll know what I mean. We get accustomed to the racket while we're there, but when we try to return, we find ourselves wondering who turned up the volume. We don't even know how noisy it is until we step away from it. Entering Hekate's cave begins the process of distancing ourselves from this noise pollution, within the collective, and within groups and relationships.

Practica: Creating an Inner Council

This activity helps you distinguish personas that are taking up room in your sacred space but shouldn't be, from those who give good counsel— your personal torchbearers, your trusted advisors. Begin by drawing a circle as described in the boundaries activity in chapter 6. Imagine a council table placed in the center. Who gets a seat at the table? Who needs to be removed? Certainly, Hekate will sit at the head of this council, but perhaps you have other deities and spirits who advise you as well. Are there ancestors and archetypes who should be granted a seat? Are there certain personas you want to be represented? Be sure to leave a seat for the self and for the shadow as well.

Practica: The Torch of Creation

We often think that the shadow contains only negative elements—pain, bad habits, and the like. However, all that is hidden or suppressed within us is also part of the shadow. The shadow harbors experiences and emotions and feelings that long for us to pull them out from the darkness and illuminate them so they can grow to their fullness. You can help this to happen by creating your own symbolic torch, whether this is a drawing or a special candle, as a source of illumination. This torch can allow you to see the potential within yourself.

Sit with your candle or image and contemplate what is hiding in your shadows that you need to pull into your consciousness. This may be latent talents, long-abandoned dreams, even hobbies and interests. What have you forgotten? What was snuffed out by those clamoring voices of others? Consult with your Inner Council for guidance. Consider this the beginning of creating your unique torch. Set aside time each week for a "meeting" with your Inner Council to discuss what you are bringing to light.

Practica: Creating a Shadow Mask Talisman

To face the shadow is a ritual of acceptance. We enter into the temenos within to explore our wounds, our fears, and the parts of ourselves that we do not like. But the shadow is also the protector of the soul when it is unsafe for our true selves to interact with the world. The shadow is thus to be honored as part of who we are, yet it is a mask that we can choose to put on or take off. This exercise can help you bring to light the hidden shadow burdens we all unwittingly carry. Go gently into this project. Light your candle, connect with your tiger's eye, do your meditation, and draw your daily cards beforehand. See this as a sacred assignment, a true ritual unto itself.

I like to craft a *mirari*, a soul-seeing mirror, in advance of doing this activity. I encourage you to do likewise. Any mirror adorned with symbols that feel right to you is wonderful. Use the mirror to see both your physical appearance and beyond, looking into your eyes to see how you are much greater than your outward body. When you see your full reflection, you view your shadow in its totality. See this body and the light within as sacred space.

With pen and paper handy, say:

Maskelli Maskello, reveal my shadow to me.

Allow your imagination to open up to the parts within yourself that are the shadow. Write down any words that come to you, or sketch images if you like. Stay with the process. When you are finished, you can add flourishes that bless the talisman with healing energy—for instance, anointing it with oil or adding flowers. Allow your creativity to flow.

Keep your mask talisman in your Cista Mystica when it is finished. Use it as a focal point for communicating with your shadow when it threatens to get carried away. As you journey through Hekate's cave, continue to spend time with your shadow mask at least a few times a month. Over time, as your light comes through, you may want to change or replace some of the words or images with the new soul keywords and images that come to you.

Chapter 9
Borborophorba: The Catharsis

Borborophorba.
Borborophorba.
Borborophorba.
Catharsis.
Catharsis.
Catharsis.
Mother of the Cave.
Eater of Filth.
Goddess of Bones.
Mother of the Cave.
Eater of Filth.
Goddess of Bones.
Mother of the Cave.
Eater of Filth.
Goddess of Bones.
Borborophorba.
Borborophorba.
Borborophorba.
Catharsis.
Catharsis.
Catharsis.

Borborophorba, one of the more unusual of Hekate's epithets, is found in The Greek Magical Papyri. It translates to Filth Eater. A few years ago, when I started sharing this role with students, it truly caused a commotion. Some were immediately attuned to this symbolism, while others balked at the idea that their beloved goddess would eat garbage. Symbolically, Borborophorba dines on the meaty offerings of our wounds and shadow, relating the journey through her cave to the experience of catharsis. Borborophorba meets us as we finish the descent. She tells us that the price of admission to the cave is our unburdening.

Beyond the epithet, there is other historical evidence linking Hekate with waste. Notably, household waste and ritual leftovers from sacrifices made to her were offered as part of a supper on the night when the moon was dark. She thus had the power to dispose of waste and excrement, as well as the power to throw it at our fears and enemies. James Hillman, in *The Dream and the Underworld*, saw her filth-eating power as representative of releasing our internal garbage:

> The junk of the soul is primordially saved by Hekate's blessing, and even our trashing ourselves can be led back to her. The messy life is a way of entering her domain and becoming a "child of Hekate." Our part is only to recognize that there is myth in the mess so as to dispose of the day residues at the proper place, that is, to place them at Hekate's altar. Ritually, the garbage was placed at night at a crossroads, so that each dream may lead off in at least three directions besides the one we have come from. Hekate, who has traditionally been represented with three heads, keeps us looking and listening in many ways at once.

The cave journey is thus "making myth out of the mess." We offer to Borborophorba what longs to die within us while retaining the hard-gained wisdom.

Each of our myths is unique, beginning with what we deliver up to death and how we perceive the Filth Eater. In the boneyard of Hekate's cave, we leave our burdens, bringing death to that which has weighed us down. Allow yourself the gift of following your intuition. The gut knows. Indeed, the word *borborygmus* refers to stomach grumbling, signs of movement of the bowels. At a spiritual level, however, this can be "gut knowing."

Catharsis and Healing

The word "catharsis" comes from the Greek word for purgation. The idea that releasing brings healing is found throughout the centuries, from Aristotle to Freud. The body, mind, and soul are believed to benefit from a thorough cleansing of what is causing us trouble.[1] The release of long-held burdens clears the way for buried emotions to surface. When we purge our traumas and our distress, we create space in which more beneficial feelings can flourish. One of my favorite quotes is both the title of a semi-autobiographical work by C. S. Lewis and the name of a poem by William Wordsworth—"Surprised by Joy." To me, this is the gift of Borborophorba.

Whenever I think of catharsis, two bits of wisdom from the women in my family come to mind. My father's mother frequently burped loudly and proudly, then said: "Better out than in." When I was upset as a child, usually over some social slight, my own mom observed: "A good cry is what you need." These two women intuitively knew of the importance of both physical and emotional purging.

Our spiritual catharsis as we cross the first gate of Hekate's cave is essential for the journey ahead, because we are creating the space to allow healing to begin. Hekate as the Filth Eater is one face of the Great Mother who accepts our waste. The Aztec goddess Tlazolteotl also ate the waste of humans, then defecated it as flowers, symbolizing the transformative power of the goddess to turn filth into gold.[2] When we encounter Borborophorba, we become aware of how overburdened we are by the accumulation of shadow debris, spiritual programming, the impacts of toxic people, and so on. She challenges us to purge all these things. Yet she also reminds us that there is treasure in all of our waste. We may go digging in it to find it, or to extrapolate the flower of wisdom. If you've ever been severely constipated, you can relate to this process in a visceral way. Consider this transition period as recovery from psychological and spiritual constipation.

The Roman goddess Cloacina, who is related to Hekate through her roles relating to roads, governed sewers. In today's world, we can focus too much on the road and ignore the sewers that run beneath them in urban areas. Cloacina, the great purifier of the Roman world, rid the empire of waste, allowing the waters to run clean. And for every sewer pipe that removes waste, there is a conduit that brings pure water. All this is going on under our feet, in the subterranean darkness. In many cultures, Underworld goddesses are associated with this type of release. They are governesses of both trash and treasure.

Miasma

Cloacina, Tlazolteotl, and Borborophorba are all collectors of what the Greeks called *miasma*. Miasma doesn't have a precise English equivalent, but we can think of it as pollution.[3] In their religious practices, these goddesses removed miasma from the home and from its occupants, often in connection with rituals dedicated to Hekate.[4] Some thought that physical diseases were caused by miasma in the body.[5] Through various practices, this contaminant was regularly removed from the body and mind, and from buildings and the environment. Some thought cultural ills were caused by miasma as well. Infectious diseases were thought to be spread by it, for example. Today we use the word "toxic" in similar ways. Miasma is thus like a toxin that functions at the archetypal level as well as the physical. It has a spirit and will of its own and activates the archetype of fear upon which it rides. All miasma is supported by fear.

Miasma is the lifeblood of complexes, which are dysfunctional clusters of thought patterns, behaviors, and associated emotions. Complexes are expressions of archetypes.[6] They work on us, demanding to take up occupancy in our lives. Complexes are often seen as negative, but they also carry positive signatures. I've long identified with the queen of swords card in the tarot. As an archetype, the illuminated Queen of Swords is decisive, driven, and in control of her powerful mind. When she sits in shadow, however, she is razor-tongued and dictatorial. As a complex, she may occupy my personality in both capacities.

Typical complexes revolve around our families. Some may have a "mother complex," which can mean that their distress is driven by the relationship they have with their own mothers, or that they are entangled in the maternal archetype. Those with a "daughter complex" may continue to define themselves within this role in the family and may be occupied by the archetype of the young, dependent woman. Complexes can constellate around the self archetypes, like the Warrior, the Mystic, or the Healer.

Personally, I have a "savior complex" that pushes me toward rescuing people. None of these are inherently problematic. But when they are activated in inappropriate ways, they certainly can cause great upset.

When we are freed from miasma, it creates a space within us that we can fill with nourishment. But if we are not careful, miasma, often regurgitations of the past, can rush right back in. Allowing joy, contentment, and peace to come into ourselves can be enormously challenging if we've lived in the filth for ages. When you are unburdened of what no longer serves, you may experience something like the phantom limb phenomenon, in which people who've lost a limb still feel it (sometimes called "ghost" limbs). This process includes releasing pieces of yourself, which you may miss, even though they were beyond repair or making you ill.

And this is also an accurate description of our psychospiritual death-bringing. We feel the pull of old complexes, past relationships, and old wounds. Exploring our boundaries and putting them in place shields us against being consumed, being filled up once again by these hungry ghosts. The only way these ghosts can get past Borborophorba is if we step outside the temenos of her cave. Like Persephone, we have an obligatory time in the Underworld. If we abandon this journey, the entire balance of our lives will be thrown off-kilter.

Dealing with our "dirt" means facing the shadow. Filth is seen as "undivine" or somehow "sinful" in our society. We've all heard that "cleanliness is next to godliness." But Borborophorba teaches us that "dirtiness" is *of* the goddess. We see evidence of denial of the importance of exploring our dirt everywhere: how removed we are from our own garbage; how sanitized the world has become. Yet garbage is part of life. Without waste, is there abundance? The feminine is inherently messy. The menstrual cycle is still seen as "unholy" in many cultures. Yet without this mess, no new life can be created. Where is the mess in your life that you used to view as sinful, but that is truly sacred?

Healing is found in the miasma; it's in the dirt of trauma, invalidation, and suffering. There is an expression that the problem is the solution, and so it goes with this journey. Denial, blame, and other avoidance strategies pull us away from the process. Borborophorba teaches us that, as we expel our burdens, we extrapolate wisdom. We find the treasure that emerges from the mess. We find it when we get quiet—in the stillness. Just as when we take medicine but don't feel its effects until after our emotions simmer down, this treasure, this healing, comes to us through dreams, synchronicities, and inner knowings.

Shame–The Hidden Infection

Miasma shows up as shame. It tells us we aren't enough and are unworthy. Shame can be the infection that's usually so hidden that we don't even know we have it.[7] Shame as the unmerited experience of deep feelings of unworthiness is often an unspoken problem that wounds deeply. Others can cause great harm by invalidating our true nature. This miasma runs right through our core. While we may be cognizant of our anxieties and fears, and of the toxic people in our lives, exposing the underlying shame takes serious excavation. But Borborophorba is a willing consumer of this insidious disease. As you go deeper into the cave, pay attention to where shame is rearing its dirty little head. Resist the shadow's desire to judge yourself for feeling ashamed, stupid, lazy, inadequate, and all the other "shame cousins." If you find yourself doing this, shift your attention toward kindness for your shame. Acknowledging its existence and power are the first steps on the way to releasing shame.

Of course, shame has a place in the lives of those who have done truly shameful things. What I'm talking about here is the rest of us who feel ashamed without any legitimate reason. I'm not talking about making mistakes and then feeling contrite, either. My focus is on chronically feeling ashamed of who we are, and for things that were done to us. Shame is such a sneaky creature that we're unlikely even to be aware that it is holding us prisoner.

We feel shame not only through personal invalidation, but also from a culture that devalues our identity. Underneath all of this is always a history of trauma. We have many wounded among us who carry a great deal of shame. While the initial escape from abusive organizations and individuals often brings respite, unless we acknowledge our shame, we often remain controlled by it. What happens on the individual level is therefore expressed in our communities as a whole. We need to confront shame at both these levels.

Shame keeps us silent. We fear that everyone will think we're idiots or crazy if we speak up. No one will believe us. That's shame talking. Shame is a specific type of fear that's related to having our sense of self violated by others. But this fear is also spread through societal views of what's acceptable.

Think of shame as a disease-infected tree that is weighed down with a variety of rotting fruit. In the garden of your life, this tree draws out all your energy and keeps you from nourishing anything beautiful. When you shake the shame tree, the spoiled fruit falls to the ground. When this happens, you can send it to the compost pile, which is a sort of temple to Borborophorba. When I shake my family tree, shame falls out. The impacts of the deep shame I've felt have been widespread across my life. Shame has often prevented me from sharing who I am with others. It took me ages to work through this.

And shame still creeps up on me—for instance, when I heard one woman deride another because her children had two different fathers. Being the Queen of Swords that I am, I'm certain my face morphed into a mask of hurt and disgust at her words, causing her to stop mid-sentence and apologize to me. I've felt the shame that others have tried to heap on me about having been married twice. But I've come to realize that, when others throw unmerited shame at us, it's usually the fruit from their own shame tree that they are chucking. They are projections—projectiles—of their own insecurities.

When we stay in any type of abusive relationship, shame plays a big role in keeping us there. Then there's the shame involved in remaining quiet, when we are either victimized or standing silent while others are. If you are triggered by reading others' stories, I urge you to examine how shame over your own experiences may be involved.

If you long to be able to speak truth in a safe environment, I need you to know that you can and you will. Start small by finding an online community of like-minded souls. You have much to contribute. We need your voice. Right now, there are too many loudmouths clogging up the dialog and minimizing the power of our conversations. Evidence for all types of shame-spreading is everywhere these days. Speaking up is the first step. If you aren't comfortable doing so, find ways of quiet resistance, like not supporting individuals whose behavior is shame-inducing in others.

Getting real about shame, rather than continuing to deny that we feel it, is the way through. Given the deep nature of shame, energetic methods like Reiki can also help remove its toxicity from our minds and our bodies. Shame gets right into our tissues. It's also in some of our DNA. Ancestral healing work may be part of your journey. Start by acknowledging your shame. Follow this with a deep exploration of its roots. Finally, enter into catharsis. Simple rituals activate your healing from shame, like sitting quietly with a lit candle to see how it mirrors your own internal spark. Work with the energy of the waning moon for help with banishing your shame.

The Gate of Catharsis

Borborophorba brings us here, where we unburden ourselves of what longs to die within us. Whether personal trauma or enmeshment with societal toxicities, all is released as an offering to Hekate as we enter her sacred cave. As we shake the shame tree, we continue to explore and enforce these boundaries. Stay with your daily practice. Take your time before this first gate, allowing your burdens to come into vision. Know that emotions can be strong during the process. You may feel angry, afraid, distressed, or slightly anxious. All these feelings are invitations to explore what they are to you. Work on developing a relationship with them. Allow them to have their say. Until you listen to them, they will continue to act up. Give them a seat at the table of your Inner Council.

Fighting emotions because they are uncomfortable is not going to make them go away. One of my go-to mantras when my emotions are strong is: Get real, feel, deal, and heal. These intense feelings are positive. Borborophorba is chomping down on your burdensome garbage. Consider your avian companion as her assistant in your catharsis, eating away at what you are releasing—picking you clean.

After this catharsis comes a hunger. These pangs are an invitation to a buffet of what truly feeds your soul. You may emerge ravenous for both physical nourishment and "soul food." You may feel exhilarated and eagerly search for meaningful nourishment. After a purge, however, we can also feel exhausted. There is no right or wrong reaction to catharsis. Stay with the emotions that come up. The sense of spaciousness, that hunger of the soul, is an invitation for your purpose to percolate to the surface. It can take time to adjust to the empty space, to learn what your soul needs to be well fed. It is from this space that you will embark on the great journey into your unique wholeness.

Of course, the road that led you to this moment is part of the map of your life. It's all a bit like home renovations—demolition creates a great mess but leads to a beautiful new environment. Trauma and pain are important parts of your "messy myth."

One of the most transformative books I have read on my personal journey is *Broken Open: How Difficult Times Can Help Us Grow* by Elizabeth Lesser. I found this book when I was utterly defeated after the end of an abusive relationship with a true narcissist. Heartbroken, I went to a large bookstore with the intention of calling forth a book that would feed my starving soul. When you experience catharsis, you begin to crave a healthy spiritual diet instead of the old junk food. Old ways of being, tired relationships, unfulfilling jobs, even your physical surroundings may find themselves on your list of dietary restrictions as you seek out what nourishes the center of your being. Go gently into making any major changes.

After cleansing the miasma, we can become acutely aware of toxicities in others. Creating space in which the healing of the deeper world nourishes us, we become sensitive to the risk of infection by toxic people around us. We all have miasma—not merely the wounds from others, but also our own shadows. Keep in mind when dealing with others that they are also wounded. This isn't to say that you should put up with their filth. Just be mindful of the fact that they are wounded, too.

You can be in close relationships with people who are toxic. Exploring your shadow inevitably leads you to become more attuned to the same issues in the people you know best. In a general sense, people can be considered toxic if their presence is generally upsetting to you, although there are broad categories of personalities that are particularly infectious. When discerning whether a person is truly toxic, keep in mind that some people are introverts, shy, depressed, or anxious. All these problems can lead to presenting characteristics that can be mistaken for toxicity.

The Shadow of Narcissism

Narcissism is a term that describes a spectrum of behaviors, thoughts, and emotions in personalities who present with exceptional confidence and self-focus.[8] A small bit of narcissism can be very adaptive. We need to be our own cheerleaders, and being somewhat self-absorbed is healthy. Narcissism becomes problematic, however, when it descends into false bravado combined with the tendency to be very bombastic. These individuals appear utterly self-absorbed and are extremely manipulative. Unfortunately, they are usually also very enchanting. At the most troubling end of the spectrum is narcissistic personality disorder, which is quite rare.

Understanding that a tiny bit of narcissism as both healthy and maladaptive deepens our ability to explore how this trait presents within us and others. A key distinction between healthy and harmful narcissism is how you feel when you are with others. Do they demand your undivided admiration? Do you feel as if you're constantly walking on eggshells around them?

But narcissism is more than a personality aspect or psychological disorder. It is also a deep archetype that is described through myths like the original story of Narcissus, who was fated to stare longingly at his own reflection but never see his own interior depths.

When Persephone, as the innocent maiden—before the great trauma that ultimately led to her triumph—is introduced in the Homeric *Hymn to Demeter*, she is being lured by narcissus flowers, which are the last ones she picks.[9] This indicates that Persephone, then still Kore, has become enthralled with the outer life. She delights in herself without any thought to her inner depths. But if all we do is pick flowers on a sunny day with nymphs, we will never answer the call of the soul. We become this young version of Persephone when we remain stuck in an adolescent version of ourselves. This primary narcissism is part of healthy development.

We need to focus on the outer self in order to understand who we are in relation to others. But this trap can be difficult to outgrow, especially in the face of the societal pressures that keep us from maturing:

Narcissism is yet another pitfall for some Persephone women. They may become so anxiously fixed on themselves that they lose their capacity to relate to others. Their thoughts are dominated by self-questions: "How do I look?" "Am I witty enough?" "Do I sound intelligent?" And their energy goes into makeup and clothes. Such women spend hours in front of mirrors. People exist only to give them feedback, to provide them with reflecting surfaces in which to see themselves.[10]

While the primary type of narcissist is stuck in childhood, the grandiose narcissist is the classic version we often see in celebrities and politicians. These are the bombastic loudmouths who can't stop telling us how wonderful they are.

Common to both primary and grandiose narcissists is an inability (or refusal) to understand the feelings of others. They also have a need to demonstrate their supposed greatness due to a poorly formed self-concept. It's easy to tell primary from grandiose narcissists because their own behavior tells us everything we need to know. But it is more difficult to identify a covert narcissist. These personalities are often far more damaging than overt narcissists because we can't quite put our finger on why they make us feel bad about ourselves. All three types feed on the attention of others, but covert narcissists get their fix by creating dependency. They rely heavily on passive-aggressive methods and convince others, especially children and romantic partners, that they need them to survive because they themselves are utterly worthless. This is a reflection of their own profound insecurity and inability to feel empathy.

Overt narcissists are out to get us. They attack, they gaslight, they lie, they manipulate, and use other forms of abuse in ways that are glaringly obvious because of their aggressive nature. At first, they may fake a caring nature, but as soon as we violate their need for control, they lash out. Contrast this to covert narcissists, whose attacks are much more subtle, yet more damaging because they use all the same tactics, but in a way that is difficult to discern. Malignant narcissists share many characteristics with psychopaths—a lack of empathy, vivid mean streaks, and a lack of restraint that disregards social conventions.[11] Both can be overly aggressive, either physically or through psychological means. Gaslighting—convincing someone they are wrong even when all evidence indicates otherwise—is a very common toxic tactic.

Both psychopaths and malignant narcissists are typically quite bold. They care little for social norms and are fundamentally unable to take responsibility for their actions. It is incredibly difficult for those with high levels of narcissism and psychopathy to change. Often, they lack the personal insight to entertain the idea that they even have a problem. The most important thing to know if you have these types in your life is that you cannot change them. All you can do is manage how you interact with them.

While we all can act a bit narcissistic from time to time, true narcissists continually demonstrate the trait in a wide variety of situations, and they always make us feel the same way—ashamed. As you move deeper into Hekate's cave, your ability to discern between truly toxic people and those who are nourishing to you amplifies. This may result in a cutting away of relationships with those who offer nothing but a steady diet of toxicity.

The Keys to Soulful Living

Exploring how people can be toxic has the potential to entangle us in the underlying archetype. We can get infected with the spirit so that we see the bad in everyone. This isn't our fault; we're dealing with incredibly powerful forces. Bringing into consciousness that toxic personalities are driven by deeper archetypes can help you to prevent infection.

Look at the events of the world these days. It's as if the spirit of Narcissus is everywhere. Yet there is much more going on if you just look beyond that shadowy reflection. By performing your daily practice, working with your shadow mask, and continuing to explore your boundaries, you can inoculate yourself against the powerful force of the shadowy aspects of Narcissus and turn toward soulful living.

Soulful living relies on three key principles: passion, kindness, and integrity.[12] All three of these are missing from, or not functioning in, shadows and the types of toxic personalities I talked about earlier. Passion is the energy of enthusiasm, courage, creativity, and curiosity. Kindness includes taking care of ourselves as well as considering that others have their own experiences, burdens, and challenges. Integrity is the enactment of our boundaries, following through, and living on the outside what we know to be true in our center. Living these principles can be subtle or audacious.

Add the exploration of these principles to your daily practice. Do a "PKI Check-Up," as we say in my school. How are you allowing each of them to live through you? How could you let them work on you more? Seeing these principles as archetypal forces and yourself as the channel through which they are expressed, provides you with a steady diet of real soul nourishment. Contemplate how your avian ally embodies them. Create symbols of them using three keys and keep them in your Cista Mystica. When times get tough, which they always will, "PKI it" for a sort of quick catharsis. This approach works well with even the most mundane tasks. I absolutely loathe cleaning the house, so I put on my Clean Sweep playlist and PKI the hell out of tidying up.

Practica: Ritual of Catharsis

This is one of the Rituals of the Sacred Cave I referred to in chapter 6. I've led hundreds of students through it, and I've adapted it here so you can do it on your own. If you are feeling a bit intimidated by the process of a formal ritual, that is perfectly normal. The previous chapters laid the foundations for this ritual, and subsequent chapters will help you with the integration process after the catharsis.

For this ritual, you will need:

- A release candle (preferably a black candle to symbolize the junk being released).

- One of Hekate's stones. Red jasper is excellent for releasing shame, especially for wounds associated with sex and sexuality. It is also a balancing and embodying stone, bringing vitality in the days after the ritual.[13] Black obsidian is the powerhouse stone that can absorb almost anything. Spend time with all the stones before the ritual.

- An offering from Hekate's garden. Agrimony, juniper, moss, sage, and yarrow are excellent accompaniments for this ritual.[14]

- Sacred oil. In *Entering Hekate's Garden*, I shared the formula for creating an Oleum Spirita, a sacred oil. Any oil that has botanical signatures of catharsis will work. Test the oil to ensure that it is safe for you.

Before you begin, determine your offering. The ritual features an offering symbolic of what you are releasing. For example, you can offer a ring that represents a past relationship or keys to a former home. It can be a piece of jewelery, a photo, an article of clothing, or whatever represents what you are releasing.

Next, create a Borborophorba altar that use images and symbols that evoke the energy of the filth-eating goddess. A piece of black obsidian is excellent for this altar, as is red jasper. I recommend using a fresh candle, which you can relight after the ritual to help with further releasing. Make certain to have your avian ally present on the altar, as it will be your guide during the journey into the cave.

When your altar is ready and prior to the ritual, purify your body with a ritual bath. A perennial favorite of mine and my students is a black-salt scrub. This rids the body, mind, and spirit of miasma, making the ritual much more meaningful. While there are many ways to make the scrub, a basic formula is to mix ¼ teaspoon of activated food-grade charcoal powder with one cup of high-quality sea salt. Cover the mixture with olive oil and blend. You can add appropriate botanicals like lavender and rosemary. Warning: you'll end up covered in black sludge, but it washes off easily with soap. My students who are brave enough to do this consistently report never having felt so cleansed and have become repeat users.

After cleansing, and about thirty minutes to one hour before you perform the ritual, anoint the inside of your ankles and wrists with your sacred oil, then place a few drops on the three meridians of the root, heart, and crown. You can repeat the process at the beginning of the ritual.

Here is a short text that you can read for your ritual. Adapt it as works best for you.

Light the candle, anoint it with the oil, and hold it at your heart center, saying:

I am on the journey through darkness to wholeness.
This light ignites the fire in my soul and connects me to the eternal torches of Hekate.

Move the candle in a counterclockwise circle three times while saying:

Through this flame, all that harms is banished.

Move the candle three times in a clockwise circle while saying:

I am protected within this sacred space from all that harms.

Return the candle to your heart center and say:

The Ritual of Catharsis has begun.
I am blessed with the power of release.

Place the candle on the altar. Anoint the root, heart, and crown with the oil (three times each) in a clockwise manner. Hold your avian ally symbol at your heart center, anoint it with oil, and say:

I call upon my avian companion, lead me into Hekate's cave.

Return the symbol to the altar, then pick up the candle and hold it at your heart center and say:

I call out to Hekate, grant me entrance into your cave.

Replace the candle on the altar and take up the offering. Holding it at your heart center, say:

I honor you with this sacrifice, Borborophorba.
I willingly bring death to this burden I carry.
I offer this . . . (Describe the offering you are giving her and why.)
Accept my sincere offering,
Mighty Goddess of Catharsis.

Envision the altar as a portal to Borborophorba's cave. See the candle flame lighting the entrance to the cave. Open your soul vision to see yourself walking through the flame into the cave. The flame becomes Borborophorba, consuming the miasma in your offering. Imagine the weight being lifted; feel the space created.

Stay with this feeling for as long as you need. If emotions come up, pour them into the candle as well. Once you are feeling lighter, see the energy of the candle shifting from consumptive to an outpouring of Hekate's wisdom. Take careful notice of any images, sensations, or feelings that come to you. A symbol will manifest.

After the ritual, spend time either crafting or selecting a physical representation of the symbol you received as a souvenir of your catharsis. Keep it in your Cista Mystica. Refer back to the tips for processing and integrating deeper-world experiences in chapter 6. You can dispose of the offering in whatever way feels right to you. Some students keep the offering in their Cista Mystica, while others bury or burn it.

Chapter 10

Skotia: The Darkness

Hail, Hekate, Mistress of the Night.
Pale Chthonic Queen,
It is to your darkness I turn
When the world threatens to consume me.
Hail, Hekate, Mistress of the Night.
Torch-bearing Goddess,
I freely follow your path,
As you light the way toward truth.
Hail, Hekate, Mistress of the Night.
Keeper of the Keys,
I take those you offer
And claim them as my right.
Hail, Hekate, Mistress of the Night.
I seek your mysteries of the dark,
Reveal your truth and mine.
Hail, Hekate, Mistress of the Night.
Guardian of Souls,
Awaken what is deep inside my darkness.

Skotia is the essence of the darkness and the depths of obscurity. In the post-catharsis terrain of the cave, she is the elemental darkness that surrounds us and fills the space we have created. But this darkness doesn't evoke the terrors of the night. Rather we find ourselves in the dark, wet womb of the goddess. It is here in the utter darkness that we enter the first stages of gestation of what we are becoming.[1]

Persephone, in her despair, refused to eat, believing that denying herself nourishment would lead to her emancipation. We've all been there—heartbroken, betrayed, and full of pain. But eventually, she summoned her strength to dine on the darkness.

Consider your interior world, that which you never share with anyone. The darkness of Skotia is like those prized secret desires and interests. I think of this deepest dark as the feeling of being safely tucked in bed, knowing that I am protected from all harm. Working with this deep darkness within awakens a similar sense of contentment. It also brings with it the wonder of our own mysteries—from why certain things light us up to our innermost dreams. Indeed, this is the dreamworld, our nightly explorations of the goddess's deeper world. As Hillman wrote, this is where we find the meaning of our lives.[2] It is where the true nourishment abides.

Diodorus Siculus, in his historical accounts of the ancient Mediterranean, mentions a temple near Memphis in Egypt dedicated to Hekate Skotia.[3] For me, living in Nova Scotia, I was enchanted when I stumbled across this obscure epithet. How did Scotia go from being a title of my beloved goddess to being the name of the place I call home? The answer is mythic, naturally. To the Egyptians, the title was one bestowed on goddesses of the night. Skotia spoke to me of the mysteries of Hekate, of her sacred darkness, of the unconscious, and of the way through darkness to wholeness.

Placing Hekate in Egypt begins with a brief detour to possible connections with the similarly named goddess Heqet (Hekat) and also Heka, who was the deification of magic. Both share the responsibility for helping to bring new life into the world.[4] So, although Heqet is not an historical antecedent of Hekate based on the available evidence, she is very closely tied to her in spiritual meaning. Moreover, Hekate, the goddess whose worship spread across the region, was well known in Egypt during the time of the great empire of the Greeks. The most striking evidence of this comes

Entering Hekate's Cave

from the collection of fragments known as The Greek Magical Papyri that inspired me to write this book.[5]

The Legend of Scota

Skotia—also known as Scotia, Scota, and even Scoti because of the different translations that have been done over the centuries—was most likely a mythic figure who had origins in the human wife of a pharaoh, perhaps even the great Tutankhamen. By the time of the ancient temple to Skotia described above, the title referred to the feminine darkness and was held in high esteem.

Legend has it that a young princess name Scota sailed north with her husband, known to the Irish as Gaodhal Glas, to the Emerald Isle when the Egyptian temple to Skotia would have been active.[6] Their descendants became the Gaels of ancient Ireland, and later the Scots. Perhaps young Scota was blessed by Hekate in her eponymous temple. We can imagine young Scota boldly venturing into the darkness of the unknown as she set foot on that ancient sailing ship destined to birth Scotland and Ireland. Perhaps she stood on the prow under the stars, feeling very alone among the sailors. Surely, she left behind a life she knew in search of a promise of brighter days.

Scota was a sovereign queen in a foreign land, going to her death in an epic battle with the Tuatha Dé Danann as she sought vengeance for her husband's death.[7] Those who know the pitch-black of grief can understand the type of darkness that can light the torch of revenge. Scota evolved over time into the figure of the Wise Woman through stories shared around the hearth. She is transformed into the Cailleach in some legends. Scotland now bears her name, possibly in reference to the valiant warriors known as the Scotti.[8] And my home became the new land of Scota, Nova Scotia.

The Primordial Darkness

The epithet Skotia has been translated into English as "black," "shadow," "night," "gloomy," and "murky." Skotia can thus be experienced as a smokey darkness created by the trail of Hekate's torches that forces us to be still—as the isolation of standing alone on our own ship, or even as the pit of despair. It is the shadow within that we can see only when we begin to go deep into our own darkness. When our complexes and working models become illuminated, we see the patterns of our lives. The absolute stillness allows us to peer through our personal unconscious into the archetypal underpinnings. These are the mysteries of the Crone—Hekate fully realized as the one who can contain all our darkness because she is the darkness itself. You may perceive her as an aged woman or not. Her outward appearance can vary based on how you need to see her. Yet Skotia is the most ancient one. The dark existed long before there was light. And it is to this primordial darkness that we return.

Skotia is not hopeless, however, for it is when we stand with absolutely nothing in the blackest of nights that we finally begin to see. The power of Skotia is to see from the soul. In this sacred darkness, which is womblike and lunar, we begin to explore our depths. We open up to our soul's vision, which perceives our inner depths and sees beyond chronological time. Skotia opens us up to the *kairos*, the eternal cyclical time of the goddess. We stretch back into the past to heal old wounds. We peer into the future to orient ourselves toward the foretold rebirth. And we stand very still in the darkness until our eyes adjust to it in all the forms she brings.

Skotia evokes the primordial darkness from which all life came. She is The Before, the ancient, the timeless. She is wisdom and kindness. Her womb birthed the universe. She appears to us in many guises. The Great Mother, of course, is light *and* darkness. She is young *and* aged. Yet when we turn inward to what is ancient within, she often comes as the Crone, with her many faces—which include the Cailleach. I personally have connected to the Crone as the Cailleach, whom Scota became.

Hail to the darkness,
Without and within.
Hail to the Underworld,
Without and within.
I honor my darkness,

I value my time in the Underworld.
Hail to Hekate who stands with me in the
Dark of my Underworld journey.
To the light of her torches,
To the gift of her keys,
To the deeper world.
Our journey is of the dark
And the Underworld.
Hail to the emotional depths
Through which we are reborn.
Hail to the dark, wet womb
From which all life comes.

There is a story, told in many different versions, about a young selkie who lost her sealskin and thus had to live on land because the man who wanted her for his wife kept her precious pelt from her. Over the years, however, caring for her husband and child couldn't extinguish her yearning for the natural joy she had felt in her shiny skin, which had allowed her to swim down into the ocean's depths. She chose to leave the darkness that wasn't nourishing her to dive back into her true self so she could swim in the deep waters that had given her life. She did this knowing that the journey back would be difficult. When she finally retrieved her pelt, however, it was dried out and brittle.

With great endurance, and in the spirit of determined despair, she made her way to the Cailleach, who told her that the only way for her to become whole again was by venturing into a cavern. After being restored by the Cailleach's tea, the selkie set out again. Once inside the cavern, she was shocked to discover that all her family had been slain there. Steadfast in her resolve to put things right, she again sought the Cailleach's advice and was told to sing a secret tune. One by one, her loved ones were reborn and her pelt—her soul suit—was restored. Reunited, the whole family danced around the fire in the cave, and then dove into the ocean depths.

The territory of Skotia is our unconscious. She is the entirety of the spirit world and the dominion of the soul. She is the feminine soul of the world. We can think that our shadow is the limit of our darkness, but it resides on the fringe of this vast realm. The shadow is shadowy. It is the projection of the parts of ourselves that we don't want to admit exist, until we have no choice but to do so. When we begin to heal the shadow, bringing to light what has been hidden too long and releasing what has kept us bound, we draw ever nearer to the unconscious. This can be a difficult passage.

Our task here is twofold—to bring the shadow parts of ourselves to consciousness so that healing can occur, and then to turn inward to the deepest dark of the soul. Through our labors, we birth our gifts as seers. We understand our dreams and connect to the spirits for their healing. The world tends to avoid the labors of Skotia, preferring the easier climes of the solar world with its quick bursts of instant gratification like those delivered by social media and online shopping. However, these labors ultimately lead us to a much easier life. We can do the hard things, especially when they lead us out of darkness. As Jung tells us:

> [O]ne does not become enlightened by imagining figures of light, but by making the darkness conscious. The latter procedure, however, is disagreeable and therefore not popular.[9]

The process is designed to be challenging. The selkie's reunion was all the sweeter because it had come at great cost. Scota's evolution into the Crone cost her life. Persephone became the queen she was destined to be only because she went into the depths of the Underworld.

When we first enter the cave, we may wonder what's going to happen. Perhaps we believe that the journey will be swift and brief. But once in the darkness of Skotia, we begin looking for the exit. This is not the time to abandon yourself, however. This is the place where you begin to see who you are and beyond. It is the undiscovered territory within.

The rules for navigating this portion of the cave are found in visions and dreams. The guideposts are the moments when you realize that you are experiencing your life from the vantage point of the soul rather than the ego. These are mysterious signals that can't be accurately described, but you will know them when you are in their presence. When we stand here in Skotia's world, we find our open hearts and strong backs. We may have been wounded in the past when we were vulnerable, so we've spent a lifetime erecting barricades around ourselves to protect the treasures of our depths. The soul calls us to return to vulnerability. This is Hekate shaking us to the core, calling us to dance in her depths.

You may have frightening dreams as you are going through this initiation. You've been building your temenos through practices and talismans. Now you begin filling it with dreams, visions, conscious awareness, and more. An empty temple longs to be filled.

As you lean into the healing of your dreams and explore your shadow, you start the process of opening yourself to the mysteries within and the flow of the Great Mother. I liken this to a purifying black fire that banishes harm, protects us, and blesses us with clarity. Look for the symbols of Hekate in your dreams. Once your eyes adjust, you'll see her more clearly than ever. You may get impatient with this process, or even reject the necessity of being open to her black fire. This essence fuels your dreams and visions. It pulsates within your soul.

The Unconscious

The deepest dark within us is the unconscious.[10] As we venture farther into the cave, the unconscious, which was heretofore inaccessible, now comes to light. The unconscious is the womb within all of us. It is a rich source of nourishment as we begin the gestational period here in the cave.

Unsurprisingly, turning toward Skotia awakens our intuition and amplifies our connection to the world of spirits. It is an escape from the harsh solar world and a return to the womb that is governed by the moon. For the darkness of Skotia is lit by the lunar torch of Hekate. The ancients understood the lunar journey inward, and the torch of the goddess represented this nocturnal light. The internal light guides us into the depths of the unconscious when we put down burdens and when we separate from the artificial light of modern society.

Jung viewed the unconscious as the container of all that which is not present in our mindscape. Thus, it includes things we've forgotten, as well as the complexes we have of which we may be unaware. Moreover, the unconscious stretches out toward the archetypes that support these complexes. We may not be aware that a certain complex is living through us until we venture into our darkness. The unconscious contains the schemas, or thought patterns, for how we understand ourselves and the exterior environment.[11] Working models are the thought forms that shape all our experiences and states of being.[12]

The deeper levels of the unconscious, because they are close to the archetypal world, speak in symbols and emotions. It is at this level that our personal unconscious links to the universal web that is the collective unconscious. Consider the threads of this to be the archetypes. The titles of Hekate I use here are evocations of these archetypes; they pull the strands into our consciousness. Hillman warned that we should resist the temptation to force this symbolic language of the deep unconscious to fit into the literalness of the rational mind.[13]

Perhaps the most striking aspect of exploring the unconscious is that our vision adapts to the dimness. We see that our shadowy aspects coexist with that which nourishes our soul. There is a distinct lack of separation in the darkness of Skotia. I liken this to the beginning of the integration of self, shadow, and soul. The ability to perceive shrouded shapes in the darkness is the gift of the soul seers—those who allow their eyes to adjust so they can receive the gifts of the deeper world as they weave together the pieces of themselves. Each night, we travel into Skotia's realm, the dream world, where her healing comes to us in symbols, cryptic messages, and fantastical plot lines. There are times when our dreams may seem easy to understand, but there is always much more to discover if we allow ourselves to peer through the haze of the dream-made-conscious.

We need the mystery of Skotia in order to venture into our unconscious, so that we can open up to our soul and that of Hekate. Seers turn to dreams for prophecies, and for the power to reveal the depths of the soul. The cards guide them in the waking world, opening their field of vision to allow them to weave their tales in their minds. At night, they look to the heavens above to understand themselves and the universe.

Vulnerability is the true gift of the seer, for if we remain shut down, there is no crack through which the glorious darkness of dreams and the brilliant light of truth can slip into our consciousness. A student of mine had taken prescription medication for years to avoid the trauma dreams she had. When the time came for her to stop taking the medication, she decided, in consultation with her healthcare providers, to enter the darkness. Her dreams returned, vivid and raw, drawing her into Hekate's healing. She dreamed of women dancing, of warrior women, and of celebrating the sensuality of the feminine. The healing came.

Becoming open is a process. Most likely, you've had to envelop yourself in armor for decades. Learning to trust yourself to know when it is time to be vulnerable and when it is not safe is a lifelong endeavor. Turn to the black flame of Skotia to see the truth of any external situation and to know when it is your soul speaking, rather than the shadow. Be in relation to the natural resistance that occurs. After all, the shadow is only seeking to protect you. These blockages we have are a result of wounding and programming. The heart gets clogged up, the root gets tangled in hurt feelings, and the mind is clouded by the duality of shadow and ego.

Keep with your daily practices. Understanding how you acquired these blockages—which are really just shields—helps you to heal them.[14] Clear quartz can help with this. Becoming unblocked reveals healthy vulnerability that is, in its essence, trusting in yourself and your goddess. When you are in her deepest dark, the power of vulnerability—of opening the mind and heart—is where her healing lies. The soul serpent, with its strong back and soft front, peers into Skotia with courage and curiosity.

The Dreamworld

When I'm asked about beginning a relationship with Hekate, my response is always to look to your dreams. Trust me, she's been trying to get your attention your entire life. Dreams can offer illumination into your own darkness, from aspects you need to heal to long-abandoned desires. They can also be about the external world, providing insight into relationships, situations, and others. Dreams are communications from the unconscious. Their symbols can evoke strong emotions. When we enter the darkness of sleep, we go into Hekate's world. As we wander in the dreamscape, our physical selves vanish into something more. We walk among archetypes, tread in the web of the universe, and stretch beyond our mortal limitations. It is a sad state of affairs that our culture devalues the importance of dreams.

Dreams of snakes are a prime example of this. Consider the serpent dream that I shared back at the beginning of our cave journey. Dreams of snakes can be upsetting, but they offer strong insight into our own darkness. Or consider my student who suppressed her dreams through medication rather than receiving support for healing through understanding her nightmares. Our dreams can certainly feel as if we are "grappling with a luminous doom," but dancing in this darkness is how we find the riches. While we can practice waking sibylika through capnomancy (divination through smoke), the cards, and other practices, we also have access to nightly dream performances that await our audience. The dreamer within you knows the way forward.

Hekate's mother is identified as Asteria in some myths.[15] Asteria governed the stars and, as such, ruled over spirits of the night, as well as astrology, oracles, and prophetic dreams. As the Mother of the Mother, she births our nightly time in the spirit world of our beloved goddess. Asteria bestowed upon her daughter governance over the dream realm. Hekate thus carries on the tasks of the night assigned to her mother. She comes to us in our dreams, at times in obvious ways, but usually in more symbolic ones. She weaves the dreams and the dreamer, pulling us deeper into our wholeness as we expand our awareness of the realities of the unseen world.

The spirits who want our attention come to us in the dreamworld. They take on the faces of people known to us, compelling us to look beyond their surface embodiment. While we may long for a dream of triple-formed Hekate, she is more likely to show up in another guise, often taking the form of mysterious women who are not known to us in waking life. This is true for all the spirits. The healing that Hekate brings us in the night both illuminates what we need to see and takes from us what we need to let go. She welcomes the darkest parts of us, which often come forth in dreams, into her own world. Nothing within us is too dark for her to accept. There is no aspect of us that can destroy the purity of her darkness, where all the detritus of our lives is welcomed and eventually reborn into a nourishing form. Dreams are thus part healing, part compost. All is fertile ground in Skotia's world, whether or not we have conscious access to what goes on there.

Hillman's excellent treatise on dreams describes how Hekate reigns supreme over our nightly adventures.[16] Moreover, he argues that we should resist the temptation to rationalize our dreams. His strong case for allowing dreams to stay mystical is compelling. We have been programmed to think that dreams are either random neural firings, "garbage," or experiences that should be reduced to specific interpretations. But dreams exist with or without our attempts to rationalize them. I urge you to allow your dreams to be what they are, for it is in their pure form that the true healing abides. Respect the mystery of the dreamworld and allow it to work on you.

Dreams speak the symbolic language of the spirit world. This is Hekate's native tongue. They are archetypal and nonrational. They are rarely literal. Dreams are the way our unconscious soul speaks to us. The dreamer within is a star-traveler who has great wisdom to share if we only listen. Typically, the characters in our dreams are aspects of ourselves rather than the actual figures perceived. We can recognize the difference by exploring whether or not the person, animal, or thing is felt as "other" or as part of us. A common figure in dreams is a frightening woman doing wild sexual things or waging wars. These archetypal images are meant to scare the life *into* us. They all represent aspects within us that have been repressed, now brought to light in the darkness of the dreamworld. The spirit realm, of which the dreamworld is part, doesn't follow the laws of human morality; it has its own mysterious laws. Hekate keeps her own rulebook, weighing out the measures of our lives as she deems fit. The laws of man simply don't apply in Skotia.

Dreams do more than just bring to clarity what we are repressing or keeping out of consciousness. They also compensate for what we lack. For example, we may have sex dreams when we are denying this aspect of ourselves. Hekate's healing will always work to achieve our unique homeostasis, the true balance that the soul desires. When we are awake, we often refuse to allow her to work on us. But when we are asleep, she uses our vulnerable state to make her point.

Most of our dreams concern what is going on right now that is important for us to know. We also have "big" dreams that are prophecies of what's to come for us—and sometimes for the collective. Knowing the difference between personal "here and now" dreams and those that are prophetic often lies in the perspective of the dreamer. We are often watchers rather than participants in prophetic dreams. Discerning the difference can be challenging—and ultimately, it doesn't matter. Look to the feeling you woke up with for help. Do you feel as if you were with that person, or do you feel as you typically do when you are alone?

Our dreams of the goddess, however she comes to us, are part of both our individual healing and that required for the planet. This is why many of us are dreaming of her now. We are at a global crossroads. When we work on understanding how she speaks to us through our dreams, we are helping shift the balance of the world. All dreams have relevance and are the sacred messages of Hekate.

Dream interpretation books can be helpful in decoding these messages, but avoid relying on them entirely. I rarely use them, but I do consult *The Dream Interpretation Dictionary: Symbols, Signs, and Meanings* by J. M. DeBord on occasion. Use books of correspondences and symbols to help you understand the content of your dreams. Jung's *Man and His Symbols* and *Modern Man in Search of a Soul* are also immensely helpful. *The Book of Symbols* from Taschen is also an excellent resource. And Hillman's *The Dream and the Underworld* is essential reading for anyone wanting to understand the world of dreams and spirits.

Emotions, Intellect, and Imagination

Jung realized that there are three aspects in the process of understanding our dreams: emotions, intellect, and imagination.[17] The emotions you wake up with are the most important clue as to the message of a dream. Make sure you record them right away before you get into the content of the dream. Did you wake up sweating, pulse racing? Perhaps you feel calm. I had a powerful dream recently in which I was leading women on a world tour and menstruating all over the globe. All this bloodshed seemed unimportant in the dream, however; it was just part of the work that had to be done. My emotions were of calm acceptance and determination. And keep in mind that the dreamworld doesn't care about your morals and judgments. If you wake up from a raucous sex dream full of joy, don't play critic. Notice the emotions, record them, and then work on understanding the other aspects of the dream.

Although Hillman cautions us against using our intellect—what he called the ego—to analyze dreams, we still attempt to make sense of them. This leads to a balancing act between trying to contort the dream into something it doesn't want to be and being able to be nourished and healed by it. Dreams use our experiences and memories as aids to help us understand their message. They can also draw certain themes and scenarios from the collective. Explore the associations that come to mind. Use free association to ask yourself what a place, event, or situation could possibly mean. Connect that with what is currently going on in your life.

Weaving together emotions and thoughts is the work of the imagination. Avoid getting ensnared by the idea that, once you wake up, the dream ends. Reenact the dream on the stage of your imagination, allowing the details to fill out, following the threads of the emotions and thoughts to paint a full picture. Connect your dreams to your daily practice. Look to the images that come through in meditation. Examine how the Enodia Oracle readings are related to your dreams (see chapter 5). There are always threads to weave together. If you are a student of mythology and fairy tales, turn to them to help you understand the mysteries of your own dreamworld.[18]

Pay attention to the symbols of the dream, for they are always there. Symbols can be highly individualized or of the collective. Note the colors, numbers, and other apparent clues. See the characters and features in the dreams as symbolic of deeper archetypes. If a house or other building is important in the dream, contemplate how the type of building is used and what it means to you. Animals often appear in dreams and are usually symbolic of their associated powers. Crows are messengers; dogs are protectors; serpents bring healing. However, you always need to layer these known qualities with what the dream means to you. Ask yourself what a symbol means to you, as well as exploring its standard definitions. Explore your memory of the dream with openness and curiosity. The symbols and characters you find there are living archetypes. Allow them to be fluid and come to you as they do.

Practica: Working with Dreams

There are many ways that you can make your dreams more accessible and more memorable. Setting the intention at bedtime to have a dream that brings you the truth, keeping a journal nearby (or your phone for recording), positioning your clear quartz close by, and adding herbs associated with dreams to a nighttime beverage or sachet can all help to create a connection between your conscious self and the dreamer within.

Go gently into your analysis. It can take weeks, months, and even years to fully understand an important dream. Spending an hour a day contemplating your dreams can be much more interesting than watching TV. Your daily practice, meditation, and all the other practices I've introduced here will help you open up to the healing of the dream. I recommend recording the details of the dream as soon as you can after waking, and then opening up to them once you've done your meditation.

If you are working on your sibylika skills, ask the dream to bring you a card that helps with its message. Sit with the dream for a while before launching into research, because external knowledge can interfere with the message. We often stuff our creative side deep into the shadow, but exploring your dreams is a creative act. And creativity is the magic of Hekate.

Acting out a dream can help make sense of it as well. If you dream of cats, act like one to shift into their energy. Bring the dream into your body to vivify it. Allow yourself to feel the emotions of the dream. If you looked a certain way in the dream, dress like that.

Practica: Meeting the Cailleach

The Cailleach is an expression of the Crone, a healing spirit that offers respite along the journey through the cave.[19] There are many tales regarding the Cailleach as the eternal wise woman and healer. Sometimes denigrated as a mean-spirited hag, this figure was seen in different ways in various locations. For instance, the Cailleach Béara (also called, Cally Berra) were goddesses of winter to ancient Celts.[20] In fact, the importance of place is central to the tales of the Cailleach, and she often appears in the historical record as based in a specific location. This connection to place signifies how deeply she is connected to the land and its people. She is of the earth itself, and this speaks to her message of reconnecting to the land, of treating the earth well so that we can be nourished.

The Cailleach Béara is the ancestress of many peoples in Ireland. To them, she is the sovereign queen who remembers the time before time, and the early eons when the earth was water. She also represented the time before the freedom of the Irish was lost. The Cailleach an Mhuilinn ("of the mill") appears in many myths as well. She is both helper and foe, a seer and shapeshifter. To the ancients who revered her, the mill symbolized the power of creation through the wheel that spun the water to create the necessary friction for grinding. The association with the mill illustrates her connection to ponds and lakes, and the grist stone represents the Wheel of Time. Moreover, her connection to millstones demonstrates her primal nature. She existed before time and created the stones and the earth itself.

This practice takes you deep into the cave to meet the Cailleach in order to access her wise healing. It is best performed at the winter solstice after the Ritual of Catharsis (see chapter 9). To perform this for yourself, set an altar that is evocative of the Crone. Stones, in particular, are offerings favored by the Cailleach. She'll be curious about your growing collection, so offer them up to her and ask her to bless them while you contemplate her.

Summon your avian ally as a companion as you journey deep into the cave to meet the ancient mother. Use your candle from the catharsis ritual to create temenos as you did then; three times banish, three times protect, and then back to the heart center (see chapter 9). While holding the candle there, call out to the Cailleach three times. There are many ways to say her name and she'll respond to your heart cry rather than to how you say it aloud. I say "Cal-EE-ack."

Now set the candle down on the altar and soften into its flame, again seeing it as the entrance to the cave. As you continue to say the goddess's name, see the flame become an eye and peer into the black iris in the middle. When you feel enveloped by her presence, she may just show you her whole face. Ask her what wisdom she would grant you.

At this point, you can ask her to speak to you through the cards. Draw three—one for guidance on your continuing catharsis, one for assistance as you move toward the upcoming soul retrieval, and a final one for your eventual rebirth and emergence from the cave.

> *I call the Stone Mother,*
> *The Maker of Mountains,*
> *Older than time.*
> *Cailleach.*

Cailleach.
Cailleach.
I call the Bone Mother,
Sheltering from storms that rage,
Gathering around her fire.
Cailleach.
Cailleach.
Cailleach.
I call the Ancient Mother.
Sharing my story,
Hearing your wisdom.
Healing is found in your cave.
Cailleach.
Cailleach.
Cailleach.

Chapter 11

Paionios: The Healer

On this new moon,
Help me, Paionios.
On this new moon,
I choose compassion, courage, and wisdom from this day forward.
Guide me, Paionios, so I may so live within your mercy.
On this new moon,
I commit to honoring the light in myself and others,
And to seeing the darkness in others and myself.
Show me, Paionios, so I can see from the soul.
On this new moon,
I dedicate myself to grace and peace.
Reveal them in me, Paionios.
Render me an instrument of love and healing.
May I be guided by your wisdom,
Protected by your strength,
And blessed by your fierce love.
I am free of limitations.
Safe, healed, and whole.

In one of the most compelling hymns in The Greek Magical Papyri, the ritualist cries out in anguish to the goddess, beseeching Paionios, the Healer, to intervene. The words speak of all the pain that befalls us, and of our desire to right the wrongs that have been done to us. I've found myself in a similar scenario, crying out for relief from the pangs of heartbreak while wanting the cause of my upset to feel the weight of their transgressions. Like the ancient prayer, my words reeked of raw pain, to which we can all certainly relate.

> *Arise, Moon Goddess, Solar Healer, Guardian of the Departed.*
> *Oh, cunning, celestial, swift, and crested one,*
> *Brave, drawing your swords.*
> *Healer, wise one, renowned, encouraging,*
> *Quick-footed, courageous, crimson.*
> *Darkness, Fierce, Immortal.[1]*

Imagining the backstory behind the speaker's despair, I was inspired to dive into the power of the epithets used. Perhaps her lover had betrayed her or harmed her child. Although there is much about The Greek Magical Papyri that will forever remain a mystery, the visceral emotions of the prayer reverberate deep within anyone who has ever been consumed by despair and rage due to the actions of another—someone once trusted, now revealed as traitor. In fact, there is nothing that begs more loudly for healing than our relationship wounds.

Paionios understands the pain that we endure because of our bonds with others. She is the one who helped countless sufferers find their way through the dark abyss of heartbreak. Just as she tended to Persephone, who was alone in her grief, she comes to us when we are in the depths of despair. The energy of Paionios is that of the compassionate wise one who restores our well-being through healing our wounds. She heals with the energy of love, trust, and unwavering support. She abides during our mistakes and waits until we are ready for her to work on us. I liken this to a healing pool in the heart of the cave. Rhodochrosite is the stone equivalent of that pool.

Healing Relationship Wounds

Many of the prayers and rituals in The Greek Magical Papyri focus on relief of suffering from the wounds that others have inflicted on us. As we have journeyed into Hekate's cave, we have been tending to these scars—old structures embedded within the shadowy unconscious whispering that we are less than, or unworthy, or that who we are is inherently wrong. Up to this point in our subterranean trek, the focus has been on deep emotional root work. Now we shift our energy toward the heart, the crossroads between our interior world and others.

The heart is also the epicenter of the energy of our physical beings. It is active, building upon the emotions of the root, yet also drawing down from the crown. When you are performing the Unifying the Three Selves meditation given in chapter 4, notice the differences between the three centers. The root feels; the heart does; the crown thinks. Consider how the three blend together to form wholeness within, working with the imagery of the serpent. Imagine the Healer holding this serpent, which is the ancient symbol used today for the healthcare profession. The serpent heals itself through shedding its skin, often while ensconced in a cave. We can be viciously wounded by snake venom, but it is also used in some curative treatments. The serpent teaches us that we have both shadow and soul, bane and blessing. Certainly, our relationships illustrate this.

The Hindu goddess Akhilandeshwari embodies the continual process of healing.[2] Known as the goddess of "Never Not Broken," she is always lovingly putting herself back together while riding down a river on a reptile. The crocodile that Akhilandeshwari rides, while not a snake, symbolizes both the powerful soul within, as does Drakaina, and also the potential of the shadow to bite back at us. Consider her crocodile as all the others we encounter as well. They help us ride the river, and also have the power to damage.

Those pieces of ourselves that we are putting back together were often bitten off due to matters of the heart. While our relationships can be the source of great comfort, they can also bring us unbearable suffering. Relationships are cocreations based on what we do, think, and feel. They are *egregores*—group thought forms that are sustained by belief.[3] They are spirits unique unto themselves that exist in a "third space" that is neither entirely of us nor of our relationship partners.[4] How each person in a relationship perceives the "spirit" of it can be vastly different. One partner may believe he or she is in a committed, monogamous partnership; the other, when asked, may reply: "What relationship?"

Relationships come in many forms, from those we have with our childhood primary caregivers, to those we build as we interact with groups and society. I spent several years early in my academic career studying the linkages between different types of relationships and well-being, with a special focus on the adolescent individuation process, when we transition from being most closely bonded to our families of origin to our relationships with friends and romantic partners. The relationship world is infinitely varied and fundamentally important to our journey.

Here, however, let's focus on relationships that include romantic love and sex. Scholars once assumed that the primary adult relationship was a committed pair-bond that included sexual intimacy. The lack of that intimacy was seen as a failure. We still see remnants of this today. I can't tell you how many times a well-intentioned person has told me: "You'll find someone" or "You need to get laid." This is because I've been uninvolved in romantic alliances for the past several years. My reply to these statements, and to attempts to "fix me up" with someone is: "Actually, no. I'm perfectly happy on my own." I tell you this to let you know that, if you're like me when it comes to such matters, you are fine. On the other hand, if you are in a committed partnership, that's great. This can be as a traditional couple, or as a friendship, or it may include more than two people.

There is a lot of collective baggage around relationships. Heteronormativity and traditional gender roles lurk everywhere in our individual psyches and in societal beliefs. Romantic love and sex are entwined with these biases. An Internet search on Persephone quickly reveals the different ways in which her relationship with Hades is understood. There seems to be a limitless supply of writings, poetry, songs, and memes interpreting their partnership. At times, she is the helpless victim, as she comes across in the Homeric *Hymn to Demeter*. On the other hand, many contemporary examinations lift up the loving relationship that they had. And of course, there is always the allure of the "dangerous man" archetype as well. But the fact that their love story has endured for thousands of years shows us the power of the Underworld journey and how romantic relationships are an integral part of our personal wholeness.

When exploring the Persephone-Hades union, pay attention to the active ingredients that led her ultimately to become not only queen of the Underworld, but also the one who makes it possible for life to exist. She is a goddess of action. If she had never eaten the pomegranate seeds, the story wouldn't have had the same outcome. This is not to say that the whole thing was her fault, but rather to point out that relationships are a result of the things we do.

Unrequited love is an example that illustrates that relationships are a creation of action. If all we ever do is think about our beloved, then no relationship can exist. Sex and other shared activities contribute to our experience and to our relationship constructs. Thus, relationships are of the heart, where our thoughts and feelings create the often gushing waterfall that propels us forward to form new ones. Whether and how we engage in such things is influenced by the models of relationships that were formed in early childhood, which typically exist outside of consciousness.

Eros and Agape

Erototokos, another epithet that comes to us from the ancient prayer mentioned earlier, means Bringer of Love. The ancient priestess called out to Erototokos to resolve her broken heart. But the energy of healing is to choose love while understanding our wounds, which are rooted in the many faces of fear. Thus, we can all relate to her fearful cries to Erototokos. This anguish of heartbreak and this healing power of love are vividly depicted in the myth of Eros and Psyche.[5]

The price Psyche was forced to pay for her incomparable beauty was to be abandoned by her father. Although she was destined to be alone for all her days, she was promised that an unseen lover would come to her every night. Although she couldn't see this lover and had been told he was some sort of monster, Psyche fell hard for him. She overcame her fear of the shadow lover and eventually tempted fate—as we are often wont to do when things are too good to be true—by revealing his appearance with a lamp. Eros fled, fearing the wrath of his mother, Aphrodite, who had instigated the whole scenario because she was jealous of Psyche's beauty.

Poor Psyche, pregnant and still innocent even after all she'd been through, attempted to drown herself, but was rejected by the water. She still had work to do. After a time, she encountered Aphrodite, who put her through a series of arduous tasks before reconnecting her with her beloved.[6] These tasks included a descent into the Underworld, where she was tempted by a box promising beauty. Believing that whatever was in the box could make her even more enticing to Eros, she peeked inside. Like Sleeping Beauty and Snow White, her curiosity forced her into a deep slumber. Eventually her prince—in this case Eros, the god of desire— liberated her. Their child was born and was appropriately named Hedone, which means "pleasure" or "joy," specifically the sensual kind, depending on translation.[7] They lived happily ever after.

In Jungian psychology, "eros" refers to desire, both in its pure form and in the murky depths of the shadow.[8] I tend to refer to eros as erotic, romantic, and sexual feelings, and use "agape" to describe the general forces of kindness, compassion, and connection.[9] Eros refers to the key of passion, and agape to that of kindness. Psyche means soul, and, in one of my favorite double meanings, also butterfly. The journey of soul and desire is thus at the heart of all our relationships. Psyche's progression from naive maiden to wise wife requires proving her dedication to Eros. She must descend into the Underworld to face her own shadow—represented by the box promising beauty—in order to confront the issues that keep us from healing into wholeness and being able to have healthy relationships.

This applies to other types of relationships as well. When we walk with Paionios through the cave, we heal our eros so that our desires become attuned to our soul. The deeper message of romantic unions—like Eros and Psyche, or Persephone and Hades—is that wholeness comes from integration of the shadow with the soul. In tarot, the Lovers card at the surface level refers to external relationships, but underlying it is the journey to wholeness within. There is an unbreakable bond between our external relationships and our interior selves.

The distress caused by the betrayal we feel in some relationships bespeaks the bonds that hold us to others. While this attachment can result in love, it can also destroy. When I consider my most nourishing relationships, the bond feels bidirectional—a continual flow of mutual support and affection. There is a soul-knowing that I am held and heard, and that I do the best I can to reciprocate. The underlying archetypes at work here are both eros—the desire for the relationship, be it sexual or otherwise—and agape—the universal flow of love. When we lack this, as the writer of the ancient prayer demonstrates, we can turn to the goddess as a source of the support and understanding we need.

The message of Paionios is that the energy of love—the strong, sure kind—leads to healing our dysfunctional relationship archetypes and relieves pain while desire for such a state of being is equally involved. Leaning into the Healer archetype, however we may perceive it, helps us peel away those layers of mistrust and heartbreak. We can become confused by societal misbeliefs about love being weak when the opposite is actually true. When we are disempowered, we become possessed by fear, not love. When we have unhealthy relationship archetypes, we abide in fear. Transmuting the root back to its sacred state of purity invokes love.

We can think of love in many different ways. In the story of Psyche and Eros, love is initially equated with sexual desire. But the Eros archetype can be expanded to the energy of any desire, both wholesome and shadowy. Agape, on the other hand, refers to the pure love energy of Paionios that is characterized by trust, mutual affection, and appropriate support. When we enter into the presence of Paionios, we are awakening to agape. Eros is the strong, emotional love we feel for another, while agape refers to a sense of willful benevolence. It is ideal when both are present, both within us and in a relationship. We see this in Persephone and Hades's mature marriage, which was characterized by fidelity and respect. It is also demonstrated in the relationship between Persephone and Demeter after she became the Underworld queen. This bond portrayed a closeness, a sense of trust, and both independence and interdependence. Neither were wholly defined by the other anymore. It was a relationship of equals.

Choosing to love while seeking to understand fear is a key feature of healing. In Hekate's cave, we are abiding in the realm of opposites. This is the space between all things, where we discover that relationships are spirits unto themselves. They have a vitality that goes beyond the individuals involved. Nobody would deny that in both Psyche's and Persephone's relationships there were serious problems. Yet they achieved wholeness by embracing this tension. Now I'm not saying that we should engage in disempowering or abusive relationships. But I am advocating for understanding that the problems we encounter in relationships can be enriching. And when we reduce these issues down to their root, they are always based in fear.

Root Damage

Understanding how our early childhood traumas damage our ability to form healthy relationships allows us to see how the past shapes the future—how our fears possess us. We have a difficult relationship to agape and eros. But when we lean into Hekate Paionios, we allow her to work on our deepest roots, which are often traumatic experiences felt early in life. It is often said that psychologists get into their line of work to heal themselves. I ventured into my research focus on attachment and health without a conscious understanding of why I was doing so.[10] My mindset as a young, single mother was to create a better life for my son, and becoming a psychologist was my means to that end. Unwittingly, I was engaging with the Healer archetype. How serendipitous that a fresh, new assistant professor who studied human relationships took me on as a trainee! The very thing that had caused me the most grief to that point was where I had landed.

Archetypes always work on us in this way. Paionios, the Healer, had had her way with me. I had always felt unwanted in my family of origin. Right out of high school, I ran off with a very damaged man who took his wounds out on me. But when I turned to psychological research, I took the first step toward healing myself. Through my early research on attachment, I learned how vital a supportive and consistent early primary caregiver was throughout the life span.[11] I became obsessed with understanding, and later developing, the impacts of this early relationship, both as a way of helping others and preventing myself from damaging my son.

What became clear over the years is that the best approach to preventing this sort of "root damage" from happening in the first place is through early-intervention programs.[12] I have learned that, while it is possible to transmute the dysfunctional root, this is not nearly as easy as prevention. Over the years, I've observed how, in my research exploring of what this root consists, I've found a consistent pattern of early adverse childhood experiences. Known as "attachment crises," these events occur when caregivers fail to provide the necessary safe and supportive environment that facilitates healthy development. Since we are here now as adults, what do we do about it? Before continuing to the answer, I need you to know that having an insecure attachment style is neither your fault nor uncommon. While about 50 percent of respondents report having what we call a secure attachment style—one characterized by trust, support, and a positive self-concept—the other half report having an insecure attachment orientation, which is the root of the surface problems.

It's as if all our healing efforts were akin to cutting off the visible part of a dandelion. But this weed is truly toxic. Underneath, the root persists when the conditions are right, and the flower reappears. And we grow the same damned dysfunctional flower again and again. That root is often traumatic early childhood experiences. The flower will respond only to the same conditions in which it took root. If we could never trust our caregivers, then our root will be drawn only to untrustworthy partners. The good news is that we can transmute the root. By this, I mean that we can reconfigure the structure of this root so that it grows flowers only in response to conditions that are nourishing to us. By developing and living our boundaries, we choose when the flower of our love blooms. Boundaries are a highly effective means of transmuting the root.

But dandelions clearly don't have great boundaries. They'll grow anywhere. They are quite easy to pick, cut, and destroy at the surface level, but they keep coming back. Consider a different plant, like mullein. It is fussy about where it grows, and its blossoms are incredibly resistant. While dandelions are indiscriminate in building relationships, mullein is particular about the environment it chooses. Because of early traumas, the dandelion doesn't know any different. It isn't aware of how beautiful it is and how much it offers the world. Trauma early in life influences all aspects of our lives. But you can begin to uncover those early roots as you engage with Paionios.

And remember. While dandelions tend to have a bad reputation, they can also be incredibly healing. They are fantastic for ritual baths. Just brew a pot of dandelion tea and add it to the bath water as it runs.

Attachment Archetypes

I've been studying close relationships for over two decades. In my approach, the root is known as our attachment orientation, sometimes called a "style." But these styles are much more than mere personality descriptions; they are actually archetypes. These attachment archetypes function largely outside of consciousness, and they have a life of their own. How many times have we decided to approach a relationship in a certain way and then some unconscious force seems to stampede over our best intentions?

Understanding attachment archetypes by bringing them into consciousness helps us to reconstruct root problems and heal root damage. There are both soul and shadow archetypes, and the attachment archetype that presses on us most plays out in all our relationships. Generally, this archetype flows into us from our primary caregivers early in childhood. Once this energy is in us, it influences all our other relationships and how we see ourselves. The mother who has a healthy connection to the attachment archetype from her own childhood draws from that in parenting her own child. She is neither a hovering Demeter, nor a self-absorbed mom who neglects her offspring.

The main soul archetype is grounded in agape and positive eros. The agape attachment archetype is constellated with a positive self-concept, feelings of efficacy in the world, and an optimistic outlook. It is the natural orientation of the soul. We can see the secure attachment archetype as nestled within agape and positive eros—although, of course, there are times when fear is experienced. About 50 percent of us are naturally in this archetype. The rest of us have the opportunity to heal into it.

The shadow attachment orientations are situated within the Phoberos archetype, and there are three different expressions. The preoccupied archetype hyper-focuses on approval from others while denying personal needs. Those enmeshed with this archetype change their personas in response to what they believe others want them to be. By contrast, those who are connected to the avoidant archetype do everything they can to stay away from close attachments. Both types are driven by insecurities about how others will treat them, learned from early interactions with their primary caregivers. Splitting the avoidant archetype into two types—fearful avoidant and dismissing avoidant—clarifies the ways it orients toward others. The fearful avoidant archetype has the same eros orientation as the preoccupied type—the desire to merge so completely with a partner that the self evaporates—but it avoids attempting to do so, unlike the preoccupied style. Those drawn to the dismissing avoidant archetype are fearful and don't desire relationships because they have shut down their basic need for connection.

Generally, we have one dominant archetypal style, although it can vary. As we heal on our journey through the cave, the Agape archetype becomes more present and the Phoberos archetypes become dormant. Also keep in mind that factors like introversion and extroversion can influence the archetypes.[13] If you are more in relation to one of the Phoberos archetypes, the energy of Paionios can help to restore your trust in yourself and others.

You can use the attachment styles inventory below to help you understand what attachment archetype is dominant in you.[14] Without overthinking, choose the archetype that best describes your general orientation toward others:

- I am usually comfortable depending on myself and having others depend on me. I don't worry much about others not accepting me.

- I want to be completely emotionally intimate with others, but I often find that others are reluctant to get as close as I would like. I sometimes worry that others don't value me as much as I value them.

- It is important for me to feel independent and self-sufficient, and I prefer not to depend on others or have others depend on me.

- I would like to be close to others, but I know that they'll let me down. I don't like being self-sufficient.

The first statement describes the soul orientation, the agape attachment archetype. If you chose this archetype, see it as a North Star guiding you toward it. The other three lean into the shadow's territory. If you chose one of those, I congratulate you for having the courage to be honest. Recognizing that we are operating from the shadow is the most important step to healing. You are well on your way to wholeness. Think of your choice as a reflection of how you are connected to the underlying archetype, and how this association influences the bonds you have, or don't have, with others.

This is a process. Don't judge your dominant archetype or choose one that doesn't actually map you. This is a powerful practice of self-revelation. I recommend using this inventory in conjunction with your daily practice, after your meditation but before your reading, which you can do afterward to find guidance for working with your attachment archetype.

The Cords That Bind

Depending on the relationship, we may need to work on repairing the cords that bind us to others, or even cutting them. These cords can get tied into tight knots that can trap us in past wounds and damage present relationships. When we work on healing the cord, either by repairing or severing it, it loosens those binding knots. Keeping in mind that relationships become spirits unto themselves, we can work on the cord from us to it to further our healing journey. When we rectify our bond to the relationship, there is potential for profound healing.

Whenever people give energy to each other over a period of time, a relationship spirit is formed. We work on our connection to this spirit. Sometimes no relationship spirit is formed—for instance, if we are the victims of violence by a stranger. Most often, however, our wounds are inflicted by people we care(d) about deeply. These thought forms work mostly outside of consciousness, whether they relate to a relationship or an event. If you have multiple relationships to work on, like many of us, start with the one that is most complex. At times, there is no salvaging the relationship. In such instances, you can perform a cord-cutting ceremony (see below).

There are two approaches to cord healing. The first is to cut your bond to the relationship. This stops the energy supply going from you to the relational spirit. Over time, the spirit withers and dies because, even if the other person is sending energy to the relationship, the spirit can survive only if both (or all) partners are feeding it. The second method is to cut your tie to a painful memory. Strong memories of betrayal, loss, and trauma can become vivid if a lot of energy is dedicated to them. Think of these memories as spirits. The former technique is recommended in complex situations and in a toxic relationship; the latter is recommended for isolated experiences—for a relationship with someone to whom you were not attached or something that transpired in an otherwise healthy relationship.

Here's an intense personal example of a binding bond I once had. I had been in a romantic relationship for only a few months when my partner ended things. It had been one of those whirlwind attachments in which neither of us was being honest—with ourselves, with each other, or with much else. I was coming out of a divorce and was incredibly lonely. This was a classic "rebound" if there ever was one. I was unbearably upset over the end of the relationship, and I felt caught up in something much greater than myself, as if we had been fated to come together and then separate.

When my partner literally sailed off into the sunset, I was bereft. As the days passed, I felt physically pulled to pieces. It was as if the bond between us were an anchor that was being pulled farther and farther away, and I was powerless to break its chain, although I kept trying. One night, I had a horrible dream in which my former partner was in grave danger as his boat endured a terrible storm. I woke with a start, discovering that the locked window in my bedroom had blown open. A few days later, I got an email from him asking if I had put a curse on him, because exactly what I had dreamed had transpired. FYI: I hadn't. That is how strong the cord was between us.

Over time, with many repeated ceremonies and deep soul work, the cord withered and eventually died. But I was so distraught that I went to a trusted medium for advice. As soon as I walked into her salon, without me having said a single word, she said that I was caught up in some past-life karmic cycle that would finally be resolved. I collapsed, sobbing, onto her lovely little table. Cords can bind across lifetimes.

Stay within your boundaries when healing or cutting a cord. Severing from a dysfunctional relationship takes time. Your daily practice can help.

Archetypes and Relationships

Our attachment archetypes represent our general orientation about ourselves in relation to others. Relationships, as cocreated spirits, are also embedded within archetypes. Approaching relationships as archetypes allows us to bring into awareness that they are much more than mere constructs. They are living, breathing entities nested within the much larger aggregate archetype. The archetypes of "marriage" or "friendship" are examples of overarching relationship archetypes. While they may have vastly different expressions at the individual level, they are part of something much larger. The personal archetypes we are connected to greatly influence our relationships. The archetype of Healer, for example, may drive us to believe that we can cure others.

We also may be embodying various other archetypes, such as the Wounded Child.[15] In studying the myth of Persephone, we see how her personal archetype is transformed. She goes from being the nameless daughter (Kore) to being Persephone (the Destroyer). But more important, she becomes Anassa Eneroi, the terrible queen who is a benevolent, yet fierce monarch. Within the story, Demeter presents a hugely different archetype. We might call her a "helicopter" mother today. She simply can't let go. Moreover, she takes on her daughter's pain as her own, something that is known as codependency in contemporary recovery language. Yet her "ride or die" devotion to Kore is admirable, representing a healthy aspect of the Mother archetype.

Myths, legends, and other stories are also archetypal.[16] When we are tethered to a relationship, we can get connected to the archetype and to the myths that inhabit it. Consider your romantic relationships. Have you been caught up in the Psyche-Eros myth and been blind to the beauty of a lover until that person left you? Did you do everything to win the person back? Have you been willful Kore, whose rebellion against the maternal figure led to great upset? The myth of Semele, the mother of Dionysus, has been working on me for the past year as my youngest son transitions into adulthood. While I've been engaging in that story, the Persephone-Hekate-Demeter myth has been equally present with me. Unsurprising that this started right when I began writing this book. A beloved student, whom I called Kore, had traveled to stay with another student, one on whom Demeter was seriously working. I found myself playing the role of Hekate, the healing mediator, between them. Learning myths and fairy tales gives us a context in which to understand our own mythic life, giving it meaning and illustrating that we are part of that great archetypal web that is the soul of the universe.[17]

Embodying Healing

What we know from the research is that early trauma and later wounds can force us into a state of chronic disconnection from our physical selves. But remember that the heart is about the body, not simply about the underlying emotions and thoughts. This may present as a defense mechanism we invoke when we are energetically trying to disappear so that we don't attract the attention of those who hurt us.[18] Physiologically, our bodies become the depositories of the pain. Bessel van der Kolk, in his seminal book, *The Body Keeps Score*, described how our physical selves hold the pain of trauma for us. The gift of Paionios is that we can greatly improve our physical and psychological health by doing the soul work. This is why relational healing, recovery from trauma, and changing the energy of current relationships are situated in the heart. It is the result of interactions with others, but it also abides in our physical beings.

One of the most demanding aspects of trauma is the effects it has on the body, including many chronic illnesses.[19] Until we work on healing the body, our journey to wholeness gets stuck. In addition, when we disconnect from our bodies, which are temples of pain, we place ourselves in a chronic state of hyperarousal, always on the alert for the next attack.[20] While the mind work we do to heal is vital—including learning to trust again—we also need to get back into our bodies. What is interesting to me is that, for as long as we deny our bodies, often numbing them through addictions and so on, those bodies continue to do all they can to get our attention. This is much like how our dysfunctional relationship archetypes continue to play out until we tend to them. No matter what the pain, learning to be in relation to it, instead of falling back on denial and other forms of opposition, is the way to healing.

Think about when the last time was that you had a pleasurable experience with your body. Even turning your attention toward this starts to pull you back into your physical self. Was it when you went for a walk in the woods? When you had fabulous sex? Perhaps dancing alone brings you joy. Pause every day as you journey through the cave to have and reflect upon bodily joy. As someone who lives with chronic pain, I can testify that daily embodiment not only heals the physical self, but also reconfigures that dysfunctional root.

Practica: Healing Bath

This healing bath gives you a fresh start. I recommend lighting a fresh candle to symbolize this new beginning. Healing through purification was a core practice of Hekate's ancient priestesses and of those in their care. When we see our accumulated relational wounds as a type of miasma, the bath becomes the sacred removal vessel. Add to the ritual by calling upon the energy of the moon phase, allowing the lunar powers to stream down into the water.

I recommend making an altar on or near your tub or shower, including stones like rhodochrosite, pink quartz, and amethyst.[21] Enter into the healing waters of Paionios to feel physical pleasure while spiritually detoxifying the root. Try adding dandelion-root tea to the water. You can also add a teaspoon of yarrow when you steep the tea. Create a luxurious bathing experience, whether in the tub or shower. You can amplify the cleansing power by using my (in)famous black-salt scrub (see chapter 9).

Practica: The Never Again Facecloth

You may want to create or choose a talisman to amplify your work with Paionios. Here's a comical story about the talisman I created the last time I got into a dysfunctional relationship. I call it the Never Again Facecloth.

After I was divorced, we moved in with my boyfriend and his two sons. This was one of those relationships that looked far better from the outside than the inside. After only six months, we mutually called off our attempt to form a blended family. For me, a huge realization was that my eros to have a blended family was driven by the shadow, not soul. I'm an independent woman who always feels caged when I live with a partner. I had succumbed to the societal demand for coupling. When we split up, we divided the household contents that we had purchased together. It was all very civilized. Except for this one facecloth.

After we separated, my former partner reported to a mutual friend that I had taken one too many facecloths. He was quite upset about this slight. Maybe I did take one more than I should have. When I heard about his complaint, I took one of these facecloths and put it on the top shelf of the linen closet, saying: "Never again." I meant that never again would I find myself dealing with a breakup from a cohabiting situation. But it meant much more as well. Never again would I deny my truth for the sake of being in a romantic relationship. To this day, over seven years later, the Never Again Facecloth sits as a talisman on the top shelf of the linen closet. It's worked perfectly. Perhaps you have a similarly unique talisman of a relationship wound that can become your own Never Again Facecloth to place in your Cista Mystica.

Practica: Cord-Cutting Ceremony

This ceremony can help you to sever cords that may be binding you to failed or dysfunctional relationships. Whatever the origin of your toxic cord situation, this ceremony will invoke the cutting of the bond. I recommend you perform this during the waning moon, if possible. To add some astrological support, perform it while the waning moon is in one of the fire signs (i.e., Aries, Leo, Sagittarius). Perform this after your daily meditation, then pull your Enodia Oracle cards to provide guidance.

For the ceremony, you will need:

- A piece of rhodochrosite to keep the energy nourishing.

- A piece of black obsidian to catch any residue.

- An image of the person (or situation) from whom you are severing.

- Some string.

- A fresh red candle to symbolize the heart.

Write an intention on the image in red—for instance: "I am completely released from the bond I have with this X (person, event, etc.). It has no connection to me." Light the candle and recite your intention, then tie the string around the image and wrap the other end around your left wrist.

Call out to Paionios to sever this attachment until you feel her presence, saying something like: "Paionios, Hekate the Healer, sever this tie."

Sit with the energy of the relationship or the painful memory as Hekate envelopes you in her healing. When you are ready, use the flame of the candle to burn through the string and cut the attachment. Feel the freeing energy. As this bond is severed, Hekate will bring forward healing imagery that replaces this toxic bond. Draw your Enodia Oracle cards for guidance.

When you are finished, thank the goddess and extinguish the candle. Remove the cord with the image attached from your home—for example, you can bury it or dispose of it in a public refuse bin.

Practica: Cord-Cleansing Ceremony

This ceremony cleanses a connection that serves you well, but that perhaps is a bit "muddied" through past hurts, conflicts, and communication troubles. This is a great ceremony to perform for people you are stuck with—someone like an ex with whom you share a child or an annoying coworker. Note that this is not designed for use on relationships where one person is currently engaging in warfare with the other. It is up to you to decide what relationship can benefit from it. The energy is of purification rather than severing.

For this ceremony, you will need:

- A piece of rhodochrosite to keep the energy nourishing.

- A piece of black obsidian to catch any residue.

- An image of the person (or situation).

- Some string.

- A fresh red candle to symbolize the heart.

- Some khernips and some juniper.

- A bowl of sacred water.

Basically, this ceremony involves igniting a banishing botanical like juniper with the flame of the red candle and then plunging it into the bowl of sacred water—for example, water that has absorbed the energy of the full moon (for clarity). The water becomes infused with banishing and clarity. Follow the steps for the cord-cutting ceremony above, but cleanse the string and the images and where they connect to you instead of severing them.

To create a lasting talisman, use images or symbols of yourself and the other(s). Cleanse the cord with the sacred water created after the plant spirit is immersed in it. Instead of disposing of the cord, keep the talisman on your altar or in the place where the two of you most often come together.

> *Hail, Hekate. Goddess of the Moon.*
> *Unconquerable ruler of land, sea, and sky.*
> *I call upon you now.*
> *Hail, Hekate. Three-Formed Goddess.*
> *Reflected in the moon's three faces.*
> *Hail, Hekate! Key Holder of the Mysteries,*
> *The secrets of the moon are yours.*
> *Release unto me the energy of the moon.*
> *I draw down the energy of your glorious moon;*
> *I seek your favor for this working.*
> *My intention is true,*
> *And my will is strong.*

Chapter 12

Psychopomp: The Soul Guide

Psychopomp

At this crossroads,
The end of a long journey.
I am no longer seduced by the past.
Nor am I fooled by the hollow promise of the well-lit path.
It is the deepest darkness that I seek.
Guided only by distant torchlight.
The Mistress of Souls, my only companion.
Each step has been my own.
I am here to reclaim what is mine.
Pieces of me that found refuge in her dark womb.
After the cruelty and violence,
Of those who preyed on my weakness.
They are dead to me now.
Slain by my will to heal.
How her Wheel has turned.
Now I keep my own keys.
I have returned home.
Into the welcoming darkness I tread.
The very heart of Hekate's realm.

Where she harbored my soul fragments.
I call them back to me.
Such sweet reunion.
Truth courses through my being,
And I am once again whole.

One of Hekate's most ancient roles is as Psychopomp, which translates as "soul guide."[1] According to the Greeks, the Psychopomp guided the departed into the afterlife, whether it was the nightmarish Tartarus or the heavenly Elysium.[2] Certain deities like Hekate and Hermes, her frequent companion, had the special ability to travel at will between the Underworld, the world of everyday life, and the heights of Olympus, so they could easily cross into the territory of the afterlife.[3]

Hekate, in particular, was responsible for overseeing the restless dead and for guiding souls to the other side. There is a special relationship between Hekate and those who have suffered great soul loss at the hands of others. She held close to her the dead who were marginalized by society, especially women and girls who had died due to sexual violence or during childbirth. In modern terms, Hekate is a trauma specialist whose darkness welcomes our fleeing soul fragments that find refuge in her cave. She tends to them until we are ready to be reunited.

Hekate Psychopomp is much more than the one who helps the earthly dead cross over the river to the other side, however. She is the midwife who assists new souls as they are born into flesh, and she reunites us with the fragments of our selves that we lose along the way. She calls us to take care of our own souls and to see the soul in all things. When we care for our own souls and seek to understand the soul in all things, it draws us closer to the archetypal web, to the very soul of the world. The shamanic and psychological practice of soul retrieval is the process of calling back pieces of our soul that were lost due to individual and cultural trauma.[4] In my own work, I act as a Psychopomp, lighting the way to the wholeness known only through the return to soul.

There is sometimes confusion about the intentions of a Psychopomp. Some view Hekate and others in this role as nefarious when their work is truly benevolent. Some fear these figures who walk between the living and the dead, especially within certain religions in which control of the soul is firmly in the hands of one God and his emissaries. But even in these traditions, there may be Psychopomps at work. The Angel of Death, sometimes called Azrael, consults his book of names and then guides the departed along their journey.[5] Our deep-seated fear of death contributes to our tendency to see Psychopomps as undesirables. When we first encounter Hekate in this role, we begin to face our own precious soul in a way that we have not yet done. It is natural to feel vulnerable when beginning the process of preparation for soul retrieval. But Hekate is a benevolent Psychopomp. She is not out to suck out your soul, but to gently guide you back to it.

Nonetheless, there are many tales of nefarious soul eaters who are confused with these more benevolent Psychopomps. We find them in African cultures, in popular vampire movies and books, and in ancient mythology—for example, in the Egyptian goddess Ammit.[6] In African traditions and in today's popular culture, these creatures take the souls of their victims, rendering them shades of their former selves. Ammit and other deities, however, dine only on the souls of the evil. There are human soul suckers, real "psychic vampires," who seem to steal the very essence out of us. Those of us who are natural empaths are at heightened risk for this because our souls shine brightly. Thus, it is vital for our spiritual health that we work on our boundaries and stay with our daily practice as we step into the energy of the Psychopomp.

Hekate's Horde

Throughout my childhood, I was plagued by nightmares featuring a figure I call "the burning man." Even now, writing about this character sends a frisson throughout my being. He never did anything to me, but he appeared in terrifying splendor, surrounded by flames at the edge of a forest in an old-fashioned, black-and-white prisoner's uniform. On occasion, I felt a similar presence late at night in spaces where I felt vulnerable to harm. I now believe that this figure is a protective member of Hekate's horde—the collection of restless souls that became associated with her role as Psychopomp. In ancient Greece, this horde was a collection of the restless dead and other spirits who found no rest in the afterlife. Unsurprisingly, Hekate and her horde evoked great fright.

The historical record reveals a correlation between Hekate's portrayal as a "queen of the unclean" and the diminishment in power of the Great

Mother goddess archetype. The mythic shift to depictions of Hekate as a terrifying specter parallels the cultural shift away from seeing the cave as sacred. This was replaced by a belief in a monotheistic God who ruled from the heavens above. As the ancient Greek writings were being translated into English during the 19th century, this view of Hekate gained force until it overshadowed all other descriptions of her as a Great Mother figure.[7] Even today, this version of Hekate persists.

Hekate's horde of spirits were credited with inflicting sickness of the mind and the body, spreading their toxins on the wind to those who weren't protected.[8] According to one myth, Lamia became a child-eating monster after her offspring were destroyed by Hera as revenge. The *laminaia* became known as spirits who feasted on children. Closely associated with them were the *empousai*, female spirits who feasted on young men. These were particularly connected with Hekate, lending some credibility to her reputation as the mother of vampires.

Contrast this to her well-established earlier role as Kourotrophos, "guardian of children." This marked a change in the societal zeitgeist, and in the localized understanding of Hekate. She was also linked by some to the *mormones*, spirits generally used to frighten children, and with Mormolyka (Frightening Wolf Mother), who was the wet nurse of Acheron. All of these ghastly characters came to be associated with Hekate. To me, however, these spirits aren't infernal. Rather they were misconstrued in public perception as a means of controlling anyone outside of the power structure. They served the purpose of preventing the souls of those who resisted the mainstream to find validation.

In particular, the so-called restless dead were typically denied a conventional burial because they did not conform to societal mores—women who had children out of wedlock, for example. The stories of Hekate and her nefarious horde were told to scare people into maintaining the status quo. Tales of Hekate's horde are found throughout folklore, influencing the common understanding of "dangerous women" and other resisters right up until recent times. The evil queen in Snow White isn't far removed from Hekate's ancient horde.

Ever since Hesiod described Hekate around 3000 years ago, our cultural energy has been obsessed with the bright light of day, denying the wonders of the darkness.[9] A truly fascinating phenomenon that I've observed over the years is the appearance of mysterious figures in dreams similar to mine, many of whom identify with characters like Maleficent. My theory is that these figures help us connect to our own souls. They are rebellious in that they live in darkness. They are lunar, rather than solar. These characters come to us in dreams to show us our own fears. We may even feel their presence at times. They are Psychopomps who can help us face our innermost fears and personal demons so that we can journey through darkness to wholeness.

You may also feel drawn to books, movies, and other media that are frightening. This is a sort of pull in the direction of allowing a fearsome entity to be your protector. These spirits may be frightening in appearance, but they never make us feel threatened. If you encounter such a being, look to your intuitive emotional reaction. If you are afraid because they are frightening, but do not feel that they are going to harm you, this is probably one of Hekate's helpful horde offering protection and guiding you toward your own soul.

Hail, Hekate,
She who stands at the threshold
Between the worlds.
I bring a fine meal
Knowing that it honors you,
And feeds creatures of this place.
They, like me, are yours.
I feel the spirits
Gathered in this place.
They, like me, are yours.
I am embraced by the darkest night,
For the moon has covered her face out of respect for you.
They, like me, are yours.
Here at your crossroads,

I am never alone,
Nor am I afraid.
I am surrounded by my kindred
Those who seek your mysteries,
And those whom you protect.
We are your horde.
Hail, Hekate,
She who stands at the threshold
Between the worlds.

Soul of the World

The tales of Hekate Psychopomp leading a spine-chilling horde are one part of the historical record. But there is much more to her history than this limited perspective. Hesiod firmly viewed Hekate as the Great Mother who governed over the Three Worlds—a goddess to whom even Zeus acquiesced. How Hekate and others like Persephone, Demeter, Artemis, and Cybele were understood was, at least partially, due to geography, and also to the spirit of the times. In the earlier historical records, the Great Mother was viewed as the one from whom all life flowed, sometimes accompanied by a Great Father figure as consort.

One of the most fascinating pieces of Hekate's history is found in a collection of fragments known as The Chaldean Oracles, which explored the structure of the universe and the meaning of life.[10] One of my favorite passages from these oracles explains that Hekate is the fire of creation:

> . . . from there, a lightning-bolt, sweeping along, obscures the flower of fire as it leaps into the hollows of the worlds. For from there, all things begin to extend wonderful rays down below.[11]

This is a vastly different version of Hekate from the one in which she patrols the night with a phantasmagoric squad. In her doctoral thesis,

Sarah Iles Johnston examined how Hekate was presented in this philosophical treatise, offering erudite context and interpretation to help understand the oracles.[12]

Here, Hekate is portrayed as Anima Mundi, the World Soul. She is the primal source from which all the universe flows. Symbolized by fire, she is the igniter of all the world. By contrast, the Great Mother is shown as a sort of outer layer that surrounds the Anima Mundi, positioning Hekate as the mediator between divine immanence and humanity. This role is akin to that of Enodia and is reflected in Persephone's story. Moreover, she can be interpreted as a cosmic Psychopomp whose work is to help humans ascend into wholeness. The World Soul is the one to whom we turn for reunification with our own souls. While The Chaldean Oracles and the writings about them are almost impenetrable in their complexity, they identify the essence of Hekate as a manifestation of the World Soul.

Our cave journey is a return to Anima Mundi, its sheltering darkness symbolic of Hekate's womb from which all life flows. To Jung, Hillman, and others like Joseph Campbell, the only way for us to achieve wholeness is through this epic adventure.[13] In Paulo Coelho's book *The Alchemist,* the hero undertakes this journey back to soul, which is always one that draws us into the mysteries of the deeper world.[14] My favorite passage from this book captures the essence of Anima Mundi:

> Listen to your heart. It knows all things, because it came from the Soul of the World, and it will one day return there.

Our individual quest to return to soul not only benefits us; it also shifts the energy of the collective:

> This is individual inner work, and yet it takes us beyond our individual self into the archetypal world where the symbols that belong to all of humanity also change and transform. Here we may discover that we are working not just with the substance of our own soul, but with the Anima Mundi, the soul of the world. The light we discover in our own depths is a spark of the World Soul, and the world needs this light to evolve. When we make this connection within our consciousness and within our imagination, we begin to change the fabric of life.[15]

Thus, the real work of our lives is this journey back to soul, traveling the path of Anima Mundi, the Great Mother. Although this spirit is known by many names, the very summoning of Hekate to mind evokes imagery of the deeper world where the soul abides.

When we engage in the care of the soul, we become our own Psychopomp, guiding the surface self back to the soul. This is one of the key constructs in Jungian psychology.[16] Jung viewed this unification process as central to healing into wholeness. Thus, the Psychopomp is the one who seeks to retrieve the soul and bring it into consciousness, guiding the psyche (soul) to light. This is thus the work of bringing the unconscious out of the shadows. When we explore our dreams, we are acting as a Psychopomp.

Jung viewed all things as comprised of his principles of anima and animus. To simplify what is intensely complex, anima—the primordial feminine principle—is the soul, and animus—the male principle—is the outer self. He further divided these into eros—love and desire—and logos—rational thought.[17] Thus, our soul retrieval is the unification of both our emotional, intuitive root and our intellectual, logical crown.

While Jung's binary classification becomes problematic at the individual level—we are all combinations of what he called female and male—it is helpful to explore the reunion of the outer self and inner world as the work of the Psychopomp.[18] The soul is not a "thing." Rather, it is a way of being in connection to the truth of who we are, our past lives, our experiences, and our deepest yearnings. It is the place we occupy in Hekate's limitless realm of the deeper world. It is not found within us, but throughout us. But it is also outside of us. Yet we tend to it as if it were an object, because this allows us to make sense (logos) out of what is essentially numinous. Our soul is our temenos and it deserves to be well tended.

The great psychologist James Hillman dedicated his life to understanding the soul, and his writings about Hekate have been profoundly influential on my teaching. Hillman asks us to see soul as a way of being in the world, a lens through which our field of vision, both physical and spiritual, immensely expands:

> By soul I mean, first of all, a perspective rather than a substance, a viewpoint toward things rather than a thing itself. This perspective is reflective; it mediates events and makes differences between ourselves

and everything that happens. Between us and events, between the doer and the deed, there is a reflective moment—and soul-making means differentiating this middle ground.[19]

Unfortunately, today there is great fear of the soul in our society. For us to embrace the care of our own souls, others' souls, and the Anima Mundi involves rebelling against mainstream culture. To see from the soul takes courage.

For centuries, the soul, along with the goddess, has been pushed out by the prevailing power structure. The work of the Psychopomp is thus often regarded with suspicion or outright vilification, and we may have become indoctrinated to this fear of our own souls. Surely, the unconscious with its strange dreams can be seen as a foreign territory where we don't understand the culture. Yet the way back to the soul leads deep into this territory. And that is where soul retrieval occurs.

When we engage in this soul work, our ability as soul guides for others often comes very clearly into consciousness. This can take on the form of healing work, mediumship, and our relationships with spirits. We see the soul loss in our culture in many ways—from out-of-control consumerism to a power structure that emphasizes the ego. The diminishment of dreams and the imagination is one of the most personally devastating weapons of the cultural war against soul. But when we learn that these are the sacred manifestations of the soul, we restore ourselves. I cannot count the times I've been asked if something is "just my imagination." My dear one, the imagination is the most important thing. Marion Woodman summed it up well:

> Kill the imagination and you kill the soul. Kill the soul and you're left with a listless, apathetic creature who can become hopeless or brutal or both.[20]

Soul Loss

The entire journey through the cave is a retrieval of lost fragments of the soul. Soul retrieval is an ancient practice found in many traditions, yet it is absent from our contemporary culture. Depth psychologists, mystics, shamans, and other traditions share a similar view—that the return to soul is the key to wholeness.[21] Here we will focus on the soul fragments that have been lost, broken off from the whole by the toxic conditioning of today's world.

Our society, in its determination to block the soul from surfacing, traumatizes us all. Given that soul is anima, the sacred feminine, we see the correlation between the marginalization of women and the denial of soul. Society says to focus on appearance and materialism, and to stay in ego mode. Hekate sings her song to awaken us to the deeper world within. She calls us to reject the false self that dwells in fear, gossip, and pettiness.

We have all done these things to fill the void when the soul is absent, and they are always characteristic of functioning from the more toxic energies of the surface self, also called the ego. But when we do the work of soul retrieval, we retreat from both the mania of society and old habits of the ego, for they always work in tandem. That is the natural process of soul retrieval occurring.

Many of us have pieces of our souls missing due to trauma. Like Persephone, we may have had our innocence taken from us. Now we reclaim it through the process of soul retrieval. We see the problem of trauma-induced soul fragmentation in different ways. Disconnect from emotions, disembodiment, and staying in relationships with psychic vampires are all symptoms. Feelings of anxiety, depression, and generalized distress always accompany soul loss. We grieve for what we don't even know we've lost until we bring the soul to light, illuminating the places that are still in darkness. Perhaps there is a specific event that comes to mind even as you read this passage. That is where your soul loss occurred. Travel back before that to see what longs for reunification.

One of the most debilitating features of soul loss is seen in the emergence of what is known as the "innocence complex." Because we have lost a piece of our soul, we are perpetually occupying the shadow of the child archetype. Instead of identifying with the playful, curious, and energetic child, we become the orphan child, constantly seeking approval from others. This complex is characterized by believing that, if we are nice enough or good enough, if we quash our desires and feign interest in things we dislike, if we put others' needs above our own, someday our prince will come and save us. We've all seen children—usually girls—who literally turn cartwheels in an attempt to seek validation. If gymnastics fuels your soul, then by all means do them. But if you're doing these sorts of contortions because of what you think others expect, go for a walk instead. When we turn inward to Hekate, we give up these futile pursuits. Persephone walked straight to her waiting throne when she was ready and claimed it for her own. She relinquished the innocence complex.

Another feature of soul loss, especially loss due to early childhood crises, is an incomplete definition of the true self, which we often experience as a listless emptiness. Simply stated, those suffering from this loss lack a strong view of who they are.[22] Their likes and dislikes are based on others' ideas rather than on their own as they attempt to fill up the empty space left by their missing soul fragments. This is often reflected in having a general Phoberos attachment orientation. Because pieces of their core are missing, they become volatile rather than stable. They may turn to misguided ways to fill the void, like self-harm practices, cutting, or addiction. These are all symptoms of what's known as borderline personality disorder, and they are also associated with PTSD. While these diagnoses may be needed at times—for clinical treatment or for insurance purposes—they are problematic because they don't address the underlying issue, which is loss of soul. This is why treatments like cognitive behavioral therapy can help us cope, but never, ever solve the root of the problem.[23] Pharmaceuticals can help us manage symptoms, but they don't address the root either. The only remedy is reunion with the missing pieces. This is how the void is filled.

Soul Retrieval

Now we stand at the gate of retrieval—the second gate of Hekate's cave. This gate offers the opportunity for intentionally calling back the soul through a transcendent ritual. You've journeyed far, with grace and grit. Enter into the mercy of Psychopomp, who has been tending to the missing fragments.

The shadow deserves mercy, not criminalization. This wrongminded idea is perpetrated by those who don't have a deep understanding of shadow healing. The shadow protects during difficult times. It releases the soul fragments into Hekate's cave, for it knows when they need to be safeguarded. The resulting gaps in our personal identity and deeper self are filled in by the shadow. While this often saves our very souls, it may also result in emptiness, addictions, distress, anxiety, depression, toxic relationships, and an inability to stand in our own power.

See yourself as the Psychopomp doing the work of calling back pieces of yourself while Hekate leads the way. When you go into soul retrieval, you enter kairos, the nonlinear time of the numinous. In my own experiences of soul retrieval, I felt as if I had been there for weeks. But when I came back, only minutes had passed.

It is natural to feel intense emotions when preparing for soul retrieval. Rest assured that I've adapted the ritual given below so that it is safe and effective. You are not alone. Hekate and her companions are there. Your avian ally is especially important during this journey. Winged creatures have long been associated with soul retrieval and are most skilled as companions for this work.

As you move through the process of soul retrieval, your returned pieces bring with them their experiences, dreams, and desire. These memories, ideas, and ways of being may be quite different from the person you are today. Talking to them with acceptance and curiosity while offering support is key for a successful reunion. Generally, there are many emotions that immediately percolate to the surface upon soul reunion. You may feel blissful, along with the emotions that you were feeling at the time of the fragmentation. Talk to your returned self as you would an old friend. I encourage you to engage in these soul sessions after performing your daily meditation and to ask the cards to reveal guidance during the Enodia Oracle.

Integrating our returned soul fragments plays out in our dreams and imaginations. These can be deeply unsettling, yet they are invitations to wholeness. Just last night, while preparing for an upcoming ritual, I had a very distressing dream in which I was trying to win back my high school boyfriend, whom I hadn't thought of in years. In the dream, I was doing all sorts of things to impress him and his family to no avail. When I ended this relationship, I was in the throes of a great family upheaval. My mother had gone to jail for serious fraud and embezzlement. My boyfriend's family, on the other hand, was the epitome of a happy and successful family. Instead of rejecting me because of what my mother had done, they increased their care and support. Simply stated, I couldn't handle their view of me as worthy, so I broke things off.

This kicked off a horrible spiral for me that lasted over a decade, although the bright blessing of my oldest son came during this period in my life. To have all this return to me in a dream was meaningful. My early attachment wounds opened the way to chronic sexual trauma in adolescence and a series of extremely poor life choices. Retrieving the pieces of myself that fled during this time in my life showed me that I was ready for the integrative healing of another piece that Hekate has been tending for me.

It is important when we are reunited with these earlier versions of ourselves to let them know that they are safe. Whenever the difficult aspects that led to the soul loss surface, it can help so much to say: "I am safe. You are safe. We are together now." We will be exploring this integration process in the next chapter in greater depth.

Empathy and Soul Retrieval

Caring for our own souls often calls us to tend to the souls of others. Soul retrieval awakens our empathy as we learn that all things have souls. We move from being unconscious of the soul in all, including ourselves, to being conscious of it. How we enact this consciousness takes many different forms, all of which honor Anima Mundi. When we interact with plant medicine or stone spirits, we enter into relation with their souls rather than their superficial qualities. The "soulness" of objects and places comes into focus, seeking to understand.

To see from the soul is to know that all the world is enchanted with a deeper meaning. This draws some to environmental work, helping to nourish the soul of our planet. Others use their sacred creativity to connect with their own souls and inspire others to do the same. Some work as mediums, connecting the living with the departed. A few are skilled at traditional Psychopompery, which is the guiding of souls between the spirit world and embodied life.

As we build a relationship with our retrieved soul fragments, empathy becomes very important. By empathy, I mean intentionally contemplating how our retrieved selves feel. We enter into this with the spirit of understanding, having a strong back and a soft front. Proceed with curiosity and compassion. Lean into the key principles of passion, kindness, and integrity to awaken your empathy.

Empathy surfaces when we put ourselves in the shoes of others, and we can do this internally as well, as we build relationships with our different selves.[24] Empathy asks us to imagine temporarily what the other is experiencing. It encourages us to put aside our snap judgments for a moment so we can try to understand others. True empathy begins with having kindness, passion, and integrity for ourselves. Empathy isn't about giving advice or solving someone else's problems. It's not a characteristic of the savior complex. Leading empathy and shame researcher Brené Brown describes it like this:

> [E]mpathy isn't about fixing, it's the brave choice to be with someone in their darkness—not to race to turn on the light so we feel better.[25]

Empathy in adulthood has a complex relationship to trauma in childhood. Some studies report that adults with severe trauma early in life are more empathetic than control participants,[26] while others report just the opposite.[27] As you walk through the process of integrating your lost soul fragments, your past trauma may influence how supportive you can be of the returned fragments. Lean into the imagery of Hekate as the benevolent soul guide, and see empathy flowing from her to all of you.

Healthy empathy seeks to understand rather than merge with another. Unhealthy empathy, on the other hand, is correlated with weak boundaries. In our genuine efforts to connect with others, we can unintentionally take on their emotions and wounds. This is harmful to us because we end up avoiding our inner life, instead adopting the feelings and thoughts of others. This is easy for those of us who are highly sensitive, caring people. But if we were deeply wounded as children, we can struggle with establishing and maintaining boundaries, based on healthy instincts that tell us when we need to escape or fight. This is damaging because it is absolutely exhausting. Taking on others' energy drains us of our own. When we bring our missing pieces back home without intentionally dialoguing from a place of empathy, we can tire ourselves out. Hold space for your reunited self.

Having a strong back and a soft front allows us to have empathy for others without becoming engulfed in their energy. It reminds us that others' feelings, experiences, and wounds are not ours to bear. Empathy doesn't include violating our own boundaries because we fear rejection. Empathy says: "I see you. I hear you. Here is what I am able to offer you." Sometimes, empathy for ourselves necessitates stepping away from other people and situations. If someone is negative, insulting, and ignorant, we can try to understand why they might be that way, but we are not obliged to correct them. That is not empathy. That is demonstrating our need to be right.

Moreover, we can develop PTSD if we take on the wounds of others. This results from something known as "secondary traumatic stress," which is often associated with caregiving. My own research has shown that secondary traumatic stress was associated with many negative outcomes, including increased depression and physical health problems. It simply isn't helpful for anyone to take on the stress of another.

True empathy has firm boundaries through which we can understand and hold space for others.[28] Only by holding ourselves accountable, with appreciation for our pain and weaknesses, can we become whole.

Here are some tips to help you develop and manage empathy with your retrieved selves and with others.

- Reply to others with specific remarks and let the speaker know that you are actively listening.[29]

- Repeat back what a person says: "So if I understand you, this is what you are saying . . ."

- Avoid story-matching. When others pour out their hearts, let them know you appreciate their trust in you rather than launching into your personal narrative. Ask them to say more.

- Affirm: "I can imagine that was very exciting/difficult . . ."

- When interacting in person, use your eyes to demonstrate that you are focused on what others are saying.

- Know who you can help *and* who you can't. It is more than enough to say: "This sounds rough. I wish I could offer more help, but I don't know anything about _____. I am happy to listen."

Practica: Soul Retrieval Journey

As you prepare for this journey, stay with your daily practice. I recommend working with shungite in the week leading up to the ritual, keeping it next to your skin, as it is strongly purifying and activating for transcendence. An amethyst can be carried on your body as well, as it is a great aid to soul retrieval. Continue to work with these stones for several days after the ritual. Arrange all the stones on the altar before the journey.

The waxing moon is the optimal phase for this journey because it carries the signature of attraction. Create an altar that evokes Hekate as Psychopomp. If you know the specific soul fragments that are missing, add symbols of them to the altar. I recommend thorough purification of body and mind immediately prior to the ritual. A healing bath with amethyst and shungite and your ritual candle can help.

Adorn your ritual candle with appropriate symbols, like torches or images evocative of the Psychopomp. You can continue to use this candle during the integration phase that follows the ritual. Starting one week before your ritual, light the candle each day before bed to activate your powers as a Psychopomp, reaching out to your missing fragments and sending them the message that your reunion is approaching. You can use words like: "Psychopomp, Psychopomp, awaken in me. I call back my soul to me." Doing this at bedtime will encourage dreams about these missing fragments. You may experience intense dreams during this week. Journaling about them will be enormously helpful.

For this ritual, you will need:

- Pieces of shungite and amethyst.

- A selection of Hekate's herbs. Damiana, foxglove, poppy, and thyme are perfectly suited for soul retrieval.[30]

- Oleum Spirita or another trance-enhancing oil or appropriate substance.

- A fresh candle to begin the process of retrieval—preferably red—in addition to the one from your daily practice.

An offering is not necessary for this ritual, as the very process of soul retrieval is a great blessing to Hekate.

Sit comfortably before your altar. Light the candle and hold your stones. Summon your avian companion. See it gently resting on your shoulder. Shift your weight onto your spine, down into your sitting bones. Relax your shoulders and place your hands in a comfortable position, but don't cross them or your legs.

You can use the visualization that follows as a guide for your soul retrieval journey. It may be helpful to record it so you can play it during the ceremony.

Picture a set of thirteen stairs deep within you. With each number, you descend one step, with your avian companion flying slightly ahead.

- On the thirteenth step, pull air in, filling your lungs slowly and letting your chest expand. Then exhale.

- On the twelfth step, pull a slow breath deep into your belly. Exhale.

- On the eleventh step, repeat the slow, deep breath, noticing any returning thoughts or images from the material world. Exhale.

- On the tenth step, dismiss these thoughts and images. Exhale.

- On the ninth step, pull your breath deep into your lower torso. As you exhale, release all tension there.

- On the eighth step, your breath reaches down through your legs to the tips of your toes, disconnecting you from the external world, wrapping you in a protective shroud. Exhale any tension you are feeling.

- On the seventh step, return your breath back into your torso, encasing it in protection—safe and secure. Exhale.

- On the sixth step, your breath wraps your chest and heart center in a shell. Exhale.

- On the fifth step, pull that powerful breath down into your right arm, right to your fingertips. Exhale.

- On the fourth step, repeat this for your left arm. Exhale.

- On the third step, bring your breath up to your shoulders and neck. Your thoughts are completely still. Exhale.

- On the second step, feel your breath activate your mind for opening the gate to the deeper world. Exhale.

- On the first step, enter Hekate's cave. Completely separated from the world of form, you are an energetic being. Exhale.

Feel your physical body resting comfortably. The air is electric, charged with incense. With each breath you become more attuned to the cave. Below your feet, the path is black as night. All around you, the red of the life force shines. There is only peace here. Secure. Safe. Alert.

You see a fire. Walk over to the fire. As you look up from the fire, notice that your avian companion is hovering in front of a set of double doors, beckoning you to join. You do, taking note of the beautiful symbols carved into the doors. You know that you are meant to open these doors, and you do. You step into a small chamber lit by candles. The presence of Hekate permeates this space. A steady determination fills you. Your avian companion rests nearby, but never out of sight.

You are guided to the center of the chamber, realizing that below your feet is Hekate's Wheel, a great spiral of which you are the center. Around you, the walls are covered with similar symbols, turning, blending together. A gentle hum comes from them. Focus your attention on the reason why you are here—to retrieve missing pieces of yourself. Release this intention into the chamber.

You notice that parts of the Wheel beneath your feet are not lit. As you look around you, you see that parts of the Wheels in the walls shine brighter. Some emerge as beautiful fragments, as keys. Your avian companion collects them, one at a time, and brings them to you. As they are presented, reach out to these keys, calling them back to you. As you grasp them, the dim parts of the Wheel under your feet light up. The energy of the keys and the Wheel surges through you. You see the Wheel within you; that is your pure being welcoming the pieces back. At this moment, your bird ally brings you a gift that is a symbol of the reunification. Allow this symbol to be what it is meant to be.

Take some time here while the reunion occurs. A pure sensation fills you. Bliss. Contentment. Joy. Pause here in this moment as your lost pieces are reunited. All your keys, your soul fragments, are together. You are the keeper of your own keys. You are the Psychopomp, the soul guide.

Now the time has come to exit the chamber. Your companion is now flying ahead once more, leading you back to regular consciousness. Pause here to express gratitude to Hekate and your companion. When you are ready, begin your return journey back to regular consciousness, to your physical being. Count up from one to twelve, with each number climbing up the steps to the Middle World.

- On the first step, you notice your feet reconnecting to their physical form.

- On the second step, your breath starts to return to the material world, as do your legs, releasing their protective shell.

- On the third step, your breath releases the shield and travels up through your torso.

- On the fourth step, your left arm returns to the material world.

- On the fifth step, your right arm does the same.

- On the sixth step, your chest reconnects to your physical heart and lungs. The eternal fire of your Inner Temple warms them both.

- On the seventh step, your breath travels up to your throat. Your voice comes back to your embodied self.

- On the eighth step, you release your crown.

- On the ninth step, your thoughts begin to return.

- On the tenth step, you begin to hear the material world once again.

- On the eleventh step, your breath is completely back to the Middle World, taking in the smells.

- On the twelfth step, you open your eyes.

Draw your Enodia Oracle cards for further guidance on integrating the returned pieces.

The soul symbol you received as you left Hekate's cave is your power object for activating your soul-guide abilities. You earned this by completing your own soul retrieval. Create or acquire a material representation of this symbol, connecting you to your Psychopomp abilities and to Hekate (and perhaps your avian companion). Keep this talisman in your Cista Mystica. Wear it or hold it whenever you wish to activate your Psychopomp skills, including those for soul retrieval and time-bending.

Practica: Carta Recupero

You can create a map to help guide your returned pieces to the here and now, and then add your imagined destination. This is known as a *carta recupero*.

Here are some questions to guide you as you create your map:

- Ask your returned pieces to describe where they come from and how things were while they were waiting for reunion. Listen with acceptance and curiosity. Offer your unconditional support.

- Guide your lost fragments to where you are now by discussing your journey since they departed. Share your experiences, accomplishments, heartbreaks, favorite things, relationships, and so on.

- Dialogue about where this map leads. Inquire about their desires, goals, and dreams, then share yours. Find the common ground in the destination.

Chapter 13

Rixipyle: The Chain Breaker

Spin and shake,
Loosen and quake.
Stomp and step,
Speak and sing.
Freedom within,
Freedom without.
Moving toward wholeness,
Liberation begins.
Coming together,
Standing strong.
Rixipyle.
Rixipyle.
Rixipyle.

The ancient title of Rixipyle was bestowed upon Hekate in The Greek Magical Papyri, translated by Hans Dieter Betz as "she who throws down gates." This meaning goes beyond the crashing of the gates to the very upheaval of the status quo. In modern parlance, Rixipyle refers to the chains that bind us—from societal norms to the shackles of the shadow. We break free of what has barred us from transcending into our own sacredness. This is the return to our wildness—not irresponsible abandon, but the natural connection to our own soul. This is Hekate and her deeper world being restored.

Rixipyle shakes us awake. Our chains don't slide off like a satin robe; they need to be shed through our own will and actions. The very notion of a gate-crashing, chain-breaking, upheaval-bringing goddess can evoke strong emotions. Freeing the wild soul always demands that we dance off the binding chains. Frenzy, resistance, and ecstasy are experienced. Shall we dance? The Chain Breaker comes with her dragon, burning down the old ways and creating a new landscape. I am reminded of Daenerys Targaryen from *Game of Thrones*. Indeed, Hekate was also called Drakaina, and this mythic flying serpent can be such an ally as we break free. Our avian companions remind us that it is time to fly free.

The Liberation

Every time we explore Rixipyle, my students report massive upheavals in their personal lives. They end relationships that no longer serve them. They walk away from abusive situations. They quit their day jobs. They even move clear across the country. This is the energy of the goddess as the chain-breaking, gate-crashing force. When we call out to Rixipyle, it is because we are more than ready to break free and break through. Perhaps before entering the cave, we were unaware of our shackles. Our load lightens; perhaps our backs straighten; we are opening up. This shifts the chains, bringing them into our conscious awareness. What once was outside of consciousness is now front and center.

Rixipyle symbolizes both the breaking of chains and the breaking down of gates. This dual role is something we can apply in our own lives. As gatekeepers, we tend to our personal temenos, being careful about whom we let in and mindful of nourishing what and who is inside. Yet we also engage in the process of liberating ourselves from the chains that others wrap around us, as well as those of our own design. The chains to which we were once numb now rattle in our ears and dig deep. Unignorable. That is the awakening of Hekate Rixipyle, breaker of chains and crasher of gates.

Rixipyle doesn't work only on the soul; she works on our physical selves as well. Itching, aches and pains, and feelings of restlessness can all ignite when she comes to us. When I was in the final stages of a relation-ship that I shouldn't ever have gotten myself into, I started to have allover unbearable itching with no physical symptoms like a rash. My only relief was to take scalding hot baths as often as possible. The bathroom was my escape from the never-ending arguments and upset. Yes, I often used what's become known as the Never Again Facecloth in those baths.

Rixipyle doesn't meander; she strives. She burns; she yearns. She turns her blazing keys toward us, reflecting all that we are and all that is possible. We can be stunned by her presence. Where has the gentle goddess gone? Instead, we stand before the bright burning one. Reflected in her image, we ignite. She is the swift bringer of truth. She speaks through her actions, which are decisive and forceful. She can be an angry goddess—we may call her Brimo, the Fierce One, another title of Hekate, Persephone, and Artemis—and she can be one who induces sacred frenzy. She is Hekate preparing a wiser Persephone to go back into the light of day.

A common side effect of this is radical changes in our behavior. We no longer give one sweet damn about what others think about what we wear. By shedding all the programming that happens to us sometime in early adolescence, we return to the person we were before society placed its chains on us. I recall reading the now-classic *Reviving Ophelia: Saving the Selves of Adolescent Girls* by Mary Pipher in my early thirties and feeling both outrage and liberation. In this book, Pipher outlines the process by which young girls' souls are caged and how they can recover from it. This is the healing of the Chain Breaker.

Rixipyle's not messing around. Stay centered by doing your daily practice; lean into the messages the oracle brings. Breaking through these chains of societal conditioning is a process. In the years since Pipher's sem-inal work, many other authors have written about the need to feel these feelings all the way through to access the healing that moves us closer to rebirth into our unique wholeness. As Pipher wrote:

> Authenticity is an "owning" of all experience, including emotions
> and thoughts that are not socially acceptable.

Rixipyle is not in the business of shielding us from strong feelings at this stage of the journey, because she has looked into our souls and found us ready.

Unbinding the Emotions

Once we invoke Rixipyle, we step out of numbness and into our power. The electricity has been turned back on. Being able to engage fully with our strong emotions is an essential part of healing. Emotions abide in the body; spin, shake and dance them through.

This brings up fury and frenzy, and our old friend the shadow can try to clamp down on the undoing by yelling louder than ever. Many emotions may be in play. Frenzy, which shows up in shadowy behaviors like over-functioning and hyper-enthusiasm, in its illuminated aspect is an invitation to redirecting the flow toward embodied expressions. These are adventures into the deeper world that allow emotions to flow freely while we maintain physical momentum—with dance or rhythmic movement, for instance.

If you've ever had your hands physically bound, the feeling of release that comes when you are unbound brings up pure emotions. The sense of liberation is unparalleled. At this stage of the journey, you may find yourself riding the Rixipyle wave, being full of enthusiasm and highly motivated to shake up your life. The dreams you've hidden for so long now demand attention.

Our ability to recognize our own emotions and those of others grows out of our early attachment with our primary caregiver. Attachment archetypes are formed based on these emotional interactions, which contribute to our general orientation toward ourselves and others. If you have challenges identifying your archetype, it may be correlated with a deficit in emotional vocabulary, a condition sometimes called *alexithymia*.[1] This troublesome condition is associated with a lack of what neuroscientists call "mirroring opportunities," and is often associated with trauma.[2] Certainly, numbing when we are bound too tightly dampens emotions, and also causes an overwhelming ricochet effect when we do feel them.

In *The Dance of Anger: A Woman's Guide to Changing the Patterns of Intimate Relationships,* Harriet Learner attributes the difficulty many women have with their anger to the gender norms about which emotions are acceptable for women to have. Rixipyle can bring up a lot of anger. We may rage against those who've bound us, from our family of origin to our present-day boss. The thing is that we are often so conditioned against feeling angry that we direct this ire back at ourselves. I think this

Entering Hekate's Cave

is why many of us are stuck, depressed, and anxious. We need to feel our anger all the way through and channel it in productive ways. I want you to stop second-guessing your anger. Listen to it instead. Give it the respect it deserves. Anger can be driven by the soul or the shadow. Anger itself is not the problem, but rather how it is working within us.

Artemis was not one for the bindings that others attempted to place on her. Even her father, Zeus, knew better than to inflict on her the sorts of shackles he liked to use, from pregnancy to being turned into an animal. One day, Artemis was celebrating her wild self in a lake when a man came upon her. Outraged—and righteously so, because he was invading her private ritual—she turned him into a stag and then turned his own hounds on him.[3] And consider Circe's rage over the men who invaded her island, or Medea's fury when she was betrayed.[4] In these myths and countless other stories, the justifiable anger of these women was viewed as contemptible. But ask yourself: If a man had done these things, would he have been seen as evil? Most likely, he would have been labeled a hero.

The shackles we bear about our emotions have deep and sharp hooks because of this cultural programming. The process of learning to give our anger the space it deserves begins with becoming aware of these social mores. This often makes us angry, creating an altar upon which all the repressed fury in our bodies can position itself. Think of this as a sacrament to Rixipyle.

Our righteous anger is a call. Often, waking fury leads to deep healing in the dreamworld. It also breaks down the gate to the deeper mysteries, like ecstatic experiences and our coming rebirth. We need to feel the power of the physical self to get connected to the limitlessness of the deeper world. Dionysus, an ancient god associated with emotions and expressions of embodiment (among many other things), sometimes appears in our field of vision as a mysterious man, perhaps even with horns. Given that, as women, we've been programmed to avoid strong feelings and to assume that being present with our physical selves is out of bounds, it makes sense that a masculine figure would appear to guide us.

Yet before there was Dionysus, there was his mortal mother, Semele, who passed on emotional abundance and embodiment to her son.[5] In this myth, Semele, who is wildly beautiful, is struck down by Zeus's wife, Hera, after he impregnates her. Hera represents the civilized woman, an unwitting agent of the patriarchy. Eventually, Semele is reborn as a goddess through the efforts of her son. In ancient rites, she was called upon to bring spiritual ecstasy to women, who called her Semele Thyone, Inspirer of Frenzy. And frenzy calls us to liberate from perfectionism and inhibitions. Without the wisdom of the soul to guide us, however, it can lead to trouble.

A shift occurs with the release of these chains, and that is that the soul can now hold presence in our consciousness. Our anger and ecstasy become momentum for change. From this vantage point, we have emotions rather than them having us. Even when the rushing tide of anger or enthusiasm seems about to drown us, the soul abides. The practice of the daily meditation awakens the soul while strengthening the polyvagal system, which is the physiological basis of the inner serpent.[6] When we see the body as attuned to the soul and the deeper world of Hekate, we can see how our past traumas and current pains are actually portals, rather than blockades to this realm, as we can commonly be programmed to believe. Rixipyle smashes that gate to dust.

The body is the soul expressed, and emotions are the fuel that links the two. We may think that all this energy will burn us out, but it actually revitalizes us since it comes from the soul rather than the shadow. Too often when we live in shadow, we are preoccupied with not feeling emotions, which leads to an amplification of our distress.[7] Liberation, as titillating as it is, can also lead to the shadow having an unprecedented hissy fit. It may scream in fear that we simply cannot do the things our souls, and our goddess, urge us to do. But anger and ecstasy combine into the superpower of courage. The boldness of liberation compels us to reclaim our wild souls.

Rixipyle offers the key of personal sovereignty. When we take the key of liberation from her, we choose to become the architects of our own journeys. No more blaming others, regardless of how much they may deserve it. I invite you to dialogue, with both the power of Rixipyle and the shadow. This liberation can lead you to many first times, including (perhaps) allowing yourself to feel your feelings all the way through for the first time.

Entering Hekate's Cave

Rewilding

Rixipyle's rebel cry reverberates as she shakes our chains loose. She offers a key she's been keeping for us until we were ready—the bravery to return to our sacred wildness. The time has come to free yourself from the shackles of self-neglect, denial, doubt, and restriction. Rewilding is an intentional practice that is driven by the Chain Breaker's momentum. It's dancing, shamanic journeying, performing rituals on the beach to bind a toxic person. And it's deeply driven by emotion. It's not sitting in your room waiting for the cards to tell you your next move. It's sticking them in your pocket as you move forward. If you haven't yet read *Women Who Run with the Wolves: Myths and Stories of the Wild Woman Archetype* by Clarissa Pinkola Estés, I highly recommend it as an exploration of rewilding, along with *Untamed* by Glennon Doyle.

Part of the process of rewilding is to embrace a spirituality that is often contradictory to the one with which we were raised. Releasing the shackles around our spirituality is part of the awakening. While I'm not here to vilify any religion, it cannot be denied that most preach a dogma based on our essential sinfulness. Women in particular are often vilified. Moreover, the most popular religions view God as male. This makes for a heady cocktail of programming.

Spiritual freedom occurs when we realize that we have a choice in what we believe and practice. This often brings forward both anger and ecstasy. You see that your parents, partners, and others perhaps view your spiritual journey with suspicion. You may try to justify your practices to them because you are full of enthusiasm, but this rarely works. The better alternative is to use your anger as a clarifying lens through which to explore spiritual programming and reserve your ecstasy for those who appreciate it.

One of my earliest memories is of sitting in a church pew on a Sunday morning in my short summer dress. The wood beneath me stuck to my bare legs. As a child, I couldn't articulate how that painful feeling of stickiness permeated my soul, but I knew that my discomfort was about far more than my sore legs. I didn't belong there, in spite of being surrounded by my family. My wild soul was completely chained. I yearned for the freedom of my beloved woods, where my imagination drew me into the deeper world.

Flash forward ten years or so, and I'm devouring every book on spirituality I can get my hands on. But while I loved many of them, and still do, I had that sticky-legs feeling again. The systems offered in these books didn't sit right with me. Jump ahead another decade, and I'm involved with a group who, although beautiful in many ways, felt like just another uncomfortable church pew. Something within me said to keep searching, so I did. After exploring yoga, Buddhism, and other spiritual paths, I found what made sense to me and left the rest for others. Each time I started feeling sticky, I vacated that pew in search of my soul's liberation.

Spiritual programming shows up as discrediting—so much so that what we know to be true ends up needing some sort of external validation. Becoming conscious of how often we do this to ourselves is a process. If you are feeling hesitant about the practices and rituals in this book, because you think that others will think they are weird or even sinful, it may be your shadow blocking you from unleashing your wild soul.

My goddesses are wild and free.
Inconvenient, independent.
Rebellious.
Resisters.
Revengers.
My goddesses are wild and free.
Hunting the wicked.
Conquering monsters.
Turning fools into swine.
Driving dragon chariots across the sun.
Shining pale moonbeams,
Burning torches.
All the stars above,
And the deepest depths.
My goddesses are wild and free.
Many faces, many moods.
They scare the life into me.

Shakers. Movers. Chain Breakers.
Dream haunters.
Screaming whispers,
Dead silence.
Enduring, changing.
Fleeing, remaining.
My darkest desires,
My brightest dreams.
My goddesses are wild and free.
Death walkers.
Truth talkers.
Troublemakers.
Impatient with fakers.
Claiming those they desire,
Casting others into the fire.
My goddesses are wild and free.
Answering my call,
Showing up uninvited.
Forever traveling their road,
Leaving behind a trail
That I choose to follow.
My goddesses are wild and free.

Practica: BE-ing Check-In

This practice involves simply pausing whenever your stress dial starts to rise and doing the BE-ing check-in that originated in twelve-step programs. Explore what is going on in your body by asking the HALT questions used in addictions recovery: Am I hungry? Am I angry? Am I lonely? Am I tired? Scan for sensations as well. Where am I holding pain in my body? Where is there tension? On a scale of 1 to 10, how much contentment am I feeling? How much anger?

You can establish this as a regular practice by adding these questions to your daily practice, so it is much easier to do throughout the day. This practice brings you back into your body. Over time, you will become attuned to it and start to do it on autopilot. Use the BE-ing approach for grounding when you are experiencing an abundance of feeling, whether you are exhausted or exhilarated. Ask yourself: What is one thing I can touch? See? Hear? Smell? What emotions do each of these things bring forward? Hang on to your garnet stone to help balance you through the shaking up.

Practica: Creating a Personal Religion

Try creating your own personal religion and including in it what feels right to you. Explore how you understand the sacred feminine, whether it's Hekate, Persephone, Demeter, or one of the other goddesses. Celebrate your stones and avian ally. Perhaps you connect to the sacred only through stones, plants, or animals. Perhaps your avian ally is your primary companion from the deeper world. If the cards or other oracular tools speak of the sacred to you, make an altar to them. Allow what is longing for expression within you to come out, breaking the chains of your spiritual programming.

I recommend Thomas Moore's lovely book, *A Religion of One's Own: A Guide to Creating a Personal Spirituality in a Secular World*, as a helpful guide to liberation. Sue Monk Kidd's book *Dance of the Dissident Daughter* inspired me to craft my own personal spirituality. In a sense, we're here together in the pages of this book because of that religion.

Here are tips on how to proceed:

- Do an inventory of your spiritual practices. Which ones feel true to you? Do you perform some just because someone told you to? Which ones do you do based on fear? Which ones bring you freedom?

- Unplug from the spiritual matrix—perhaps for a day, perhaps for a year. As long as you are digesting others' opinions, you'll have a hard time connecting to what you already know to be true.

- Create space for the new in your life. Give up someone that you don't like but stick with because you don't want to be lonely. You'll never make new friends until you release the ones you've outgrown.

- Collect objects that speak truth to you, whether it's a beautiful crystal or some pebbles found on the shore. There are no right or wrong ways to create altars, so arrange these objects into your own personal expression of spirituality.

- Detach from spiritual consumerism. Adopt a buy-nothing policy for your next ritual. Or, better yet, do one with absolutely no external objects. You are the only required ingredient in magic.

- Read perspectives that are different from your own. This also applies to podcasts and videos. Try out new ideas like new outfits; if it doesn't fit, take it back.

- Express your spirituality through creativity, whether it's baking a cake or painting your toenails. Create an altar that is an external manifestation of how you see the sacred in your soul. Do what feels spiritual to you. Creativity and programming cannot coexist.

Chapter 14

Anassa Eneroi: The Death Queen

Hail, Hekate,
Anassa Eneroi, Queen of the Dead.
She who commands all spirits,
And keeps the keys of souls.
Come, I call upon you.
Hail, Hekate,
The Supreme Empress,
Bringer of death,
And giver of life.
Come to me now.
Reveal yourself to me.
You who knows the secrets of all living and dead,
Mighty Anassa Eneroi.
I come seeking your mysteries
Of death and rebirth.
With you as witness,
I bring death to that which no longer serves.
Bless it with your eternal power,
Take my burden now.

My words are my offering,
And my soul cleansed in your presence.
I am your follower and witness to your power.
Rebirth shall take place; this cannot be denied.
I implore you this very night.
Hail, Hekate,
Anassa Eneroi, Queen of the Dead.
As I speak it, it becomes so.

*—Inspired by the Hymn to the Waning Moon
in The Greek Magical Papyri (IV. 2241–2358).*

Anassa Eneroi is the calm comfort of the stillness after a period of great suffering. But she is also chaos, the whirring energy of the Wheel. She is both the Moirai, who know the Wheel's mysteries, and the Furies (*Erinys*), who can be seen as correcting things when fate is interrupted by wrongdoers.[1] She controls the guardian of the Underworld, Cerberus, keeping him in line. Covered in the serpents symbolic of the Great Mother, she represents the soul serpent within and the endless cycle of the ouroboros.[2] She offers succor to unquiet souls.

The raging voice of Anassa Eneroi shrieks at those who cause pain. But it also beckons the wounded to her protective horde. Her voice gives rise to great discomfort, shaking us from our living death. This call of hers vibrates us to the core, leading us to come to life and dance our way down her road toward her great cauldron of rebirth that awaits beside her throne of bones.

In the ancient rites of Eleusis, the final stage of the journey through the cave was rebirth.[3] There has been much speculation about the details of this ceremony and all the rituals related to it.[4] What was the ultimate meaning of life and death that was revealed to participants? Those who journeyed through the cave faced Anassa Eneroi, the Death Queen, where they learned the answer to this question. I suspect that it was the journey itself that revealed the answer—much as ours has throughout the preceding chapters, moving us from the initial ritual of catharsis through soul retrieval to the final stage of rebirth.

Persephone, as Hades's consort, bore the title Anassa Eneroi, as did her close companion, Hekate. The epithet was applied to Hekate in the tale of

Jason when Medea, flushed with love for the soldier, journeyed to the temple to craft a spell to render him invincible. She called upon her mother to bless her talisman, created using the power of Prometheus, crying out to "Brimo, Kourotrophos, Nyktipolis, Chthonia, Anassa Eneroi."[5] These appellations translate to "Fierce, Guardian of Children, Night Wanderer, Underworld Goddess, Queen of the Dead."[6]

We know, as Medea did, that Hekate is both giver of life and the one who rules over the departed. She is both benevolent and terrifying. It can be difficult for us to wrap our minds around the destructive aspect of the goddess, however, due to our societal conditioning. We may have been trained from birth that women are only nurturers, and that the power over life and death resides solely in a remote, masculine God who is purely "of the light." In this construct, the mysteries of the darkness, including death, are to be avoided at all costs.

Many have written about the connection between darkness and fear of the sacred feminine.[7] We live in an age when the goddess is emerging from her cave, bringing with her the mysteries of death. That life is a great, eternal wheel that marks the perpetual cycles of gestation, birth, decline, death, and rebirth may have been what the initiates at Eleusis realized. When teaching the mysteries of rebirth, I have found that some students eagerly anticipate the process, while others are understandably intimidated at the prospect. Anassa Eneroi, as the one who holds power over the dead while watching over their souls, can have a strong allure to us. This is a potent archetype that activates our natural fear of physical demise while offering the possibility of being born anew within an incarnation.

I am the one whom they call Life, and you have called Death.[8]

The duality of the goddess as both life and death reaches its apex here. Her illuminating torches have led us through tears and joy. Now we stand at the foot of her throne. Having moved beyond seeing her solely as creatrix, we know that she is Mother of All, including the dead. One of my favorite descriptions of Hekate was written when the force of the Great Mother was newly awakening several decades ago:

In the dark of the moon, small covens awaited Her near drooping willow trees. She appeared suddenly before them with Her torch and

Her hounds. A nest of snakes writhed in Her hair, sometimes shedding, sometimes renewing. Until the new moon slit the sky, Hecate shared clues to Her secrets. Those who believed understood. They saw that form was not fixed, watched human become animal become tree become human. They witnessed the power of Her favored herbs: black poppy, smilax, mandragora, aconite. Awesome were her skills, but always Hecate taught the same lesson: without death there is no life.[9]

Death, the night, magic, and mystery. They are all illuminated by Hekate's torch as we bravely approach her as Anassa Eneroi.

These are keys that we stretch out to grasp, but that are always just out of reach. We struggle to comprehend the cyclical nature of her universe, where the deeper world is but a step away from our mundane one. To lean into her death mysteries is to seek her gifts of the spirit world—to become an oracle and a Psychopomp, and to tame our own hungry ghosts.

The Death Queen

To the ancients, her role as Enodia, goddess of the road, was entwined with her association with the dead, for they believed that the restless dead wandered at night. To have her favor was insurance against being victimized by the terrors of the night. Hekate guided the departed to the afterlife and tended those unable to rest well. She doesn't occupy the throne of the Underworld, which is Persephone's domain, but rather acts as intermediary.

Beginning in the heyday of ancient Greece, amplified during the Roman Empire, and growing throughout the centuries until now, Hekate's features were contorted until she became purely a "dark" figure. She has been described as the eater of men's hearts, and as the drinker of blood. In ancient cultures, these characteristics originally corresponded to the natural rhythm of life and death. But in a world increasingly obsessed with solar pursuits, they have been vilified.[10] When we face Hekate as Anassa Eneroi, however, we see that her terrifying aspects play an important role in the natural cycle. Her bull horns are symbols of the uterus. She drinks blood so that she can regenerate it into healing energy. She cleaves the earth to allow her sacred darkness to return, freeing us from being possessed by artificial light. This is restoring the sacred feminine to Great Mother status—she is both illuminated and shadow. Life and death. Creation and destruction.

These frightening images of Hekate may scare the life back *into* us. Our journey through the cave quelled the hungry ghosts who possess us, healed the wounds and memories of trauma, released the grip of the shadow over us. Hungry ghosts like these demand constantly to be fed, yet they are never satisfied.[11] They are the restless dead within us, forever wandering the night. At the throne of Anassa Eneroi, we lay them to rest one final time in preparation for our emergence from the cave. Grief, despair, and heartbreak don't feel like treasures when they sit heavily upon us. Moreover, the joy that accompanies the deep work of the cave is equally important. True initiation—for that is what rebirth is—comes only when we learn that the heartaches exist alongside the triumphs.

We find great contentment when we enter into the mysteries of the Death Queen. Whenever we connect with our cards, perform our meditations, and engage in deep rituals, we are approaching the mysteries of Anassa Eneroi. Witches have long been associated with death, the feminine, healing, and the liminal. The witches' broom itself is associated with communing with ghosts and spirits and is a symbol of the Death Goddess.[12] Some of us are called to work directly with the departed through mediumship, but all of us have encounters with the dead. At times, they come to us in our dreams, the nightly death, where they speak in their symbolic and emotional language. We bear the DNA of the dead, reminding us that death is always part of us. For some, this inheritance is troublesome. We can suffer from ancestral wounds that were never directly inflicted upon us. Yet these are all gifts of the Death Queen.

When we look to the Great Mother as the one who presides over death and the dead, we have an opportunity to see the possibility of new life. I well remember being told by my father when I was pregnant with my oldest son that a woman is never so close to death as when she is pregnant. Honestly, this didn't help. I was very young and already scared to death about pregnancy, birth, and becoming a mother. I was haunted by nightmares that something would go horribly wrong. Yet my father was correct. Birth and death form a crossroads, a sort of portal where new life can emerge—or not. How many times do we feel something growing inside of us that longs to be born, yet we deny it the nourishment it needs to come into the world?

I see the parallels between my dad's observation and the deeper structure of the universe. I also understand how I've denied the largeness within me the loving care she deserves. For years, I felt a force greater than myself gestating inside me—a force that I, on occasion, nourished through spiritual practices. But I spent more time trying to abort this spirit within me than giving it the care it deserved. I tended to quit whatever I was involved with in an attempt to "appear normal." There is a particularly sad-looking photo of me at my youngest son's baptism. I'm wearing a suit in a certain shade of brown that most definitely didn't work with my complexion. I remember that, when I opened the photos from the photographer, I simply stared at this woman and asked who she was. The day I stopped dressing in a manner that I believed would make me pass as "normal" was certainly an informal rebirth ceremony. My soul is expressed by wearing black, and so I do. The Death Queen can act upon us in these seemingly small ways if we only let her.

Anassa Eneroi is the regenerating force that pulses through the universe. She abides in the spaces between life and death while ruling over the Three Worlds. She is both breath and the lack of it. Her special guardianship over children as Kourotrophos—especially girls and women—illustrates the connection of the feminine to the totality of the natural cycle. Since we live in a culture that denies the dark, death, and the feminine, we suffer from an illusion of separation between life and death. Yet the departed often are very much alive to us. This contradiction between what our culture dictates and what we know to be true creates a tension within us.[13] This tension can be deeply felt while we are on the cave journey. As we face Anassa Eneroi, it becomes clear that it is time to let go of societal rules about spirits, death, dying, and so on. We turn instead to the truth of the Death Queen.

In her Master's thesis, Angela Hurley points out that:

> Hecate was always associated with death but as a natural stage of life, not as a negative opposition to life. These stages are also closely linked to the stages of the harvest because in early Greek society the harvest, and vegetation in general, meant life and carried a

veneration. Through time, there is a correlation between a waning reverence for harvests, and the life cycles associated with it, and Hecate.[14]

To see time as cyclical, to know that death is both end and beginning: this is the final stage before we bring death to our former selves and our encumbering baggage.

To become the one who stares the Death Queen in the face, seeking her mysteries, is brazen. It is knowing that it is time for the largeness inside of you to come into the world.

Persephone, Orpheus, and Eurydice

In the Homeric *Hymn to Demeter*, Persephone is the queen of the Underworld, at least for part of the year. Hekate is not depicted as ruling over Hades's domain, but as occupying her own cave. We see here the separateness of Hekate from the vast terrain of the subterranean realm of the dead. She occupies a chthonic space that is uniquely hers. When Hekate guides Persephone from her Underworld throne to launch spring, Persephone reverts to Kore. She is reborn.

Persephone's story starts out as one of catharsis, casting off her immaturity and perhaps even her vanity. Hekate helps her navigate the transition to Underworld queen, and then returns her to the land of the living. Persephone did not languish during her time as Hades's queen. Instead, she became Anassa Eneroi, ruling with passion, kindness, and integrity over the souls in her domain. Her loss became her power. She was victorious over the deaths she endured. With Hekate's wise counsel, she accepted her fate and leaned into it.

As Anassa Eneroi, Persephone is a benevolent dictator—always fair, but very firm. One particular legend tells how she granted a boon to Orpheus, the gifted poet-musician.[15] In this story, we find that trusting the Death Queen is required. Persephone's sympathy for Orpheus for having lost a loved one is part of what allows her to give him permission to regain his bride. Orpheus had fallen madly in love with the beautiful nymph Eurydice. Shortly after they were married, Eurydice was killed by a poisonous viper as she was fleeing from a shepherd, Aristaeus, who was in hot pursuit. Heartbroken, Orpheus used his musical talents to sing his way through the Underworld until he stood before the thrones of Hades and Persephone.

Undoubtedly, Persephone is sympathetic to the plight of Orpheus and Eurydice because of her own deep mourning for her former life. All were deeply moved by Orpheus's grief; even Cerberus, the fierce three-headed dog who guards the gates of the Underworld, was subdued. Persephone and Hades grant Eurydice freedom from the Underworld on one condition: Orpheus cannot look back at her as he leads her back to the surface. But Orpheus couldn't help himself. He looked back at her just as they were about to emerge from the Underworld. Eurydice was immediately sucked back in, forever lost to the land of the living.

A question that has plagued me is: Why did Orpheus look back at the last minute? There was no reason for him to do so. Unlike most of the other gods, Persephone and Hades were known to be trustworthy. They had permitted Orpheus into the afterlife and allowed him to leave again, which was prohibited to the living. Was it his desire for Eurydice that drove him to turn around? Or was it doubt?

Have you found yourself in a similar position? During a meditation, have you pulled yourself back before venturing too far astray from your physical body? We can sometimes feel as if we are going into the mysteries, as Orpheus did—treading where mortals fear to go. And we can sometimes question the healing of the dreamworld, disabuse synchronicities, and avoid our daily practice. And all these can be expressions of the demon of doubt. An entire multimillion dollar industry focused on "scientifically" proving the existence of these phenomena thrives because we let ourselves doubt what we know to be true.

The Greeks used the term *daimon* to refer to spirit, differentiated from *psyche*, the soul. All things have daimons, from people to plants. Words and feelings can take on their own daimons. They are living entities that seem to have a will of their own. There may be times when, acting as your own Anassa Eneroi, you need to bring death to these troubling spirits, which can include relationships and situations. We have our own restless spirits to contend with that often plague us with mistrust. These are all our demons to bear until we choose to bring about their demise.

Ancestral Healing

We are the embodiment of a thousand dreams, and we stand on top of an eternal bone pile. In a way, we function as Anassa Eneroi over our own lineage. What is shockingly absent from mainstream culture is veneration of the departed. Even Halloween, once a time for connecting with ancestors, has been thoroughly commercialized. Yet still, there is the presence of death in many of our Halloween festivities—from children in cute ghost getups to decorations of skeletons. We have an urge to connect with death. Intentionally honoring the departed can be beautiful.[16] We can also connect with "ancestors of spirit," those with whom we feel a kindred bond, in spite of a lack of blood ties. This can include writers, celebrities, and other figures. Whatever memories we have of those of our flesh who have departed this world—whether troubling or beautiful, or more likely both—we are a result of their lives.

There is increasing scientific evidence to support just how profoundly we are shaped by our ancestors' lives.[17] The descendants of victims of atrocities often have memories of the crimes perpetrated against their forebears, even when they have absolutely no conscious knowledge of these events.[18] Epigenetics research has consistently shown that children of trauma victims have altered stress systems and an increased likelihood of a vast array of health problems, even when they were not directly exposed to trauma.[19] The key to healing this trauma is to reconnect to our ancestors through both practical and spiritual techniques, like honoring them with rituals, learning their stories, and exploring our dreams.[20] The dead are always with us. Ancestors are powerful allies, coming to us in our dreams and sending us signs. We even may feel their physical presence. And this is true not only for our biological forebears but also for those with whom we share a spiritual lineage as well.

Studies have revealed a remarkable correlation between descendants' problems and their ancestors' experiences.[21] From extremely specific complaints like a chronically sore arm to widespread disorders like fibromyalgia, our forebears' trauma has profound impacts on our lives beyond their genetic contributions. With Hekate as our guide, we can lean into exploring the lives of our ancestors by learning about their journeys using both everyday and mystical means.

Shame and other associated emotions like anger and fear are also transmitted through blood ties. Although I have long taught about the impacts of ancestral trauma, it wasn't until a few years ago that I learned just how precise the wounds across generations can be. Part of my healing of my maternal ancestors has been to research my mother's parents. My mom was raised by her maternal grandmother and aunt. Almost nothing was ever spoken of my mom's mother. I had only a vague memory of her dying when I was four years old. My recollection is that my aunt, who raised my mother, told me she died from drinking "too much Pepsi." When I became curious as a teenager, my inquiries were shut down. After years of badgering, my great-aunt finally revealed the name of my mother's father.

A few years ago, I convinced my sister to go on a trip back to our ancestral region. I had done some research on the name of my grandfather, so I knew he had died during World War II. On a rainy August afternoon, we stumbled into the tiny basement that housed the local museum to look for answers. We discovered quite a bit about our mother's family and got a good lead on the family for our grandfather as well. But only dead ends resulted when we tried to connect with my paternal relatives. I was very disappointed that the identity of my grandfather remained a mystery.

A few months after this, I dreamed of a mystery man who had been wounded in battle in his left side. My oldest son was born with an exceptionally large birthmark on his left side that reminds me of a collection of islands. Since childhood, he's suffered from intense pain in this area. We've sought out all manner of healing, from allopathic remedies to traditional healing, all to no avail. If my dream was ancestral, it may provide an explanation for my son's inexplicable condition. Whether or not the dream was ancestral, it was certainly a message from the deeper world that created a channel for helping my son. I crafted a healing talisman for him and set the intention for ways to bring him relief to manifest. The next morning, without forethought, I picked up a certain over-the-counter analgesic that we hadn't tried before. It was as if I were led there by the spirit of my unknown ancestor. This finally brought him some relief. Pay attention to those ancestor dreams and allow them to guide you to healing.

The restless dead within, and without, are often incredibly resentful. This is partially due to the unfinished business that causes these spirits to wander. Both personally and in my professional life, I've observed that this resentment can be absolutely deadly.[22] It's also one of the most difficult "hungry ghosts" to lay to rest. Resentment is insidious. We can believe that we've progressed in our healing, yet still carry deep grudges. It's entirely possible for resentment to linger long after catharsis and soul retrieval have occurred. I know in my own life, resentment was the last burden I shed on my journey toward wholeness. Resentment requires a "once and for all" approach. It is like a giant stone blocking the exit from the cave. That is resentment.

Complaining that life is not fair and focusing on how our flawed upbringing ruined our lives are symptoms of resentment. Shifting from this state, which I believe is the last stand of the shadow, occurs over time. When we bring resentments into the light of day, we burn away their power. Exploring how resentment may still be working on us begins with asking ourselves if we are feeling that life is unfair. Recurring dreams with themes of being left out, lost, or unable to find things are also signs of possible lingering resentment. Discussing these issues with your Inner Council can help greatly to resolve them (see chapter 8).

Clear quartz is excellent for letting go of resentment.[23] Since resentment is a particular "hungry ghost" for me, I have two beautiful specimens right on my kitchen windowsill. One is a classic point, and the other is an open geode, resembling a cave. I envision the point as piercing through the thought traps I can fall into when I feel resentful toward someone who has disappointed me. I ask the stone to help me understand how resentment is involved. Then I use the geode as a container for releasing the resentment. Another technique that is most healing is to have a conversation with the person for whom you carry resentment. This practice can also be used when you want to contact the deceased for other purposes. I've also long associated rainbow moonstone with the deepest mysteries of the sacred feminine, particularly her role as Death Queen.

Kalos Thanatos

To the ancient Greeks, *kalos thanatos* was the beautiful embodiment of a good death. Thanatos and his brother Hypnos, god of sleep—born of Nyx in most tales—together represented the nightly departure from the physical into the dreamworld and even permanent demise.[24] Thanatos could bring a beautiful death—one with peace and honor. This was important because, if death was not honorable, the soul could become severely distraught and end up haunting others.[25] The journey of the cave is a long, beautiful goodbye to the person we used to be. It is most honorable to choose to honor the soul.

However, a beautiful death is not one without filth, pain, and suffering. We often think that the best way to die is to go peacefully in our sleep, thus avoiding these things. Yet, as Hekate teaches us, it is in the undesirable stages of dismemberment where we find the greatest treasure. We learn of our compassion, our courage, and our endurance. Without suffering, there is no need to lay to rest what longs to die.

Hekate is the great unquiet that we find in the utter stillness of the dead of night. This silence screams at us to stop living as if we were already in the hereafter while ushering in a host of hungry ghosts. She is *psychais nekuōn meta bakcheuousa*—"raging among the souls of the dead."[26] To answer the cry of the Death Queen brings the realization that we are much more than this particular embodiment.

You heeded the goddess's call when you entered her cave. Now the adventure is at its end. This is where you stand before Hekate on her throne of bones and find both humility and pride. The widening field of vision that the cave journey brings applies not only to our lives, but also to the mysterious order of the universe. We are small cogs in Hekate's Great Wheel, but we have a vital role to play in her grand scheme. Congratulations for your progress; take pride in this moment.

As your guide along this journey, I have taken great care not to glamorize the necessity of spiritual dismemberment, death, and rebirth. But this has been a challenging and messy journey. Old ways of being are the offerings we place before the Death Queen. Habits, relationships, and even entire lifestyles are laid on the sacrificial altar. The price of being a liberated soul, bathed in truth and reflecting Hekate's illuminating fire, is to sacrifice all that bound us. There is freedom in death, and there is the promise of new life. Death brings us great discomfort. We have all lost loved ones. Perhaps you've borne witness to someone close to you who had a horrible demise. And our hearts have been shattered in myriad other ways.

In psychodynamic psychology, "thanatos" refers to the death instinct, while "eros" is associated with the creative life force.[27] But this death wish

Entering Hekate's Cave

can be used as a rationale for risk-taking behavior, from addiction to engaging in daredevilry. I propose that thanatos—or Thanategos, to use the precise title given to Hekate—is invoked in this way only when this instinct is denied, thereby becoming associated with shadow rather than illumination. We can push the inevitability of death down so deep in our consciousness that it only leaks out in ways that undermine our soul's journey.

We began with the Ritual of Catharsis to address both our own eventual demise from this life and the need to allow the past to rest in peace because it draws fear of death out of the dark (see chapter 9). It is ironic that we see such things clearly in the dark of Hekate's cave only if we refuse to see the shadows on the walls—the specters of the past, the ghosts of who we once were, the shades of those who have wounded us, and, yes, ancestors and other spirits. From the soul's perspective, death is both ending and beginning. While it is natural to fear our own pending demise from this incarnation, as we stand before Hekate Thanategos, we see beyond this one life. When we glimpse the Great Wheel in which we abide, we see the threads that connect us to past and future embodiments. It becomes evident that Freud and his followers missed an important part of the death wish, which is to know what lies beyond this life. Misguided though it may be, we have a drive as strong as hunger to seek the transcendent.

We also have a fear of answering the demands of the psyche, which is the will of Hekate for each of us. Think back on how you felt before beginning the cave journey. Were you truly alive? To be the bold one who lives from soul is to be reborn every day. Many walk this earth already dead. They cover their ears to Hekate's screeching, ignore the rattling of her keys, and stay in their cages. But as James Hollis tells us: "Death is only one way of dying; living partially, living fearfully, is our more common, daily collusion with death."[28] This waking death is a symptom of a culture that denies the Great Mother or reduces her to a purely saccharine caricature. We are living in the aftermath of this individual and collective disaster. Woodman describes the consequences:

> In our collective neurosis, we have raped the earth, disrupted the
> delicate balance of nature, and created phallic missiles of mass
> destruction. Ironically, in our desperate attempt to keep death at bay
> (or prevent dissolution, from the point of view of the ego) we have

brought ourselves to the brink of extinction. So long as we deny the Great Mother and refuse to integrate her as Goddess in our psychic development, we will continue to act out neurotic fantasies and endanger our very survival as a species.[29]

By completing your cave journey, you not only heal yourself, you also contribute to the awakening of the Great Mother across the globe. You are working to restore the planet.

There are well-documented cases of people who were literally were scared to death—mortified—by trauma. On a physiological level, we can become trapped in a "freeze state" due to the trauma.[30] On a psychological level, we may become phantasmagoric unto ourselves, trapped in the chronic stress response elicited by being victims of inescapable trauma— truly restless spirits who are chained to the past and unable to live in the present. Hekate shrieks at us, rattling her keys, until we awaken from this false death. Undoubtedly, her raging appeals bring all our emotions to the surface, including anger. Through our fury, we can rectify the injustices by cutting cords and having difficult conversations where possible, and by laying to rest the rest. With our anger transmuted to agape and our positive eros restored, we can march deeper into the cave until we stand at the throne, behind which the illuminated pathway out awaits. By healing the hungry ghosts we were, we lay them to rest with love. That is kalos thanatos.

The Dance of Bones

There are times when we walk along the Mother Road calmly, minding our own business here in the cave. And then there is the dance that Anassa Eneroi awakens in us when she cries her death-call. In this dance, we are shaken into spinning wheels that disintegrate our old selves. Hekate herself is the leader of this dance—screaming and raging, eating hearts to replenish her powers, and leading the horde of souls. The image of death as a dancing specter who can arrive at anytime and with no notice is found across time and cultures.[31] Woven into this dance are the Psychopomps, the healers, and the spirit speakers who willingly two-step with the spirits associated with death. But this Dance of Bones—this *Danse Macabre*, as it is often called—has been reviled by our society.

The patriarchal obsession with God the Father, who offers the promise of heaven rather than the cool embrace of the Underworld, punishes those who enter the mysteries of the hereafter. In this tradition, communicating with the dead is, at best, frowned upon, and, at worst, a crime. But Anassa Eneroi offers us the key that opens the doors to this spirit dance hall. We honor her when we join in the Dance of Bones. It is primal and eternal. Wild beyond the restrictions of man. It beckons us to leave behind our former selves, our egos, and our limited perspectives. But it also encourages us to see that, by being our own Psychopomps, we can throw wide the doors to the entire dance hall. Dreams of the departed, sensing a presence, and communicating with the dead are natural consequences of our cave journey.

As we dance to Hekate's wild song, we may experience spontaneous spiritual dismemberment. It is all very civilized to prepare for the Rebirth Ritual (see below), yet I passionately believe that performative rituals are just formal recognition of the inexplicable initiations we have without any warning. There have been at least three times when I have been completely dismembered in the dreamworld. If I had to choose the one that was the most personally healing, I would choose the one that occurred while I was speaking at a conference on women's health. After my talk on the impacts of taking care of someone with PTSD before a large audience of First Nations women, I was standing in the lunchtime buffet line. A lovely woman asked me to hold a stick she had so she could get a can of soda. As soon as my fingers touched her stick, I felt a frisson go through my entire being. While sipping her soda, the woman looked knowingly at me.

Later that day, I was trying to make sense of the address of a psychic I was scheduled to visit. This woman appeared again, asking me what my trouble was. I replied that I had an appointment with a psychic and was having trouble understanding her address. She informed me that the psychic lived in Vancouver, Washington, and I was in Vancouver, British Columbia. The two locations are several hours drive apart. The woman said that she could help me, and we arranged to meet at sunrise the following day. That night, I had a horrific dream in which a large demon was ripped out of my heart center by a kindly woman. Scared back to wakefulness, I noticed that the wall of curtains hiding the windows was blowing from a nonexistent wind. I went to the lobby in search of this medicine woman.

She never showed up in person, and I have never been able to track her down using the name or phone number she gave me.

In another dream, a vicious hawk tore me to pieces all night long. I woke up feeling as if I had been in a car wreck and was completely detached from everyday life for hours. When I went out on the deck to try to right myself, I found a small animal that had been ripped apart. After each of these dreams, I emerged battered, but reborn.

Hekate seems to watch these rituals from a safe distance. This reminds me of Persephone's journey. She must go into her own cave, either chasing her soul-goose or because of Hades's scheme. I do not long for the deep rebirth of death and dismemberment, but I find myself craving the more comfortable dance with spirits, intentionally letting die what no longer serves. These are the true initiations of Anassa Eneroi.

Hekate does not lead us astray. She calls us out of our living-death stupor by means that are both mortifying and vivifying. To trust in her is to learn to trust ourselves. This is a great recovery from our early wounds, which taught us that we were unworthy and that those in charge of caring for us could not be relied upon. With each step we walk along the Mother Road, with each new key we claim, we are healing from these wounds. We are learning to face Hekate Thanategos.

Transcending the tertiary limits of egoic consciousness is mandatory for healing into wholeness. To face Hekate Thanategos is to admit that we desire to glean her mysteries. Without this trust, our work in the deeper world will always be superficial at best. Our meditations will bore us, the cards won't speak truth to us, and our sacred creativity will be lackluster. If we cry out to the goddess, as I imagine the sorceresses of The Greek Magical Papyri did, we feel as if our efforts fall on deaf ears.[32] But when we trust in our ability to go deeper and in the forces we work with, and in Hekate herself, we can achieve transcendence.

Hail, Anassa Eneroi. Hail, Kore.
Death. Life.
She who spins the Wheel.
Keeper of time,
Mistress of the moon,

Entering Hekate's Cave

That rises and sets in her cave.
Dark Mother, grant me entrance
Into your secret lair.
Shine your torchlight
To the inner chamber
Where your eternal cauldron
Of rebirth resides.
I come, as has been so since before time,
To be undone,
Reduced to my soul fire,
To be rebuilt in truth.

Practica: Rebirth Ritual

I liken this process of awakening to a giant cauldron that stands right in front of the Death Queen herself. The moon rises and sets in it, and it is guarded by her powerful companions. At this stage of your journey, you may well be feeling ready to give birth to the new you. The largeness inside of you may be ready to burst forth.[33] This ritual can help you shed your old life and emerge reborn.

This ritual is best performed during a full moon. I recommend adorning yourself with a key to symbolize opening the gate to your new life. If you create a sacred cord as part of the practice given in chapter 15, you can add your key to it. Cleanse your body following the recommendations given for the previous two rituals (see chapters 9 and 12).

Before you begin, create a rebirth altar that reflects bringing death and beginning a new phase. Include symbols of both. You may want to create a special shrine to your avian companion in honor of its diligent support during your journey. Set the altar with all thirteen of Hekate's stones. Obsidian is an excellent ally for rebirth, and I recommend placing it at the center of the arrangement, next to a piece of selenite, which will help invigorate your new life after the ritual.[34] Moonstone is a stone of initiation and wholeness, and you can adorn yourself with it to signify the completion of your journey.

Start with your daily practice as you prepare for this ritual to keep yourself grounded and centered. You may want to look back at your record of the rituals and practices you've experienced throughout your cave journey and spend time with the symbols in your Cista Mystica.

To perform this ritual, you will need:

- All thirteen of Hekate's stones.

- Rebirth botanicals like aster, birch, lavender, mugwort, oak, pomegranate, and rose.

- Oleum Spirita or another sacred oil that opens the way to the transcendent.

- A "new life" candle (*phos vita nova*)—a white candle adorned with symbols appropriate for rebirth. I recommend not lighting it until the ritual.

- An offering to Hekate as an expression of gratitude for guiding you through her cave.[35]

Standing before the altar, call out to your avian companion to accompany you into the cave this final time. Once it is perched on your shoulder, petition Hekate, saying:

Hail, Hekate, bringer of death, and begetter of life.
I light this sacred candle to signify my intention of being reborn.

Light the candle and perform the three-step process of purifying, protecting, and blessing that you used in the previous rituals. Then say:

I anoint myself with this oil to open myself to the ritual.

Anoint yourself with the oil, then take up the offering, saying:

I offer this (say what it is) as a token of gratitude for guiding me through your sacred cave.

Call on the archetypes, using their full names. As you speak each name, take up the stone that corresponds to the archetype, then return it to its place on the altar:

Triformis, the Transformer.
Drakaina, the Awakener.
Enodia, the Guide.

Propylaia, the Gatekeeper.
Chthonia, the Guardian.
Borborophorba, the Catharsis.
Lampadios, the Light,
Skotia, the Darkness.
Psychopomp, the Soul.
Paionios, the Healer.
Rixipyle, the Liberator.
Anassa Eneroi, the Bringer of Rebirth.

When you have finished calling on the archetypes, say:

Guide me into your cauldron so that I am born anew.
My intention is pure, my will strong, and my heart true.

Soften your gaze into the candle, allowing it to become the entrance to the cave. Venture in, feeling excited, confident, and ready for what is to come. Envision Hekate atop her throne, surrounded by her companions. Allow them to be who they need to be for you.

Feel the encouragement and safety. See Hekate and her companions guiding you toward the cauldron. Draw near the cauldron and add the herbs, then climb in. The water, full of herbs, is steaming, yet not too hot. It gently washes away your skin, scrubbing you clean down to the bones. As this process occurs, instead of feeling reduced, you feel larger, more yourself. Everything that is no longer part of you is being removed.

As you emerge from the cauldron, Hekate's companions welcome you back and weave you anew from the essence of your soul. Don't rush through this. Feel the process as you are reborn. Every cell, muscle, organ, hair. All created from your true essence. Allow the process to progress gently, supported by your allies who are weaving you whole.

When you are finished, Hekate descends from her throne to bless you by kissing you on the top of your head and hands you a symbol that is the key to your new life. She opens the way out of the cave. Walk through the opening she creates, returning to your physical body.

Take your time with this process. As you return, notice the physical sensations. Move slowly upward from your feet to your crown, disconnecting from the deeper world. Reconnect to the physical by feeling the floor beneath you, opening your heart center to your material surroundings, and stretch your crown back up toward the Starry Road. Gently, when you are ready, record your impressions.

Practica: The Empty Chair

The Empty Chair technique is an effective practice from clinical psychology that is also found in mediumship practices.[36] The difference is a rather fine point of distinguishing between pure imagination and dialoguing with a spirit. Don't get caught up in this distinction. Spirits speak through your imagination for the most part, although you may also have sensations of a presence or see an apparition.

If there is an ancestor, living or dead, with whom you have unfinished business that has led to resentment, this technique can help loosen the grip of the grudge. If you want to have a conversation with any ancestor, regardless of whether or not there is intentional healing to be done, it is helpful to create an altar on a table beside the person's chair including objects symbolic of him or her and those that welcome in spirits. Be sure to include a fresh candle.

There are two basic methods for having this conversation. One is to write a letter beforehand, or otherwise prepare what you are going to say. The other is to set the intention to bring forth the spirit of the person. Arrange two chairs and set up the altar beside the one for your guest.

- Set a timer for fifteen to twenty minutes. Spirits can sometimes overstay their welcome. Firm boundaries work best with them.

- Create sacred space as described in chapter 7 to ensure that you are free from harm and protected from intrusions. Yarrow is excellent for the sacred smoke component.

- When you are ready, light the candle and start the timer.

- Get comfortable in your chair and awaken your soul serpent.

- See through the eyes of the soul, turning your attention to your guest. Visualize the person as best you can. Smell the person; feel his or her presence. You can keep your eyes closed through the practice if you wish. This can be immensely helpful.

- Welcome your guest into your temenos and explain your goal.

- Either read your letter or ask questions to get the discussion going.

- When it is your guest's turn to speak, do not resist whatever comes through to your mind screen. It is your guest speaking, not you. Listen without recrimination. Use the principle of kindness to filter your reactions.

- When the conversation is over, record your experiences. See how your opinion of the person has been transformed by allowing him or her to speak instead of listening to the old looping thoughts you had before.

If you wish to repeat the conversation or use the technique with other ancestors, I recommend not treating this like speed-dating. Space out the sessions, especially if you are new to mediumship practices.

The Empty Chair technique is a fabulous way to hone your mediumship skills. You may already have been developing them if you've been working with the daily Enodia Oracle in chapter 5. Cartomancy is often the gateway to communicating with the deceased. What may be missing is consciously connecting the messages that come through in the reading with your dreams and synchronicities during the waking hours. Seeking these connections levels up your mediumship skills. The more you see how all is part of the endless web, the better you become at traveling this Wheel of the deeper world.

Chapter 15

Kore: The Reborn

Kore.
Kore.
Nameless One.
Endless One.
Returning.
Emerging.
Spinner of Seasons.
Bringer of Becoming.
Opening.
Growing.
The Creator.
The Destroyer.
Take my hand.
Show me the way.
Kore.
Kore.

Just as Persephone emerged after her time in the Underworld, so do we. The journey through darkness to wholeness accomplished, we now come forth into the light of a new day. Like Persephone, we may not have been given a choice over what led us into the depths, but also like her, we chose to learn how to reign over our pain. We emerge from the cave changed and whole. Wiser, stronger, better. Poised at the threshold of a new way of living from the center of our being.

This marks our return to Hekate's garden—the solar realm, where magic and mystery abound in the plants, stones, and animals that are our allies. The garden of the goddess is also home to our beloveds. It is a place for nourishing relationships and cultivating a life rooted in the wisdom of the goddess. Here in her garden, we cultivate a life that has deep meaning, from our paid work to our daily sacred practices.

In the tales of Persephone, there is little told of the time between her entry into the Underworld and her ascension. We can imagine that Hekate pulled her into the cave so that she could adapt to her calling. During this period, she transformed from the naive maiden to the sovereign queen. She became wholly/holy. And here we are, thousands of years later, still benefitting from her journey and using it as a template for understanding our own.

Like Persephone, we emerge back into the vibrancy of the Middle World. Our return from our labors below illuminates the lives of others. We become the ones spreading vitality. No longer the ones who live without intention, we apply the subterranean wisdom to how we engage with the physical world. Walking the world with a strong back and a soft front, we demonstrate our principles of kindness, passion, and integrity.

We are Persephone—the benevolent sovereign who emerges from the cave full of joy and enthusiasm for a new journey. Like her, we can extend the self-nourishment we learned in the subterranean world to others while maintaining strong boundaries. The physical world offers us love, responsibility, accomplishment, and satisfaction. Persephone's exuberance at returning to the world of mortals can become our own curiosity and enthusiasm. She earned her joy during her Underworld time, and so have we. It is our right to find contentment, to take pleasure in the gifts of the world, and to love fiercely.

Tempering the ebullience of our return is Demeter, who reminds us that there is real work to do. We are planting the seeds given to us in the cave, because these will ultimately yield the wholeness of our souls. This is how we grow the garden that surrounds us on this new journey. Selenite is our "magic wand," helping us bring into the world all we've been waiting to bring.

The Reborn Queen

In the course that led to this book, we explore the meaning of the "initiated maiden" as we emerge into wholeness. Consider how the young Persephone got caught up in the web of fate and then made decisions that seemed bad at the time. Down she went as consort to the Lord of the Dead. She grieved mightily and did all she could to avoid having to go down to "Hadestown."[1] But it was in her difficult downward spiral that she found her power.

One of the strongest lessons of our cave journey is that we learn to keep the wealth from our painful past while releasing the burdens. I liken this to becoming an "initiated Kore," one who is hopeful, yet wise. Kore is not a proper name, but simply a noun that means "girl."[2] Thus, before Persephone descended, she lacked any identity of her own. The same is true for us as we forge our own identities when we examine our interior world, from practicing natural magic, to exploring our dreams, to experiencing the rituals. As you weave these pieces together into your unique cloak of wholeness, allow the natural optimism of becoming the "initiated maiden" to take root.

The epithet Kore was often assigned to Hekate and to other goddesses besides the young Persephone, including beloved Artemis. In *The Orphic Hymn to Hekate*, she is called Kore, and other texts, like The Greek Magical Papyri, reinforce this title:

> I went down into the cave, and I have been initiated.
> I saw the things down below—Kore, Anassa Eneroi, and all the rest.[3]

This passage comes from the enchantment designed to protect the speaker from harm. It begins by having the practitioner say that she is Ereskigal, and she is not taking any guff. This figure speaks as the initiated Kore who has done her time in the Underworld and isn't about to be victimized again. That is the wisdom of the initiated.

Hope flows throughout the cave journey—hope of a brighter day, of healing, of being able to live from the center of our beings. This is not the ignorance of Persephone before she was initiated; it is the intentional choice of being hopeful.

Hope and the Moon

When I consider my own personal wholeness, both hope and the moon appear like a braided cord that weaves all the pieces together. The moon has always been my companion, the one to whom I've revealed all my secrets. When nobody else was there, the moon listened to my troubles and offered me solace. I talk to the moon every night, even when it's hidden behind clouds. Hope and the moon are threaded through the memories I have of both joyful times, like midnight skinny-dipping on the blue moon—the third full moon in a season that has four—and some that are deeply painful.

When I consider the hope of wholeness, I am reminded of a night when I raged against this feeling. With tears streaming down, I raised a fist to the moon and screamed: "Damn hope!" But no matter how bad things have been, there has always been a spark of hope inside of me that simply refused to go out. At the time, I had realized that I had, once again, ended up in the wrong romantic relationship. I had sought wholeness from the relationship, rather than having the courage to find it within. I keep the Cyndi who hung her hopes on external sources at the table of my Inner Council and ask her what she thinks from time to time. But now I hang my hope hat on the things that reflect what I know to be true in the center of my being.

The initiated know that hope, contentment, happiness—whatever you want to call it—comes from tending our internal soul fire. For me, that fire is bonded to the moon. I have found greater joy in dialoguing with the moon than in any man-made experiences. Persephone, Hekate, and other goddesses who wielded torches were also identified with the moon.

In mythology, the Maiden is often linked with the moon, particularly in its waxing phase. She is potentiality. Yet the growing crescent has more darkness than light. The journey to wholeness, symbolized by the full moon, illuminates what lies in darkness. As you emerge from the cave, walk into the light of the growing moon, seeing it as a talisman that will guide you forward. Always listen to her wisdom, for it is that of your own soul.

Lunar goddesses were often seen as solitary figures wandering the night. Moreover, they were sometimes depicted as virgins. To the ancients, however, the female virgin was one who was virtuous in all ways. We can interpret this as living the keys of kindness, passion, and integrity. Artemis was a virgin who maintained her independence.[4] Even her father, Zeus, knew better than to try to control her. Evoking Artemis into this last chapter brings her sexual freedom to the forefront. You may be called by her to break free from restricting ideas about gender and sexuality. Indeed, in the ancient view of virginity, having sexual relations, especially with others of the same gender, was not off limits. Thus, Artemis has rightfully become a queer icon for her gender-role crashing and sexual freedom.[5]

Whatever feels hopeful and right to you, run toward it as the moon gets brighter. Years ago, I wrote an article about Hekate as a guardian of the marginalized, citing the historical evidence that she had been a goddess associated with the outcasts of society.[6] Since then, the article has helped many find their way within Hekate's horde. I imagine all of us on the "Hekate bus" are driving toward our common destination of wholeness and singing a most hopeful song. There will always be those who lash out at us because they wish they had our hope, our audacity, and our courage of spirit. If your optimism is running low, look to the moon. She'll tell you to be more you, whatever that looks like for you. And she'll tell you not to waste your time on those who are driven by fear to cause upset. One of my all-time favorite graphics that I've created is of the full moon reflected on the ocean. It bears the caption: energy flows where attention goes.

Authenticity and Sweet Freedom

A famous ancient statue that scholars believe to be Hekate is known as the Running Maiden of Eleusis.[7] In this work, the goddess is moving in one direction, yet looking in the other. This piece has been interpreted in many different ways. Some posit that it portrays the Maiden escaping Hades; others say it depicts a nymph lighting the way. I believe it to be Hekate guiding the journey through the mysteries. She needs to look back to make sure we are following her torches as she lights the way forward.

Another way of looking at this is by examining the dichotomy between being the one created by others and being the one who is self-made. When we follow Hekate's torches into the light, we are allowing her to show us that the code of our soul was written long before we entered this life.[8] Even though the Moirai may have woven our thread for us, it is our choice how we follow that thread. When we enter the cave, we choose to weave in the dark, and then in the light. When we emerge from the cave, we embrace our authentic selves—dark, light, and all the rest. We become the weavers of our own mythic narrative, in tune with the deeper weaving of the Fates.

The definition of authenticity that fits best for me is the one given by Brené Brown:

> Authenticity is a collection of choices that we have to make every day. It's about the choice to show up and be real. The choice to be honest. The choice to let our true selves be seen.[9]

Being authentic doesn't mean that we force ourselves on others or that we walk around cavalierly spewing our deepest secrets to strangers. Authenticity is going through life with a strong back and a soft front. It is knowing who is worthy of our truth, and who's a waste of time. Real authenticity flows from living our lives as sacred; seeing ourselves as temples and honoring the soul however it feels right for us.

True authenticity has a difficult relationship with shame. A simplistic approach would say that they can't occupy the same space, but I happen to think they can. Part of the problem with toxic positivity is that many of the "experts" make it seem as if we do one thing—write one entry in the journal, carry one stone, do one meditation—and then, just like magic, our shame vanishes. When this doesn't happen (and it never does), we end up being shamed for our efforts not working, whatever they were. But true authenticity is a process of consciously uncoupling from shame with kindness, passion, and integrity.

Shame is the currency of the shadow. I consult with mine once in a while because she is the expert on shame and my underlying fears. Talking to your shadow when you feel triggered by someone or something is an excellent practice in authenticity. Ask yours what is so activating so that you can help diminish the distress. Those outside of the power structure are often made to feel shameful for simply showing up in spaces where they preside. The natural self-questioning, talking to the shadow within, is portrayed by those in power as evidence of the "imposter syndrome," which is such a vilifying label.[10] But you're not the one in the wrong if you feel unheard and unwelcome in these circumstances. They are the problem. You have much to bring to these places, although it is certainly understandable if you find it daunting. Only through finding and speaking from our truth can we bring change to this world. Our authenticity fortifies us as we walk through the uncertainty of today's cultural landscape. Becoming who you are inside on the outside creates a sense of inner safety—a sense that, no matter what happens, you can survive.[11] Because the curious thing about authenticity is that it gives us the power to overcome just about anything and inspires others to become better.

Persephone and the Bull

There once was a wild bull named Cerus who terrorized the good people of the land. His rampages were brought to the attention of Persephone, who had recently returned to the living world to initiate spring. She calmed Cerus, rendering him a docile creature who was completely subject to her charms. Riding on his back, she brought bounty to all the world. When she returned to the Underworld, Cerus became the constellation Taurus.

This bull's name may be connected with the personification of luck, who was called Caerus.[12] The name is also related to the concept of kairos, the eternal time of the gods. This gives some context to the story. Persephone emerges from the Underworld and literally rides on the back of opportunity rather than letting fate remain wildly out of control. Luck occurs, after all, when preparation meets opportunity.[13] Whereas mythic bulls usually ravage women, here the goddess tames the creature.

Within the context of the agricultural world back when this myth was created, this symbolized Persephone's power to bestow blessings by leaning into the natural order of kairos, or fate. This myth speaks of how we cultivate our inner wildness so that it becomes a source of power rather than a hindrance. The Persephone myth cycle speaks, above all, to our need to reconcile our savageness, what we can see as aspects of the shadow, with our civilized selves. Persephone's bull came to embody the characteristics most associated with the benefits of the sign of Taurus—calm, caring, fertility, structure, and stability. Taurus is a symbol of reliability and stability.

The question we can pose to ourselves is: How do I train my inner shadow-bull to become an ally like this? This story demonstrates how the initiated maiden uses her creative force to navigate life successfully. Through the wisdom she gained in the Underworld, she understands how to use her power to control both her inner beast and the ones we encounter along the journey. How different Persephone became after her time down below!

Persephone loses her innocence at the hands of false prophets and treacherous princes. We reclaim her gifts as we emerge from the cave. Children are full of curiosity and creativity. Brimming with wonder. They have a sense of where they want to go, whether it is going out for an ice cream or grand schemes of who they will become. Perhaps Persephone had big dreams for her life before she began her Underworld journey. Maybe we did as well. Now is the time to begin again, to pursue those dreams the way Persephone vitalizes the world every spring. Drawing from youthful energy invigorates us. It is the enlivening energy of authenticity that gives momentum to our journey down Enodia's road. We lean into our largeness, allowing ourselves to blossom while nourishing the land for others.

Society is both fascinated and repulsed by the feminine energy that Persephone embodies as Kore, the Eternal Child. Our culture celebrates the beauty of young women—large breasts, flawless skin, and an impossibly slender figure—and there is enormous pressure to maintain a youthful appearance. The rise of social media has only made this stereotype more powerful, and our patriarchal society has certainly done nothing to diminish that power. This stereotype has forced many young women to remain stuck in immaturity and to indulge in infantile behavior. On the other hand, we see how some young women have reacted against societal norms and worked to change the world through their courage and enthusiasm, continuing to embody the curiosity, determination, and joy of Persephone as she comes into her own power.[14]

As James Hillman put it, "growing down" is a key of the illuminated journey.[15] Being too adult robs us of our joy and creativity, but being enchanted by youthful stereotypes denies us the "strong back" of discipline. Our task, now that we have traversed the cave, is to become the reborn Kore. How can we bring her energy to the journey ahead? By holding space within ourselves for being, and becoming, both Kore and Crone (and all the archetypal faces of the goddess) while mothering our own lives and the lives of those important to us with the fierce love that Persephone bestowed from her throne.

To love as the emerged Persephone is to claim the keys of kindness, passion, and integrity. Persephone is the one who pieced her heart back together after it was torn apart. Her love is the fiercest of all because it knows both the soaring heights of ecstasy and the depths of loss. She knows how to dance the spiral with her bare feet in the earth, celebrating the totality of love. She has become whole by journeying through the darkness and now emerges into the sunlight. She has become open to the mysteries of the natural world, and is a lover of all that is born from Hekate's great cauldron. She lives in the state of awakening that the journey has brought her.

This passage speaks to how our daily practice connects us to the agape energy that simmers within and emanates from all the universe. Persephone is now awake to her own desires, pursuing them with the vigor of youth, but with healthy boundaries. As uninitiated young women, we can be seduced by false prophets who promise much but deliver little. Without an awareness of how to manifest our soul's mission, we can fall prey to infatuation, thinking it to be true love.

Now is the time to accept, with the initiated love that is whole and true, the times when we were naive, rash, or even ignorant. The past is truly in the past now. We can look to it with affection, perhaps even chuckle over our mistakes. We have the understanding that comes from broadening our gaze to see that we are living the many myths I've shared throughout this book. Perspective is a gift of the cave—to see that we did the best we could and that others were doing the same. This is not to say that we are not responsible, nor does it infer that the ones who wounded us get off scot-free. As the wise Kore, we can see the other side of the story. We know that we are walking a road woven for us by great Hekate and her daughters. To trust in the mystery of life is the most potent blessing of Hekate's cauldron. Trust is the path to transcendence. That is the journey of the Reborn One.

Practica: Crafting a R-E-A-L Talisman

A R-E-A-L talisman is one that assigns words to each of these letters as correspondences to whatever you are working on. I encourage you to craft one as you embark on this new life and to make one whenever you feel called to do so. If you are manifesting a job that is aligned with your authenticity, the acrostic might include: Reliable, Employment, Authentic, and Local (if you don't want to move). If your desire is to start your own spiritual enterprise, it might be something like: Realizing an Enterprise that is Abundant and Loving. You get the idea. Then choose symbols that represent each word in the acronym—a heart for love, dollar signs for anything to do with money, an eye for clarity and vision, and so on. You can do this in a color whose signatures match the meaning of the word. Look in your books on symbols for inspiration.

Next, choose your disks—these can be everything from lids of jars or cans to handcrafted tiles. Make sure that you can put a hole in each one through which you can weave the "thread of the Moirai." Put the symbol on one side and the corresponding letter on the other, and then thread a piece of string through the hole. I like to add bits of botanicals as well. Bay leaves are always a good addition to any manifestation magic.

Bring the corded charms together into one, and then tie them with three knots around the grouped cords. As you tie the first knot, say:

By knot of one, this work's begun.

Move on to the second, saying:

By knot of two, this shall be true.

Finish up with a final knot, saying:

By knot of three, the truth is free.

Change up the incantation to suit your needs.

While you are crafting the talisman, consider how different this process is compared to the earlier cord-cutting and cord-cleansing ceremonies. Keep your talisman close by. I have the original one I made seven years ago hanging beside my desk. Whenever I start to slide into shame, I connect with it. I make a new one for specific projects and when I feel as if I am at a crossroads.

Hekate's Cauldron of Rebirth

So deep I ventured into Hekate's cave
That I came upon her cauldron,
From which the moon rises and sets.
Tended by her closest companions,
Those midwives calling me to this place.
Will I enter the cauldron?
It has already been decided,
When I began this deathwalking journey.
My path of transformation into
Wholeness.
Here is the final destination.
She who is the true me
Emerges,
Taking the hand of my shadow self.
Fear not, beloved.
Healing is found in Hekate's cauldron.
Through the smoke purified,
Flames burning away all pain.
Washed in the truth of moon essence.
Born anew.
The whispers of her companions surround me now,
As does pale Hekate's horde.
Persephone silences them.
She knows the work is mine to do.
Artemis protects me with her fierce arrows,
While the Dark Mother watches from her throne,
Here in her sacred chamber.
Yes.
I climb into the cauldron.
Washing the wounds,
Easing off the skin of the past.
Cleansing my aching body,
Until at last all that remains
Is my soul.
Persephone lifts one finger.

The horde take all I have discarded.
Persephone and Demeter, countless others
Step forward,
They work swiftly,
Weaving me back into form
Using my soul thread.
I am reborn from their labors,
Here in Hekate's cave.
Out of the cauldron, I rise.
Persephone smiles,
Demeter is watchful.
The midwives hold their breath,
And the horde is still.
Behold, I am reborn.
Queen Hekate beckons me come,
As I walk toward her,
The moon adorns me,
Casting about my being
A robe of pure light and the darkest night,
Anointing me with the red fire of her torches.
They sear me with power,
And my hands now hold
The keys of my own soul.
Wisdom and truth,
Sovereignty,
Peace.
Wholeness.
Hekate hails my rebirth
While opening the way for me.
I boldly venture forth into the light.

Conclusion

It's not important at all how you understand Hekate, or what your spiritual beliefs may be. Hekate is the spirit of the interior life. While I call her by this name, the feminine spirit of the deeper world has thousands of names and thousands of manifestations, from saints to goddesses. Hekate transcends all names and mythologies. She is the essence of anima, the feminine soul of the world that lives within each of us.

Above all, know that there are times when we simply acquiesce to fate. In our modern world, which is fixated on the individual as all-powerful, we fail to grasp that we are in a never-ending dance with Hekate and her deeper world. It is our mission to lean into the wholeness of this dance. Thank you for trusting me to guide you through darkness to wholeness. If it ever gets to be too much, you will always find welcome in the safe harbor of the cave.

Let's end with the wise words from one of my most beloved and insightful students, who has become a true "soul sister" to me:

> It took years, and a complete underworld journey, to understand
> what Persephone's journey meant. First, I left the company I started,
> and an industry I cared for. Suddenly there was nothing to do but
> reflect. I considered how everything I'd done was driven by market
> forces, or other people. What would I do on my own? I wrote a
> book. I started grad school. I even forged a knife, relishing the scars
> I received as I worked. With all this came much unmaking. I left my
> partner of ten years, disrupting our lives, and secured my first solo
> apartment since college. I investigated my desires, connecting me to
> larger desires in life. I began prioritizing time over money in career

decisions. I lost friends. I learned where I begin and others end. Faced with the chaos of my new cosmos, I felt fear. But as I passed from Kore to Persephone, I finally heard her voice: to change is to transgress. Sometimes you must eat the fruit. This is my gift from the Underworld. The cost was high. The reward was my power.

Appendix A
List of Practica and Rituals

Chapter 1
Threefold Ritual
Ritual Incantation
Working with Stones
Quotidia Candle Ceremony

Chapter 2
Self Reflection

Chapter 3
Triple Goddess Altar

Chapter 4
Unifying the Three Selves Meditation

Chapter 5
Creating a Crossroads Altar
The Enodia Oracle

Chapter 6
Processing Encounters

Chapter 7
Know Your Limits
Your Personal Magical Circle

Endnotes

Introduction

1. For a detailed discussion on the differences between the Hero and Heroine journeys, read *The Heroine with 1001 Faces* by Maria Tatar.
2. Susan Cain's *Bittersweet: How Sorrow and Longing Make Us Whole* explores the benefits of not being happy all the time.
3. Hans Dieter Betz (ed.), *The Greek Magical Papyri in Translation: Including the Demotic Spells,* Vol. 1 (1997).
4. From the Hymn to the Waning Moon, The Greek Magical Papyri, IV, 2280–2285.

Chapter 1

1. *The Archetypes and the Collective Unconscious* in *Collected Works of C. G. Jung*, Vol. 9, Part 1. See also *Collected Works of C. G. Jung* (48) and *Man and His Symbols*.
2. Apostolos N. Athanassakis and Benjamin M. Wolkow (translation, introduction, and notes), *The Orphic Hymns*.
3. You can explore how Hekate can be connected to the months and seasons in *Keeping Her Keys*.
4. I highly recommend the workbook by Douglas Bloch and Demetra George, *Astrology for Yourself: How to Understand and Interpret Your Own Birth Chart*, to begin your studies of the heavens.
5. Use books of correspondences and symbols like those offered from Llewellyn to help understand the symbols. Jung's *Man and His Symbols* and *Modern Man in Search of a Soul* are also very helpful. *The Book of Symbols* from Taschen is excellent, as are the Esoterica books from the same publisher. I also recommend *The Woman's*

Dictionary of Symbols and Sacred Objects by Barbara G. Walker, although it can feel a bit dated.

6. Judika Illes's *Encyclopedia of Spirits: The Ultimate Guide to the Magic of Fairies, Genies, Demons, Ghosts, Gods and Goddesses* (2009) is a wonderful compendium of spirits.

7. *Seventy-Eight Degrees of Wisdom: A Tarot Journey to Self-Awareness (A New Edition of the Tarot Classic)* by Rachel Pollack is a wonderful text on the cards.

8. *Blackthorn's Protection Magic: A Witch's Guide to Mental and Physical Self-Defense* (2022) is a great resource if you are concerned about all forms of personal safety.

9. I recommend Ted Andrews's classic text, *Animal-Speak*, to learn more about the standard characteristics and possible healing of your avian companions, along with the fabulous Taschen's *Book of Symbols*.

10. C. G. Jung and C. Kerényi, translated by R. F. C. Hull, *Essays on a Science of Mythology: The Myth of the Divine Child and the Mysteries of Eleusis* (1941).

11. Jan N. Bremmer, *Initiation into the Mysteries of the Ancient World* In Münchner Vorlesungen Zu Antiken Welten (2014).

12. You can find prayers to Hekate in *Keeping Her Keys,* and there is an entire chapter dedicated to the hieros pyr in *Entering Hekate's Garden.*

Chapter 2

1. For a detailed discussion of Hekate as Keeper of Keys, see Sarah Iles Johnston's *Hekate Soteira.*

2. Joseph Campbell, Safron Rossi, and David Kudler, *Goddesses: Mysteries of the Feminine Divine (The Collected Works of Joseph Campbell).*

3. Yulia Ustinova, *Caves and the Ancient Greek Mind: Descending Underground in the Search for Ultimate Truth* (2009).

4. Barbette Stanley Spaeth (ed.), *The Cambridge Companion to Ancient Mediterranean Religions* (2013). Daniel Ogden, *Magic, Witchcraft, and Ghosts in the Greek and Roman Worlds: A Sourcebook* (2002).

5. Johanna Best May, "Religion of the Roadways: Roadside Sacred Spaces in Attica," Bryn Mawr College, Doctoral Dissertation (2015).
6. "Mystery Cults in the Greek and Roman World" by Kiki Karoglou is a great short summary.
7. To delve deeper into the exploration of consciousness, I recommend Rupert Spira's *The Nature of Consciousness: Essays on the Unity of Mind and Matter.*
8. Marion Woodman, *The Pregnant Virgin: A Process of Psychological Transformation.*
9. Erin Woo, "Teenage Girls Say Instagram's Mental Health Impacts Are No Surprise" *nytimes.com.*

Chapter 3

1. E.g., Erich Neumann, *The Great Mother,* and Marija Gimbutas, *The Language of the Goddess.*
2. "The Triple Goddess and the Queen," *medusacoils.blogspot.com.*
3. Adapted from The Greek Magical Papyri, IV, 2441–2621.
4. *The Alphabet versus the Goddess: The Conflict between Word and Image* by Leonard Shlain is a fascinating study on the relationship between the goddess and the world, both natural and civilized.
5. Sorita d'Este, *Circle for Hekate—Volume 1: History and Mythology* Avalonia; (London: Avalonia, 2016).
6. E.g., Image XVI-XVII: Hecate as a triple-headed goddess, with her three heads as a dog, a wild boar, and a horse. *jstor.org/stable/community.11674120.*
7. E.g., Jean Shinoda Bolen, MD, *Goddesses in Older Women: Archetypes in Women over Fifty.*
8. *jstor.org/stable/community.11674120.*
9. *Shamanic Journeying: A Beginner's Guide* by Sandra Ingerman is a great place to begin exploring modern shamanism.
10. More on this can be found in *Demeter and Persephone: Lessons from a Myth,* by Tamara Agha-Jaffar (2002).
11. Stephen Ronan (ed.), *The Goddess Hekate.* (Hastings, UK: Chthonios Books, 1992).

12. Eckhart Tolle, *The Power of Now: A Guide to Spiritual Enlightenment*.

13. "What Does It Mean When They Say the Universe Is Expanding," Everyday Mysteries, *www.loc.gov*.

14. James Hollis, *What Matters Most: Living a More Considered Life*.

15. John H. Lee, *Growing Yourself Back Up: Understanding Emotional Regression* (2010).

16. Go deeper with the therapeutic model on which the Pyriboulos Council is based in *Internal Family Systems Skills Training Manual: Trauma-Informed Treatment for Anxiety, Depression, PTSD and Substance Abuse* by Frank Anderson, Richard Schwartz, and Martha Sweezy.

17. Thomas Moore, *Dark Nights of the Soul: A Guide to Finding Your Way through Life's Ordeals* (2005).

Chapter 4

1. Drakaina comes from The Greek Magical Papyri, "Mare, Kore, dragoness, lamp, lightning flash, star, lion, she-wolf."

2. Glenys Livingstone (ed.), *Re-visioning Medusa: From Monster to Divine Wisdom* (2017) is a beautiful compendium of insights and art for exploring Medusa.

3. Read Chanel Miller's *Know My Name* for an excellent narrative on healing from sexual violence and being "medusaed."

4. Tarana Burke, *Unbound: My Story of Liberation and the Birth of the Me Too Movement* (2021).

5. Gurmukh Kaur Khalsa, Dorothy Walters, Andrew Newberg, MD, Sivananda Radha, Ken Wilber, and John Selby, *Kundalini Rising: Exploring the Energy of Awakening* (2007).

6. Kevin J. Tierney and Maeve K. Connolly, "A Review of the Evidence for a Biological Basis for Snake Fears in Humans," *link.springer.com*

7. "The Cognitive Neuroscience of Human Decision Making," *citeseerx.ist.psu.edu*.

8. Peter Gay, *Freud: A Life for Our Time* (London: W. W. Norton and Company, 2006).

9. Marianne Williamson, *A Return to Love: Reflections on the Principles of "A Course in Miracles."*

10. Joan Halifax, *Being with Dying: Cultivating Compassion and Fearlessness in the Presence of Death* (2009).

Chapter 5

1. Sarah Iles Johnston, *Restless Dead: Encounters between the Living and the Dead in Ancient Greece.*
2. Maria Mili, *Religion and Society in Ancient Thessaly.* See also Myrina Kalaitzi, Paschalis Paschidis, Claudia Antonetti, Anne-Marie Guimier-Sorbets (eds.), Βορειοελλαδικά: *Tales from the Lands of the Ethne. Essays in Honour of Miltiades B. Hatzopoulos.*
3. Sofia Petrogianni, "The Cult of Deities of Eastern Origin in the Black Sea Region." Master's Thesis, International Hellenic University.
4. Sophocles, *Fragments*, trans. Hugh Lloyd-Jones (Loeb Classical Library No. 483).
5. Daniel Ogden, *Magic, Witchcraft, and Ghosts in the Greek and Roman Worlds: A Sourcebook* (2002).
6. Homer, *The Odyssey*, trans. Emily Wilson. See also Ovid's *Metamorphoses: A New Translation by Charles Martin* and Madeline Miller's modern retelling of *Circe.*
7. I wrote more about these stones in my book *Keeping Her Keys.*

Chapter 6

1. See Sorita' d'Este's *Circle for Hekate: Volume 1* for a list of sources of Hekate as Propylaia.
2. Aynur-Michèle-Sara Karatas," *Key-bearers of Greek Temples: The Temple Key as a Symbol of Priestly Authority*" (2019).
3. For more on Hekate as Propylaia read A. Zografou, *Chemins d'Hécate: Portes, Routes, Carrefours et Autres Figures de l'Entre-Deux*, Kernos Supplément 24 (2010).
4. A. Seiffert (2006), "Der sakrale Schutz von Grenzen im antiken Griechenland—Formen und Ikonographie," Dissertation, Julius-Maximilians-Universität Würzburg (2006).
5. AMS Karatas, *Key-bearers of Greek Temples.*

6. Sarah Iles Johnston, *Hekate Soteira: A Study of Hekate's Roles in the Chaldean Oracles and Related Literature* (1990).
7. I explore the mythology and symbolism of Circe and Medea extensively in *Entering Hekate's Garden*.

Chapter 7

1. One of the books that has most influenced my way of thinking about the self is *Anatomy of the Spirit: The Seven Stages of Power and Healing* by Caroline Myss.
2. Simon Hornblower and Antony Spawforth (eds.), *The Oxford Classical Dictionary*
3. Douglas Stone, Bruce Patton, and Sheila Heen, *Difficult Conversations: How to Discuss What Matters Most* (2010).
4. Matthew McKay, PhD, Jeffrey C. Wood, PsyD, and Jeffrey Brantley, MD, *The Dialectical Behavior Therapy Skills Workbook: Practical DBT Exercises for Learning Mindfulness, Interpersonal Effectiveness, Emotion Regulation, and Distress Tolerance* (2019).
5. Oxford English Dictionary Online.

Chapter 8

1. "Hieros pyr" is a masculine epithet, hinting at Hekate as Anima Mundi transcending the confines of gender.
2. E.g., Erich Neumann, *The Great Mother*.
3. These two terms are explored in depth in *The Red Book: Liber Novus* by C. G. Jung, with forward by Sonu Shamdasani (ed.).
4. *Dark Nights of the Soul: A Guide to Finding Your Way through Life's Ordeals* by Thomas Moore explores this in fabulous detail.
5. Jean Shinoda Bolen, MD, *Goddesses in Older Women: Archetypes in Women over Fifty*.
6. Individuation is a central tenet of analytical psychology. See C. G. Jung's "The Relations between the Ego and the Unconscious" in *Collected Works, Vol. 7*.
7. Margaret S. Mahler.
8. My earliest research explored the transition from adolescence to adulthood. See for example, "Attachment Styles, Social Skills and

Loneliness in Young Adults" coauthored with Enrico DiTommaso, Lynda Ross, and Melissa Burgess in *Personality and Individual Differences*, Volume 35, Issue 2.

9. Roger Brooke, *Jung and Phenomenology: Classic Edition.*
10. Marion Woodman and Elinor Dickson, *Dancing in the Flames: The Dark Goddess in the Transformation of Consciousness.*
11. This archetype's connection to the divine feminine was explored by Toni Wolff and has since been articulated by many others, although we often call it by another name.
12. Marie-Louise von Franz in *On Divination and Synchronicity.*

Chapter 9

1. "Catharsis in Psychology and Beyond," *primal-page.com/cathar.htm.*
2. "Tlazolteotl," *en.wikipedia.org.*
3. *Oxford English Dictionary.*
4. Stephen Ronan (ed.), *The Goddess Hekate.* (Hastings, UK: Chthonios Books, 1992).
5. Carl S. Sterner, "A Brief History of Miasmic Theory," *www.carlsterner.com*
6. Marcus West "Complexes and Archetypes," *thesap.org.uk.*
7. Refer to Brené Brown's excellent work on shame, such as her TED Talk "Listening to Shame" at *ted.com.*
8. Dr. Susan Schwartz, "How to Love a Narcissist."
9. Diane J. Rayor, *The Homeric Hymns: A Translation, with Introduction and Notes, Updated Edition.*
10. From *Goddesses in Everywoman: Powerful Archetypes in Women's Lives,* by Jean Shinoda Bolen, MD.
11. Christopher Patrick and some of his colleagues published an extensive literature review in which they argued that psychopaths were people who expressed elevated levels of three basic traits: meanness, disinhibition, and boldness.
12. Explore kindness in this amazing book: *Dare to Be Kind: How Extraordinary Compassion Can Transform Our World* by Lizzie Velasquez. When I consider passionate thought leaders, I think of Elizabeth Gilbert. Her book *Big Magic: Creative Living beyond Fear* was absolutely instrumental in me being able to accept my unique "big

magic," and to be able to share it with others. An excellent guide to living with integrity is *The Way of Integrity: Finding the Path to Your True Self* by Martha Beck.

13. Red jasper from *The Book of Stones: Who They Are and What They Teach*, Revised Edition by Robert Simmons and Naisha Ahsian.

14. Learn more about botanicals of release in *Entering Hekate's Garden*.

Chapter 10

1. Michelle Obama's book, *Becoming*, is a great companion at this stage of the cave journey.

2. James HIllman, *The Soul's Code: In Search of Character and Calling* (1996).

3. The Britsh Critic and Quarterly Theological Review, Vol. IV. *play.google.com.*

4. There is some debate about any possible connections between Hekate and Heka. Dive into the discussion at *quora.com.* "Is the Greek goddess of witchcraft Hecate related to ancient Egyptian Heka magic?"

5. Hans Dieter Betz (ed.), *The Greek Magical Papyri in Translation, Including the Demotic Spells, Volume One* (1997).

6. "Scota: Mother of Scotland and Daughter of a Pharaoh," *ancient-origins.net.*

7. "Tuatha Dé Danann," *en.wikipedia.org.*

8. "The Pharaoh's Daughter Who Was the Mother of All Scots," *scotsman.com.*

9. C. G. Jung, *Alchemical Studies*, par. 335.

10. C. G. Jung, *Psychology of the Unconscious* (paperback, 2003).

11. Jeffrey E. Young, Janet S. Klosko, and Marjorie E. Weishaar, *Schema Therapy: A Practitioner's Guide (1st Edition)* (2006).

12. John Bowlby, *A Secure Base* (paperback, 1988).

13. James Hillman, *The Soul's Code: In Search of Character and Calling* (1996).

14. Michael Singer's *The Untethered Soul: The Journey beyond Yourself* is wonderful for exploring how to become unblocked.

15. "Asteria," *theoi.com.*
16. James Hillman, *The Dream and the Underworld.*
17. C. G. Jung, *Dreams* (from Volumes 4, 8, 12, and 16 of *The Collected Works of C. G. Jung)* foreword by Sonu Shamdasani, translated by R. F. C. Hull (2010).
18. Erich Fromm, *The Forgotten Language: An Introduction to the Understanding of Dreams, Fairy Tales, and Myths.*
19. Sorita d'Este and David Rankine, *Visions of the Cailleach: Exploring the Myths, Folklore and Legends of the Pre-Eminent Celtic Hag Goddess* (2009).
20. Leanne O'Sullivan, *Cailleach: The Hag of Beara* (2009).

Chapter 11

1. Adapted from The Greek Magical Papyri, IV, 2241-2358, Hymn to the Waning Moon.
2. Axel Michaels, Cornelia Vogelsanger, and Annette Wilke, *Wild Goddesses in India and Nepal,* proceedings of an international symposium, Berne and Zurich, November 1994.
3. Egregore, *theosophy.wiki.*
4. Karin Ikas and Gerhard Wagner (eds.), *Communicating in the Third Space* (2009).
5. Jean Shinoda Bolen, MD, "Transitions as Liminal and Archetypal Situations," *mythicjourneys.org/passages/july2005/transitions_bolen.pdf*
6. "Myth of the Week: Psyche and Eros," *madelinemiller.com.*
7. "Hedone," *theoi.com.*
8. "Eros is a questionable fellow and will always remain so. . . . He belongs on one side to man's primordial animal nature, which will endure as long as man has an animal body. On the other side, he is related to the highest forms of the spirit. But he thrives only when spirit and instinct are in right harmony." From "The Eros Theory," *Collected Works* 7, par. 32.

   "Where love reigns, there is no will to power; and where the will to power is paramount, love is lacking. The one is but the shadow of the other: the man who adopts the standpoint of Eros finds his compensatory opposite in the will to power, and that of the man who puts the accent on power is Eros." From "The Problem of the Attitude-Type," ibid., par. 78.

"An unconscious Eros always expresses itself as will to power." From "Psychological Aspects of the Mother Archetype," *Collected Works* 9i, par. 167.

9. "Jungian Agape," *feelingmywayalong.blogspot.com,* September 2009.
10. Cyndi Brannen, *scholar.google.ca.*
11. "Attachment Styles, Social Skills and Loneliness in Young Adults," *semanticscholar.org.*
12. Cyndi Brannen Caregiving, "An Alternative Framework for Understanding Women's Caregiving Stress," *scholar.google.ca.*
13. Daryl Sharp, *Personality Types* from *Studies in Jungian Psychology by Jungian Analysts* (1987).
14. Kim Bartholomew and Phillip R. Shaver, "Methods of Assessing Adult Attachment: Do They Converge," *scholar.google.ca*
15. Although I don't agree with everything she says, I find Caroline Myss's work on archetypes to be helpful. *Archetypes: A Beginner's Guide to Your Inner-net* (2013) can be very helpful in exploring the archetypes at work in us.
16. James Hollis, PhD, *The Archetypal Imagination* foreword by David H. Rosen (2002).
17. Volume 1 of the Collected Works of Marie-Louise von Franz: *Archetypal Symbols in Fairytales: The Profane and Magical Worlds* (2021).
18. Bessel van der Kolk, "Overcoming Trauma—The Body Keeps the Score," *medium.com.*
19. Gabor Maté, MD, *When the Body Says No: Exploring the Stress-Disease Connection* (2011).
20. James S. Gordon, MD, *The Transformation: Discovering Wholeness and Healing after Trauma.*
21. See Nicholas Pearson's *Crystal Basics: The Energetic, Healing, and Spiritual Power of 200 Gemstones* for details about these stones.

Chapter 12

1. *Dark Nights of the Soul: A Guide to Finding Your Way through Life's Ordeals* by Thomas Moore contains an excellent discussion on Hekate and the soul.
2. For a short summary of the Greek ideas about the afterlife see "The Concepts of Heaven and Hell in Ancient Greece," *greekreporter.com.*
3. Sarah Iles Johnston, *Restless Dead: Encounters between the Living and the Dead in Ancient Greece* (1999).
4. For more on soul retrieval, read Sandra Ingerman's *Soul Retrieval: Mending the Fragmented Self.*
5. Azrael, *britannica.com.*
6. Ammit, *ancientegyptonline.co.uk.*
7. For example, *A New Classical Dictionary of Greek and Roman Biography, Mythology and Geography* (1884) by Charles Anthon. Available at: *archive.org.*
8. Johnston, *Restless Dead* (1999).
9. Hugh G. Evelyn White (trans.), *Hesiod, the Homeric Hymns, and Homerica,* (London: William Heinemann Ltd., 1941).
10. Mead, G. R. S., The Chaldean Oracles; (Theosophical Publishing Society, 1908).
11. Chaldean Oracles, Fragment 34.
12. Sarah Iles Johnston, *Hekate Soteira.*
13. Joseph Campbell, *Pathways to Bliss: Mythology and Personal Transformation* (The Collected Works of Joseph Campbell) foreword by David Kudler (ed.) (2018).
14. Paulo Coelho, *The Alchemist* (25th anniversary edition) (2015).
15. From *The Return of the Feminine and the World Soul* by Llewellyn Vaughan-Lee.
16. *The Collected Works of C. G. Jung,* Volume 9, Part 1.
17. For a discussion on anima and animus, listen to *This Jungian Life* podcast, Episode 076—"Animus and Anima," *open.spotify.com.*
18. For a great critical discussion on Jung's approach to gender, listen to *Medicine Path* with Brian James, MPP57 "Thomas Moore: Care of the Soul," *open.spotify.com.*
19. From *Re-Visioning Psychology* by James Hillman.

20. Marion Woodman, *Bone: Dying into Life.*
21. "Indigenous Knowledge and Shamanic Ways: Inner Journeys and Soul Retrieval," *psychospiritual.org.*
22. See *The Inner World of Trauma: Archetypal Defenses of the Personal Spirit* by Donald Kalsched.
23. *Dark Nights of the Soul: A Guide to Finding Your Way through Life's Ordeals* by Thomas Moore discusses the problems with mainstream psychology.
24. Roman Krznaric, *Empathy: Why It Matters, and How to Get It* (2014).
25. Brené Brown, *Dare to Lead: Brave Work. Tough Conversations. Whole Hearts.* (2018).
26. "Elevated Empathy in Adults following Childhood Trauma," *ncbi.nlm.nih.gov.*
    Brooke Nawrocki, "The Correlation between Complex Childhood Trauma and Adult Empathy Outcomes," *csustan.edu.*
27. *The War for Kindness: Building Empathy in a Fractured World* by Jamil Zaki (2019) is an excellent exploration of empathy.
28. "Active Listening: Connect with a Partner through Empathy and Understanding," The Pathway to Happiness Program, *ggia.berkeley.edu.*
29. Learn more about botanicals and soul retrieval in *Entering Hekate's Garden.*

Chapter 13

1. Susan David, *Emotional Agility: Get Unstuck, Embrace Change, and Thrive in Work and Life.*
2. For more on mirror neurons, see "Mirror Neurons, Embodied Emotions, and Empathy" by Ferrari and Coudé, *https://www.sciencedirect.com/science/article/pii/B9780128053973000061.*
3. Read more about Artemis's wrath at *press.rebus.community/mythologyunbound/chapter/artemis.*
4. Cyndi Brannen, *Entering Hekate's Garden: The Magick, Medicine and Mystery.*
5. For more on Semele, see *journeyingtothegoddess.wordpress.com.*

6. Stephen W. Porges, *The Polyvagal Theory: Neurophysiological Foundations of Emotions, Attachment, Communication, and Self-Regulation* (Norton Series on Interpersonal Neurobiology).

7. *Burnout: The Secret to Unlocking the Stress Cycle* by Emily Nagoski and Amelia Nagoski is full of fantastic advice for managing everyday stressors.

Chapter 14

1. Andrew Delahunty and Sheila Dignen, *Adonis to Zorro: Oxford Dictionary of Reference and Allusion*.

2. Erich Neumann, *The Great Mother*.

3. R. Gordon Wasson, Albert Hofmann, and Carl A. P. Ruck, *The Road to Eleusis: Unveiling the Secret of the Mysteries* (2008).

4. For example, *The Immortality Key: The Secret History of the Religion with No Name* by Brian C. Muraresku with Graham Hancock (2020) explores in depth the role of psychedelics in the rituals of Eleusis.

5. I discuss the mythological maternity of Medea in *Entering Hekate's Garden*. See also *Prometheus: Gods and Heroes of the Ancient World*, 1st Edition, by Carol Dougherty (2005).

6. Apollonius Rhodius, *The Argonautica* Book 3, trans. Rieu, at *theoi.com*.

7. E.g., Demetra George, *Mysteries of the Dark Moon: The Healing Power of the Dark Goddess*; Tamara Agha-Jaffar, *Demeter and Persephone: Lessons from a Myth*; Marion Woodman, *Bone: Dying into Life*.

8. George W. MacRae (trans.), *The Nag Hammadi Library—The Thunder, Perfect Mind*.

9. From *Lost Goddesses of Early Greece*, by Charlene Spretnak (1978).

10. Demetra George, *Mysteries of the Dark Moon*.

11. I highly recommend *In the Realm of Hungry Ghosts: Close Encounters with Addiction* by Dr. Gabor Maté for understanding how they can consume us.

12. Marija Gimbutas, *The Language of the Goddess* (London: Thames and Hudson, 2001).

13. Dive deep into the history and mystery of how culture views death in *Restless Dead: Encounters between the Living and the Dead in Ancient Greece* by Sarah Iles Johnston. Includes a detailed section on Hekate and the dead.

14. Angela Hurley, "An Examination of the Malleable Representation of Medea," master's thesis presented to the faculty of the Graduate School of Arts and Sciences, Brandeis University Graduate Program in Ancient Greek and Roman Studies (2018).

15. Christine Scarfuto, "The Myth of Orpheus and Eurydice," *wiki .uiowa.edu.*

16. Mallorie Vaudoise, *Honoring Your Ancestors: A Guide to Ancestral Veneration.*

17. *It Didn't Start with You: How Inherited Family Trauma Shapes Who We Are and How to End the Cycle* by Dr. Mark Wolynn is an excellent guide to understanding intergenerational transmission of trauma.

18. E.g., "The Intergenerational Trauma of Slavery and Its Aftermath," by Gilda Graff, *The Journal of Psychohistory*; Winter 2014; 41, 3.

19. Martha Henriques, "Can the Legacy of Trauma Be Passed Down the Generations?" *bbc.com.*

20. Wolynn, *It Didn't Start with You.*

21. Wolynn, *It Didn't Start with You.*

22. An excellent discussion on the impacts of resentment can be found in an episode of *This Jungian Life*, Episode 153—"Chronic Anger: Trapped in Resentment" at *open.spotify.com.*

23. Nicholas Pearson, *Crystal Basics: The Energetic, Healing, and Spiritual Power of 200 Gemstones.*

24. E. M. Berens, *Myths and Legends of Ancient Greece and Rome.*

25. I recommend *Restless Dead* by Sarah Iles Johnston for an in-depth exploration of death practices in Ancient Greece.

26. See Johnston, *Restless Dead.*

27. Danielle Star, "The Death Drive in Psychoanalysis: Decoding Three Prominent Theories from Spielrein, Freud and Klein." Carleton University (2018).

28. James Hollis, *What Matters Most: Living a More Considered Life.*

29. Marion Woodman and Elinor Dickson, *Dancing in the Flames: The Dark Goddess in the Transformation of Consciousness.*

30. Stephen W. Porges, *The Pocket Guide to The Polyvagal Theory: The Transformative Power of Feeling Safe.*

31. See *Restless Dead* by Sarah Iles Johnston.

32. There is some evidence of women being involved in The Greek Magical Papyri; see *Women and the Transmission of Magical Knowledge in the Greco-Roman World: Rediscovering Ancient Witches* by Miriam Blanco Cesteros (2017). In *Magikê Technê. Formación y consideración social del mago en el Mundo Antiguo. researchgate.net.*

33. With gratitude to Sue Monk Kidd's amazing novel, *The Book of Longings,* for planting the seed of largeness inside of me.

34. Robert Simmons and Naisha Ahsian, *The Book of Stones: Who They Are and What They Teach,* Revised Edition, (2015).

35. You can read my recommendations for offerings in *Keeping Her Keys.*

36. "Unfinished Business: Emotion-Focused Therapy and 'Empty Chair Work'" for an overview of the Empty Chair technique in emotion-focused therapy, including a handy worksheet that you can adapt, *goodmedicine.org.uk.*

Chapter 15

1. If you haven't listened to or watched "Hadestown," I highly recommend it.

2. Aynur-Michèle-Sara Karatas (2019). "Key-Bearers of Greek Temples: The Temple Key as a Symbol of Priestly Authority," Kleidouchoi nei santuari greci: la chiave del tempio come simbolo dell'autorità Sacerdotale by Aynur-Michèle-Sara Karatas in Rivista di Storia delle Religioni, 13, (2019).

3. Adapted from The Greek Magical Papyri (LXX, 4–25).

4. Jean Shinoda Bolen, *Goddesses in Everywoman,* 30th Anniversary Edition (2014).

5. "Artemis Is the Queer Girl Goddess BFF of Your Dreams," *autostraddle.com.*

6. "Hekate, Guardian of the Marginalized," *academia.edu.*

7. Charles M. Edwards, "The Running Maiden from Eleusis and the Early Classical Image of Hekate," *jstor.org*.

8. James Hillman, *The Soul's Code: In Search of Character and Calling*.

9. Brené Brown, *The Gifts of Imperfection*.

10. Ruchika Tulshyan and Jodi-Ann Burey, "Stop Telling Women They Have Imposter Syndrome," *hbr.org*.

11. If you haven't read *Man's Search for Meaning* by Viktor E. Frankl, I urge you to do so.

12. The Taurus Myth, *gods-and-monsters.com*.

13. Attributed to the Roman writer Seneca, but Oprah Winfrey also said it.

14. Malala's Story, *malala.org*.

15. Hillman, *The Soul's Code* (1996).

About the Author

Social psychologist Cyndi Brannen teaches and writes from the crossroads of modern life and the deeper world from her coastal cottage in rural Nova Scotia, where she lives with her two sons. After a successful career in academia and healthcare, she transitioned to focus on reclaiming the sacred feminine after she became convinced that mainstream psychology was not sufficient to lead to personal wholeness. Her work focuses on personal healing through depth psychology, herbalism, rituals, meditations, and exploration of the deeper self. She founded the Covina Institute, a soul school dedicated to the pursuit of wholeness through structured programs of study and transcendent experiences. Her books include *Entering Hekate's Garden,* *Keeping Her Keys,* and *True Magic.*

Dr. Brannen describes herself as a seeker of the divine within and the mysteries of the deeper world. Her quest to understand both have led her through years of studies in depth psychology, comparative religion, mythology, gender analysis, and feminist scholarship. Along the way, she has studied many esoteric teachings, including astrology, herbalism, energetic healing, shamanic techniques, divination, mysticism, and mediumship.

Brannen's former career in health research and academia brings to her teaching and writing an expertise in evidence-based self-help programs in maternal depression, PTSD, and various childhood vulnerabilities. Her doctoral training explored personality characteristics, interpersonal relationships, and well-being. Her expertise in areas of well-being include loneliness, attachment, romantic relationships, social skills, and coping skills. She brings all these practices to her interpretation of the archetypes of the witch and the goddess for contemporary seekers on the journey through healing to wholeness.

Learn more at *keepingherkeys.com*.

To Our Readers

Weiser Books, an imprint of Red Wheel/Weiser, publishes books across the entire spectrum of occult, esoteric, speculative, and New Age subjects. Our mission is to publish quality books that will make a difference in people's lives without advocating any one particular path or field of study. We value the integrity, originality, and depth of knowledge of our authors.

Our readers are our most important resource, and we appreciate your input, suggestions, and ideas about what you would like to see published.

Visit our website at *www.redwheelweiser.com*, where you can learn about our upcoming books and free downloads, and also find links to sign up for our newsletter and exclusive offers.

You can also contact us at *info@rwwbooks.com* or at
Red Wheel/Weiser, LLC
65 Parker Street, Suite 7
Newburyport, MA 01950